R. H. PARR studied history and law at C
with a double first, and became a sol
of London. She has spent thirty-five y
ranging from large corporates to High
spectrum of clients and problems. Since 2002 she has specialised in
advising charities and social enterprises and she runs training seminars
for trustees. In 2008 she set up her own law firm, which has brought her
true professional satisfaction and a good reputation in the charity sector.

A Devonian who has lived in Somerset since 1981, she is a former
President of a Dorset agricultural society. Rosemary is a trustee of
a national charity, founded by far-sighted Victorian ladies in 1859, that
supports women's professional training.

The death of her daughter Sophie from cancer in 2009 caused her to
find out more about her unknown grandfather, who also lost a daughter
to cancer, and to write her first book *A Shy and Simple Warrior*, an
account of the turbulent half-century of history that determined his life.

Rosemary enjoys playing tennis, singing in a choir, crewing on
a sailing ship, trekking in Nepal, and painting watercolours.

A Shy
and
Simple Warrior

R. H. Parr

To Neville
— with love,
Rosie.

SilverWood

Published in 2015 by SilverWood Books

SilverWood Books Ltd
14 Small Street, Bristol, BS1 1DE, United Kingdom
www.silverwoodbooks.co.uk

ISBN 978-1-78132-385-4 (paperback)
ISBN 978-1-78132-386-1 (ebook)

British Library Cataloguing in Publication Data
A CIP catalogue record for this book is available from
the British Library

Set in Adobe Garamond Pro by SilverWood Books
Printed on responsibly sourced paper

In memory of my mother and my grandmother
For Ida and Sophie

Their lives are as interesting as yours and mine, even if nobody has written about them...collectively, if not as individuals, such men and women are major historical actors. What they do, and think, makes a difference. It can and has changed culture and the shape of history and never more so than in the twentieth century. That is why I have called a book about ordinary people, the ones that are traditionally known as the common people – *Uncommon People*.

Eric Hobsbawm

Contents

Foreword

History is about people. For 143 years until 2010, the Royal Navy engaged its Artificers, the 'Think-Do' people, as the innovative engineers who found solutions to its technical problems. They would then use their skill of hand, honed over years of training and experience, to keep their ships in fighting order, so often bringing them and their crews home safely.

Rosemary Parr tells the story of how the Navy slowly came to terms with its dependence on committed engineers, and she brings it together through her grandfather George's remarkable career in the first half of the twentieth century. She covers the Navy's significant engagements during those eventful years, all through the eyes and involvement of this shy and simple warrior, George Lancaster, with his deep love of both the Navy and his family.

This is a heart-warming story of which we can all be proud, and a rare reminder of how the Navy moved from Victorian times into the modern world.

Rear Admiral John Burgess
CB, LVO, CEng

Preface

I never knew my grandfather; he died over seven years before I was born. I knew my grandmother, Ida – I was seventeen when she died. I'd heard, half-listening, my mother's memories of her father, George Lancaster. I was aware that his father had come to Devon from Lancashire, and that George, born in Devonport, had died a few miles away in the Crownhill district of Plymouth, where I grew up. I'd looked at the photographs of him – a fair-haired man of short stature, kindly-looking, probably rather quiet and reserved, not particularly memorable.

For me, a student of history at university, the name 'Lancaster' had more historical resonances – a Saxon county town, powerful medieval earls, the Wars of the Roses, the Duchy of Lancaster, a World War Two bomber.

The catalyst to my exploring George's unknown life was a common bereavement. Seventy years after his daughter died of cancer in July 1939, I too lost my daughter Sophie to cancer, both of them dying in their mid-twenties. While I was able to adopt a range of coping strategies, George and Ida never had the freedom to choose how to cope. History gave them no such options. One month after the death of their daughter, Neville Chamberlain announced that Great Britain was at war with Germany, and a year later the Lancaster family was suffering the Plymouth Blitz.

I began to think for the first time about the lives of my grandparents; to understand how their characters were formed and what gave them the strength to survive and cope in such a different historical landscape with an identical family tragedy.

George and Ida were both born in Devonport in the 1880s, during the 'long peace' enjoyed by England throughout the reign of Queen Victoria. They were to live, along with their generation, through a half-century of world wars and massive social and economic change.

I especially wanted to explore the experience of George, whose adult working life spanned forty-five years from 1901 to 1945. He left no memoirs, and all my relatives who had known him had died. But I'd never before looked through my late mother's family papers. My starting point was George's large collection of postcards from his overseas travels as a sailor – cards from Italy and Austro-Hungary, Christmas greetings from Estonia, views of Cuba, Bermuda and the Niagara Falls, and messages from Jerusalem and Japan. I then found forgotten photo albums, club magazines, George's 'China Station' diary, letters home to his daughters, his sketch books.

These fragments of memory opened other paths of research. I discovered that George's career in the Royal Navy had taken him across the Mediterranean from Gibraltar and Malta to the Middle East, and to the Americas, the eastern Baltic, Asia Minor and the Far East. In the Great War he fought at the Battle of Jutland in 1916, when he and most of his crewmates were miraculously rescued from their sinking cruiser, HMS *Warrior,* in the North Sea.

After that war, his ships were deployed to countries – Russia, Turkey and China – where armed nationalist movements were filling the void created by the collapse of empires. He served through a period marked by two world wars, imperial display and decline, a global pandemic, civil wars, communist revolution, sectarian atrocities, the Great Depression, the coronation of an emperor and a monarch's abdication. George's life was touched, and often more than touched, by all these events.

Was this Lancaster, as described by one of his less perceptive commanding officers, just a 'shy and simple' man, of no consequence beyond his family and my gene pool? Or was he one of Hobsbawm's 'Uncommon People' – one of the millions of battle-scarred and stoical men and women, inured to separation, privation and death, whose combined contribution in peace and war in the first half of the twentieth century gave us, their grandchildren, the relatively stable and prosperous post-war world of its second half?

Rosemary Parr
Wanstrow
June 2015

Liverpool to Devonport

An engraving published by the *Illustrated London News* on 15 September 1872 shows a view from the sea of the Three Towns of Devonport, East Stonehouse and Plymouth.

Across the picture stretches the large natural harbour of Plymouth Sound, with the park of Mount Edgcumbe on the Cornish side, Drake's Island in the centre, and Mount Batten on its eastern waterfront. From this bay over the centuries, many historic voyagers have set sail, including the medieval Black Prince, the great Elizabethan seafarers, Captain Cook, Admiral Nelson and Charles Darwin on HMS *Beagle*. It was here in the Sound that the captured Napoleon was kept imprisoned on the *Bellerophon* before being taken to exile on St Helena.

In the engraving, the River Tamar, marking the border between Devon and Cornwall, is full of two- or three-masted sailing ships, ferryboats and other smaller craft. Only a few of the vessels have funnels, showing that they are powered by the new steam engines. Spreading up the Devon bank of the river are the naval dockyards and town of Devonport, overlooking the waters at the mouth of the Tamar known as the Hamoaze. In the distance to the north lie the tors of Dartmoor.

The year after this view was published, a young naval recruit from Liverpool came to Devonport. George Lancaster had been born in Everton on 18 February 1858, and in July 1873 he joined the Royal Navy at the age of fifteen as a Boy, Second Class. He spent his first four days as a sailor on HMS *Eagle* as it brought him from Lancashire to Devon for training, arriving in Plymouth Sound on 11 July 1873.

Sailing in past the Eddystone Lighthouse, as the ship came around the Breakwater and into the Sound, George saw ahead of him Plymouth Hoe, where Drake played bowls before going to defeat the Spanish Armada. To the east of the Hoe, he would have sighted the historic Barbican, from where the Pilgrim Fathers set sail to America in the *Mayflower*. Above it stood the massive Citadel army barracks, built by Charles II, with the guns facing the town to deter the Puritan townsfolk from rebelling again as they had done against his father in the English Civil War.

In front of him, George could see a scene of expanding urbanisation and industrialisation, with the numerous churches and chapels of the Three Towns, their railway stations, factories, warehouses, markets and quays. As HMS *Eagle* sailed past Millbay Docks into the Hamoaze, he saw on the starboard side the Royal William Victualling Yard which supplied the Navy's ships, the Royal Marine Barracks and Royal Naval Hospital at Stonehouse, and Admiralty House at Mount Wise, all confirming the role of the port as a major naval and military base. Ahead of him up the Tamar he may have glimpsed the Torpoint chain ferry and Brunel's Royal Albert Bridge at Saltash, carrying the railway into Cornwall.

George Lancaster was a long way from home. His father, another George, was a merchant seaman in Liverpool, whose father William Lancaster had also been a mariner, according to his son's marriage certificate. At the age of thirty-one, George senior had married Eleanor Spencer in December 1852 at St Michael's Church in Liverpool. She was twenty-one, the daughter of a shoemaker called Peter Spencer and his wife Mary, and she had been born in Gibraltar. Peter, a former soldier, had been based there with his regiment, the Twenty-third Foot, when in 1831 his wife Mary had given birth to Eleanor, their eldest child. On their return to Liverpool, the Spencer family lived in Denison Street.

This street no longer exists, but it was a road off Bath Street in Liverpool 3, just behind the Prince's Dock and near the Pier Head. It is known in the history of Liverpool as the street where the public health reformer Kitty Wilkinson (1785–1860) lived.

Kitty, a poor Irish migrant from Derry, had worked in the Lancashire cotton mills and as a domestic servant in Liverpool, and had then set up as a laundress in rented accommodation in Denison Street. In 1832 there was a cholera epidemic in Liverpool. Kitty, realising that cleanliness was a vital protection against disease, allowed local residents to use her boiler and yard to wash their clothes and bedding in boiled water, giving them chloride of lime to destroy infectious bacteria. Denison Street became the site of the first washhouse for the poor, and Kitty Wilkinson would have been well known to Eleanor Spencer and her family as their neighbour when they lived there in the 1840s.[1]

George Lancaster and Eleanor Spencer had both grown up in these tough, poverty-stricken streets by the docks of mid-nineteenth-century Liverpool. The Spencer family probably washed their clothes in Kitty Wilkinson's boiler when disease was prevalent. Kitty also used her house in Denison Street as a school for poor children living in the surrounding slums of Liverpool, many of them homeless. As a child, Eleanor Spencer herself may have received some elementary lessons at Kitty's neighbouring house.

After their marriage, George and Eleanor – usually called Ellen – lived with the Spencer family in Denison Street, and George continued to work as a seaman on merchant ships carrying cargoes to and from the great commercial port of Liverpool. Ellen's first child, Mary Ellen, was born in 1854, followed by a son, William Charles, in 1856. As their family grew, George and Eleanor Lancaster moved from Denison Street to nearby Everton, still one of the poorer districts of the city. Their third child, George, our future naval recruit, was born here on 18 February 1858, and baptised on 6 June 1858 at St Peter's Church in Everton.

Two years later Ellen was a widow at the age of twenty-nine. Her husband George died in 1860 aged thirty-nine, leaving her to bring up Mary Ellen, aged six, William, aged four, and two-year-old George on her own in very tough circumstances. The 1861 census records Eleanor Lancaster as the 'Head of Family' living with her three young children at 18 Boardman Place, which was just east of Scotland Road, in the St Martin district of Liverpool. She was working as a laundress.

In 1865 Eleanor married again, to a widower called Benjamin Edge, whose first wife Harriet had died in 1862 leaving him with four daughters and two sons. Benjamin was from Shropshire and worked in Liverpool as a labourer in an ironworks or on the docks. Eleanor lived with Benjamin and his children at various addresses in Everton over the next three decades, and in 1866 she gave birth to another son, James Edge.

On the date of the 1871 census, her sons William and George Lancaster, aged fifteen and thirteen respectively, were also living with the Edge family in Cornwall Street, Everton. Eleanor's daughter, seventeen-year-old Mary Ellen Lancaster, was that year working in service as a live-in maid for the Bradley family in West Derby, Liverpool.

Her younger brothers, William and George, may have found it difficult living with a stepfather and several stepsiblings, as within two years both of them had joined the Royal Navy. Their own father and paternal grandfather had been mariners, and even if this were not an instance of running away to sea, the prospect of a naval life was perhaps more enticing for both of the Lancaster brothers than staying with their stepfamily in the impoverished streets of Everton. It was probably also a necessary route to a livelihood for both of them, given that Benjamin Edge had so many of his own children to feed.

Eleanor stayed in Liverpool for the rest of her life. After being widowed for a second time, she went to live with her son by Benjamin, James Edge. James was a coal carter and lived with his wife and young family at 1 Roger Street in West Derby, Liverpool. The 1891 census of the family records Eleanor, then aged sixty, as a 'Knocker Up' – which means she had a paid job walking along the streets and knocking on doors and windows to wake people up in the mornings to go to work, at a time when few had alarm clocks.

Eleanor Spencer/Lancaster/Edge died in 1893, aged sixty-two. She'd had a hard life, and in the latter part of it she probably had little contact with her two sons, William and George Lancaster, after they had gone to sea and been sent to Devonport. But George retained one tangible memory of his mother which has survived for some 150 years and is now kept by her great-great-granddaughter. It is a small china cup, cream-coloured, without its handle and its glaze now cracked, the name 'Spencer' in gold lettering on its side.

After Boy Second Class George Lancaster arrived in Devonport on HMS *Eagle* in July 1873, he was transferred to the hulk of HMS *Impregnable*, one of the last big wooden-walled warships, which was permanently moored off Cremyll in the Hamoaze for the training of young naval ratings.

George served as a naval rating during the long period of peace enjoyed by Great Britain in the nineteenth century. Apart from the Crimean War and other relatively minor colonial wars, the country did not engage in any major conflicts between the defeat of Napoleon in 1815 and the Boer War of 1899–1902. But life in the Royal Navy for the sailors of the 'lower deck' (the collective term for all non-commissioned crewmen, including petty officers) was still very tough during Queen Victoria's reign. The pay was low, the hours were long, and discipline was harsh.

On *Impregnable* the traditional daily routine began at 5.30 a.m. with the shave-headed and barefooted boys sanding, hosing down and drying the decks, a process known as 'holystoning'. This was followed by further cleaning of the ship, physical drill and rifle drill, the boys having to perform all their duties properly and at the double or risk a blow on the ear or cuts with a lash from their seniors. The boys were trained to climb up the rigging and balance on the high wooden yards of the tall-masted training ship, showing no fear, and to walk out above the sea on the bowsprit, an instructor behind them ready to strike a boy with a rope's end if he slowed down or faltered.

The boys had little contact with the ship's commissioned officers as all their training was given by petty officers. But the team work which the lads had to learn through hoisting up the sails, hauling on the halyards, lowering boats and raising the anchor built the sense of comradeship so vital to the efficient operation of the ship. When they were not on duty there was certainly bullying and fighting among the boys, but they also became part of the ship's company. They developed the sense of belonging to a family, which many of them, like George and William back in Everton in the Edge household, had previously lacked.

During the day the ratings would be mustered on deck for inspection and prayers, put in classes for instruction in seamanship, and sent on gunnery exercises or sometimes ashore to a rifle range. In the evening after roll-call there would be some free time for the boys in their dark, squalid quarters below deck before they had to sling up their hammocks between the guns and lamps out at 9 p.m..

The food given to the seamen, including the traditional hard tack biscuits, was poorly prepared, sparse and not particularly nutritious. Typical fare was bread, corned pork and tea for breakfast at 8 a.m., a midday meal (dinner) of meat (mutton or beef), suet and potatoes, bread and jam at teatime and a supper of corned beef, bread and dripping, with a basin of cocoa. The men had to eat the food with their fingers as knives and forks were regarded as a luxury. Table cutlery was not issued to the lower deck until the 1900s as part of Admiral Fisher's reforms.

When George joined up, flogging was still a punishment for sailors, as was the birching of boy seamen in front of the ship's company. If a few ratings behaved badly, collective punishments would sometimes be imposed on the whole crew, such as the stopping of leave. George and the other boys training on HMS *Impregnable* knew that the penalty for disobeying orders, breaking the terms of their leave or fighting would be six or twelve strokes of the birch, a punishment which was given to boy sailors until 1906, when it was replaced by caning. The flogging of adult sailors was suspended in 1879 and never resumed, but it was not formally abolished until 1949.

George may well have committed minor misdemeanours as a boy rating, but there is no indication on his service record that he was ever put under punishment or supervision for disciplinary reasons or poor performance. From the start of his service and throughout his career, his character is marked by officers as 'VG' (very good) on his naval record, which in fact meant that George met the normal standards expected of all Royal Navy ratings.

He lived a peripatetic life as a young sailor. After his initial training at Devonport on HMS *Impregnable,* he was posted in February 1875, aged seventeen, to HMS *Cambridge*,[2] a wooden-walled gunnery training ship permanently moored in Plymouth Sound, and he became a gunnery specialist. He returned to HMS *Cambridge* several times, and also served on many other ships, ones with splendid names such as *Boadicea, Undaunted* and *Renown,* and particularly HMS *Defiance,* to which he had many postings.

Sailors in the Victorian Navy spent most of their time at sea, with little time ashore. But the 1881 census, taken on 3 April that year, records the twenty-three-year-old George as a seaman from HMS *Cambridge* who was resident that night as a lodger at the Sailors' Rest and Institute at 56 Fore Street, Devonport. This was the hostel for sailors that had been opened by the philanthropist and temperance campaigner Agnes, or 'Aggie', Weston[3] in May 1876, offering them a place to eat and a bed for the night. They were also encouraged to refrain from alcohol and take the pledge of teetotal abstinence. No doubt the men were grateful for some home comforts, but in return one young rating recalled that he was 'made to sing hymns while a woman played the piano'. George's brother, William, is also recorded in the 1881 census, aged twenty-five, as a crew member of HMS *Audacious* in Devonport, working as a 'yeoman, stores'.

On 2 May 1886, the twenty-eight-year-old George married Emma Elizabeth Bayley,[4] aged twenty-three, at the Morice Street Wesleyan Chapel in Devonport. Emma had been born in 1863 in Wadebridge, north Cornwall, the daughter of a blacksmith, Joseph Hercules Bayley, who came from Devonport and later returned there. At the time of their marriage, George Lancaster was a Seaman RN on HMS *Defiance* and Emma was living with her parents at 17 Canterbury Street, next to Mount Wise Barracks. Her blacksmith father no doubt obtained a good deal of work from the stables and horse-yard at these military barracks, from the adjacent dockyard and on the ships and boats in the busy harbour at Mutton Cove just around the corner, at the bottom of James Street.

The newly-married George and Emma rented accommodation from a butcher called Mr William Cole at 26 Martin Terrace, Morice Town, in the northern part of Devonport. They took some rooms in this three-storeyed Victorian terrace house on the long, busy Keyham Road between Albert Road and St James Place.

Although living in a town of naval dockyards and military barracks, George and Emma began their married life in the England of 1886, a country still enjoying the peace of Victoria's reign as the Queen approached her Golden Jubilee. But on the national scene there were ominous signs of social and political fracture. In February 1886, the Liberal Leader, William Gladstone, was elected Prime Minister for the third time, and his first Irish Home Rule Bill was the most controversial issue that summer. Gladstone wished to grant Ireland, then ruled by the British, a measure of self-government, with a devolved Irish assembly exercising limited powers. The bill was bitterly opposed by the Ulster Protestants, who feared rule by the Catholic majority in Ireland, and with the support of the Conservatives and anti-home rule Liberals the proposed law was defeated in Parliament. Gladstone called another General Election in July 1886, which he lost. The enduring issues of Irish nationalism and devolution for countries within the United Kingdom would dominate British domestic politics for the next century, and beyond.

In the community of Devonport, the debates over Irish Home Rule probably seemed very remote from the experiences of George and Emma and their neighbours. In 1886 the topic of real interest to local people was the foundation that autumn of the Argyle Football Club, the association football team later known as Plymouth Argyle FC. The club played its first match on 16 October 1886 against a Cornish team called Caxton, and lost 2–0.

George and Emma's eldest son, George Samuel Lancaster, was born on 4 February 1887. Emma gave birth to little George at home, as did most Victorian women at a time when there were no antibiotics and there was a real risk of infection in hospital maternity wards from germs on doctors' hands and unsterilised instruments. Only women whose labours were likely to be difficult would go to the local voluntary hospital, and in 1905 a survey showed that over 95 per cent of mothers still gave birth at home. Emma was probably assisted at the baby's delivery by her mother, or she might have hired a woman who worked in the community as a nurse and who could administer chloroform, the only form of pain relief then available. Her husband was certainly not present and would most likely have been away at sea on his ship, *Defiance*.

Baby George was baptised on 23 February 1887 in the Parish Church of St Mary, his baptismal record showing 26 Martin Terrace as his address. Emma became pregnant again within two months, and George's sister Ellen Emma (named after her Liverpool grandmother, and often called Nell or Nellie) was also born at home in Martin Terrace on 27 January 1888.

Part of the terrace, including number 26, still stands in 2015, looking quite dilapidated, next to what is now called St Martin's Terrace car park, which has replaced the remainder of the terrace, long since demolished (perhaps following bomb damage). Across the road, behind the North Dockyard wall and the Victorian clock tower, are the huge sheds of the frigate refitting complex in the privatised dockyard now operated for the Ministry of Defence by Babcock Engineering.

George and Emma's third child, Joseph Hercules, named after his maternal grandfather, was born in 1890, and by 1891 they had left Martin Terrace. The national census, taken on 5 April 1891, shows that Emma and the three children were back in the south of Devonport at her parents' house at 17 Canterbury Street while George was away at sea. It was a crowded household, for Emma and her three children shared the small terraced house with her parents, Joseph and Emma, her four unmarried brothers and sisters, plus a married sister living there with her husband and baby son.

A photograph of the three Lancaster children taken at this time shows three-year-old George, with blond hair, wearing a sailor suit and holding a naval straw boater, a rather plump curly-haired little Ellen, aged two, and baby Joseph lying between them on a large bearskin rug.

A fourth child, Alfred George, was born in 1894, and by the late 1890s the Lancaster family had moved up the road from Emma's parents to a house at 8 Canterbury Street. Although he is shown as the householder in the Plymouth Street directories of the time, George probably rented the house from the manorial landowners, the St Aubyn Estate, as it was very unusual for men of his social class to buy houses in the late nineteenth century.

Canterbury Street linked Prospect Row and Mount Street, and it was just a street away from the Devonport Guildhall in Ker Street and the adjacent Devonport Column. These buildings were erected in 1824 to commemorate George IV's decree that the town be renamed Devonport instead of its former name of Plymouth Dock. This followed a petition to the King from the proud inhabitants who sought independent status for their increasingly prosperous main port of Devon. Both the Guildhall and Column were restored and reopened in 2012.

Canterbury Street was also just a few hundred yards east of the dockyard wall in James Street, and a similar distance north of the Mount Wise Barracks, which was a depot for army ordnance and military engineers. The high limestone wall to these barracks still stands in 2015 at Locks Walk, although Canterbury Street has long since disappeared under the post-war housing development of the 1950s and 1960s.

The Lancaster family lived in one of the many rows of small terraced houses in the centre of this late Victorian working-class community, where livelihoods depended on employment in the armed forces or in the dockyard as shipwrights, fitters and boilermakers, working as mariners and boatmen in the local harbours, or in allied trades such as plumbing and carpentry. Since becoming a Chief Petty Officer in the Royal Navy in 1893, George could rely on a secure income, but Emma was always dependent on her husband giving her a sufficient allowance from his pay to feed and clothe her growing family. She would have no control over his money, and had none of her own.

Devonport's main commercial thoroughfare was Fore Street, leading from the dockyard gates past the Sailors' Rest and up to the Granby and Raglan Barracks. It was always busy with pedestrians, handcarts and horse-drawn carriages and wagons, and lined with community halls, hotels, shops and public houses. But Emma was able to do her daily shopping in her immediate locality, as Canterbury Street intersected with Pembroke Street, where nearly all the premises were shops, hotels, pubs or lodging houses.

Emma bought the family's food and household supplies from the many victuallers (general stores), grocers, dairies, bakeries, butchers or fish and tripe shops in Pembroke Street. There were boot- and shoemakers at numbers 7 and 26, and she could buy fabrics, hats and clothes at the draper's shop at number 49. She could go to the hairdresser round the corner at number 20 Pembroke Street, and obtain medicines from the chemist at number 22. Lamp oil was purchased from the merchants at number 64, furniture was sold by dealers at numbers 80 and 107, and if times were hard there was a pawnbroker at number 91.[5]

When home on leave, George senior could drink at one of the many beer houses in the street or at the Royal Sovereign Inn on the corner, buy his tobacco at the nearby tobacconist's shop and get papers from the newsagent at number 39.

While their menfolk travelled overseas on tours of duty, there was little need for the wives of Devonport to go any distance from their houses, where they would be fully occupied every day preparing meals, cleaning, washing and laundering, and labouring at their many household chores in an age before any electrical appliances eased their burdens.

Emma could enjoy some recreational activities, such as taking the children to the nearby Devonport Park. Some thirty-seven acres of land was laid out as a park in 1858 for the purpose of healthy recreation by the public. In 1894, the Council extended it and improved the landscaping and walks with more park benches, a bandstand and pitches for cricket and rugby. The Lancaster family also went for occasional trips on pleasure boats from Mutton Cove, and visited the new Plymouth Promenade Pier below the Hoe, opened in May 1884.

Sometime in the 1890s, George and Emma commissioned two formal portrait photographs of themselves which the photographer then colourised, a common technique in those days. They show a bearded George in his naval uniform, wearing a medal, with the insignia of a gunner on both of his lapels. Alongside is a similarly formal photograph of his wife, wearing a high-necked dark dress and blue collar with a brooch and earrings. Both of them are unsmiling, perhaps rather nervous and worried by this new experience of being photographed, but anxious to present a suitable appearance for posterity.

Another formal family photograph, probably taken in the late 1900s, is of an older George, still with beard, and Emma with their four grown-up children, George, Nell, Joe and Alf. The parents again both appear as rather severe-looking figures in this photograph, as father George does in later surviving family snaps of him.

An explanation for their stern demeanour may be found in the 1901 Census record, which refers to them as having seven children, including three deceased infants. Emma's seven pregnancies had resulted in an infant mortality rate which was not uncommon for the times.

School and Apprenticeship

In 1892, George and Emma's eldest child, George Samuel, aged five, went to the local infants' school, the Mount Street Board School, which was around the corner from the Lancasters' home in Canterbury Street.

George's generation of pupils was more fortunate in their schooling than their parents had been. The Elementary Education Act of 1870, the work of the Liberal MP William Forster, established formal schooling for children aged five to ten in England and Wales, with later legislation making elementary education compulsory in 1880 and free of charge in 1891.

At the age of seven, in 1894 George left his infants' school to attend the Stoke Public School in Keppel Place, Devonport, which had been founded in 1819 for the education of forty boys from the Stoke Damerel parish. Following the building of three extensions after the 1870 legislation required councils to provide education, by 1890 the Stoke Public School had been divided into Lower and Higher Departments and provided education for some 500 boys and 300 girls. Five-sixths of the pupils were children of men employed by the Admiralty, who would have included naval crew, such as George's father, and dockyard workers.

The school's Approved Scheme of Instruction included lessons in English, arithmetic, geography, history, elementary science, algebra, Euclid (geometry) and shorthand, with additional instruction in drawing, singing and physical training. In the Higher School the older pupils were also taught mathematics, French, Latin and natural science. This curriculum was in line with the 1870 Education Act's objective of preparing working-class British children in the maintained schools for work in an increasingly industrialised economy, enabling Great Britain to compete with the growing manufacturing nations across Europe and the rest of the world.

The pupils' literary education was not neglected. They engaged in frequent poetry recitations, learning by rote the verse of well-known poets, including Sir Walter Scott's *Waterloo* and *The Lady of the Lake,*

Longfellow's *The Wreck of the Hesperus*, Macaulay's *Horatius,* and other poems such as Southey's *After Blenheim* and Bayard Taylor's *A Night with a Wolf.*

George was a good pupil, and at Christmas 1900, aged thirteen, he was awarded a prize by the Stoke Public Higher School for 'Special Progress, Form VII, Class 1'. The prize was an adventure story set on a Pacific island called *The Secret of the Fire Mountain* by K.M. Eady. His school prepared boys for the dockyard apprentice examinations in April each year, and George was working for this examination, which he would sit a few months later in April 1901.

He also attended the Sunday School at St John's Church in Duke Street, Devonport, where for attendance and good conduct he was awarded Certificates of Merit and annual prize books, including *Tim's Troubles* by M.A. Paull at Christmas 1897 and a book called *Almost a Hero, or School Days at Ashcombe – A Tale for Boys* in December 1900. This tale by Robert Richardson is set in a late-Victorian public school similar to Rugby School, which features in the contemporary novel *Tom Brown's Schooldays*; the sort of school which boys from George's very different social background may have read about with some envy.

Many of George's contemporaries in Devonport attended the Royal Military and Naval Free School in King Street, a maintained voluntary school that provided elementary education from the age of seven to fourteen for the sons and daughters of soldiers, sailors and other mariners in the town, with separate schools for boys and girls.

The log book for the Royal Military and Naval Free School for the years 1895–1901 survives,[6] and it gives a fascinating insight into life in Devonport schools at significant times in the last few years of the long reign of Queen Victoria, when George was a boy.

The number of pupils at the Boys' School was between 300 and 370, but the daily attendance levels varied dramatically. The Headmaster, Mr Steed (annual salary £226), frequently records in the log book his concerns over poor attendance owing to sickness, truancy and trivial reasons. Despite the 1880 legislation making education compulsory, many parents regularly kept their older children out of school to do paid work to increase the family income. The log records eighty boys absent on 20 March 1896, more than 100 absent on 25 May 1897, and on 15 September 1897 some 220 pupils did not attend school.

Mr Steed had a staff of only nine teachers, many of whom took leave of absence themselves from time to time owing to illness or to take professional exams, or to move to other posts. The classes were large, and judging by some of the Head's comments, some teachers clearly found it difficult to keep discipline or to obtain the expected level of results in the regular examinations in the Three Rs – reading, writing and arithmetic.

Problem parents were also a challenge, even in those deferential days. On 25 January 1899, the Headmaster had to reprimand one of the parents, a Mrs Linton, who had 'most unwarrantably assaulted' a teacher called Mr Nicholls over some grievance regarding her son. Unsuitable staff also had to be removed. In June 1901 a new assistant teacher called Mr Kendall was suspended and then sacked by Mr Steed following complaints of his ill-treatment of boys, which must have been extreme given the harsh standards of school discipline at the time.

Despite these problems, the annual reports of Her Majesty's Inspectors on the school were consistently positive. In 1896 their report read: 'The discipline and order are very good and the instruction is highly efficient'; in 1897: 'The school is very well-conducted, the order and tone being highly satisfactory and the instruction methodical and intelligent'; in 1898: 'Euclid [geometry] is somewhat weak in the first stage, but in general the results of the examinations in specific subjects are good'; in 1900: 'The school continues to be very ably managed and taught'.

In the town of Devonport, with its Royal Navy port, the dockyard and three army garrisons, the ethos of the armed forces' service for the Crown and Empire was very strong in the community. This is reflected in the number of times the log book records the school closing to mark events of local import or to celebrate national holidays. On 14 October 1896, the Royal Military and Naval Free School closed for the inspection of troops at the nearby Brickfields parade ground by Lord Wolseley. The school also closed every year on 28 June to celebrate the anniversary of Victoria's Coronation Day, and on 20 May for the Queen's birthday.

On Tuesday 22 June 1897, every school in Great Britain closed for Queen Victoria's Diamond Jubilee celebrations, an event of great national rejoicing. The following Saturday, 26 June, Edward, the Prince of Wales, inspected the Jubilee Fleet Review at Spithead: the largest ever assembly of naval power, with twenty-one battleships, fifty-three cruisers, thirty destroyers, twenty-four torpedo boats and many more small craft.

On 25 August 1897, the pupils of the Royal Military and Naval Free School had the afternoon off for the Devonport Regatta, and the school closed again on 18 October 1899 so that the pupils could attend the launching of the battleship HMS *Bulwark* from the dockyard. The closure on 1 October 1900 for the Parliamentary election is understandable. More surprising is the one on 3 July 1899, when the school had a day off 'on account of a large number of tea parties and Barnum & Bailey's Show' – the circus had come to town!

There were more serious reasons for a day's closure of the Devonport schools. At the turn of the century, the Boer War of 1899–1902 between the forces of the British Empire and Dutch settlers (the Boers) in South Africa was in progress, and many local men from the army barracks in Devonport went to fight in that conflict. The Royal Artillery and the Army Service Corps from the Granby Barracks and infantrymen from the Raglan Barracks near the Brickfields were all sent to the war. Royal Navy ships transported soldiers and equipment to and from South Africa and brought back home the injured, many to the General Military Hospital at Stonehouse.

Naval crew from HMS *Doris* were also involved in action against the Boers, and eleven of them were killed. Their ship returned to Devonport with a captured Boer artillery gun, which was later mounted and unveiled as a memorial to them in the grounds of the Military Hospital. The gun can still be seen in Devonport Park.[7]

In March 1900, British forces relieved the siege of Ladysmith in South Africa, and at the Royal Military and Naval Free School, the Headmaster, Mr Steed, addressed his pupils on this event and then closed the school, granting the children a day's holiday to mark the occasion. Two months later, on 21 May 1900, the school closed again to celebrate the relief of Mafeking, another cause for great national rejoicing.

On such high days and holidays, Emma Lancaster had a rare opportunity to leave her domestic drudgery in Canterbury Street and take her children on an outing on a horse-drawn omnibus or, even more exciting, one of the new electric trams recently introduced to Plymouth and Devonport.

On 22 January 1901, Queen Victoria died, aged eighty-one, after a reign of over sixty-three years, truly the end of an era for the people of Great Britain and its Empire. On 1 February, the day before her funeral, Mr Steed addressed the older boys and the girls from the associated school on the Queen's death. Later that day he recorded the following account in the log book:

> The funeral of Victoria our beloved Queen taking place tomorrow it was thought appropriate to impress on the elder boys and girls something of the overwhelmingly sad importance of the occasion. The children quietly assembled during the afternoon in the Boys' School and a short address was given them by the Hd. Master upon the great bereavement that had befallen our country and the Empire. The children then sang 'Peace, perfect peace' and 'O God our help in ages past' very reverently and after receiving a memento of the mournful occasion in the shape of a printed card bearing the portrait of the Queen they filed out with touching sadness. The short service deeply impressed both teachers and children.

In looking back to the stability of Victoria's reign, and forward to the uncertainty of the future, the words of this eighteenth-century hymn, often sung at state funerals, would have comforted staff and pupils alike at this momentous point in British history.

> *O God, our help in ages past,*
> *Our hope for years to come,*
> *Our shelter from the stormy blast,*
> *And our eternal home.*

Three months after the death of Queen Victoria, in April 1901, George sat the examinations for a dockyard apprenticeship, which he passed. After leaving the Stoke Public Higher School, he was apprenticed at the age of fourteen as a trainee fitter in Devonport Dockyard, becoming a 'yardie'. His Articles of Apprenticeship, dated 26 June 1901, are signed by him and his father, George Lancaster, recording their address as 8 Canterbury Street in Devonport. George senior, now aged forty-three, had joined the Royal Fleet Reserve in Devonport on 1 March 1901 and was no longer serving away at sea.

The Royal Dockyard at Devonport had been building warships for over two centuries. Following the accession of the joint monarchs William III and his wife Queen Mary II to the throne in 1689, King William had ordered the building of a new dockyard in the West Country, and his Surveyor of the Navy, Edward Dummer, had found a suitable site on the Devon side of the Hamoaze.

Dummer, a naval engineer and ship-builder, supervised the construction of the new dockyard, including the first successful stepped stone dry dock in Europe, and in the eighteenth and nineteenth centuries the dockyard was the main employer in the Three Towns. The monumental Royal William Victualling Yard, designed by the civil engineer Sir John Rennie, was also built between 1826 and 1835 in nearby Stonehouse on a sixteen-acre site. This was named after the then reigning William IV, known as the 'Sailor King', whose statue still stands over the impressive gateway, and the yard supplied the ships of the Royal Navy with food and stores until 1992.

Young George's six-year course of apprenticeship was no doubt a tough induction into working life in a period when the dockyard was still building warships. In that first decade of the twentieth century, the changing international situation was producing a demand for many much bigger and more powerful battleships. It was to be the era of the 'dreadnoughts'.

Queen Victoria was succeeded by her eldest son, who became Edward VII – and it was from Victoria's grandson Wilhelm, the nephew of Edward VII, that there came a new threat in the form of growing German imperialism.

The Royal Navy ships of the Home Fleet, the Atlantic Fleet and the Mediterranean Fleet, along with the ships based in the Caribbean, the Indian Ocean and on the China Station in the Far East, ensured that the sea lanes of the British Empire across the globe were kept open and that Great Britain's commercial interests were supported. The Royal Navy underpinned Britain's colonial rule throughout the nineteenth century and for much of the twentieth century.

In 1889 the Naval Defence Act established the principle of the 'Two Power Standard', whereby the Royal Navy's fleet had to be maintained at a strength larger than the combined fleet of the two other largest navies in the world. Over the next twenty-five years expenditure on the Royal

Navy would greatly increase, doubling between 1900 and 1913 so that naval spending constituted over half of the total defence budget. Such was the importance of its navy to the British Empire.

The Prussian victory over France in the Franco-Prussian War of 1870–71 and Chancellor Bismarck's unification of several German states into the new nation of Germany produced a young, ambitious and economically strong country, its universities and industries forging ahead in science and engineering. Germany now wished to establish its own world empire to rival or surpass that of Great Britain.

In 1888 Wilhelm succeeded to the German imperial throne as the Kaiser. Wilhelm II was an insecure, unstable and militaristic individual who wanted to challenge Great Britain's global maritime supremacy, maintained by the Royal Navy since Nelson's victory at Trafalgar in 1805. In common with many naval strategists across the globe, Wilhelm was deeply influenced by a book published in 1890 by an American naval historian, Alfred Thayer Mahan, called *The Influence of Sea Power upon History*. This espoused the concept of the geo-political power of nations being determined by battles between huge fleets of heavily armed battleships and cruisers. The Kaiser was convinced that Germany too could advance its territorial claims through the creation of a strong naval force.

In 1898 and 1900 Germany passed its Navy Acts, by which the Kaiser and his Secretary of State of Naval Affairs, Admiral Tirpitz, planned the creation of a new Navy comprising thirty-eight battleships, twenty armoured cruisers and thirty-eight light cruisers, plus many other coastal vessels.

Following the accession of Edward VII in 1901, the threat to Britain of the German naval ambitions was increasingly recognised and the race between the two nations to build more powerful and faster ships was under way. Germany already had the most powerful army in Europe, but in 1904 Germany's military budget was 35 per cent lower than Great Britain's; a decade later, largely as a result of the doubling in size of the Kaiser's navy, that budget was 40 per cent higher than Britain's.

After some years of being run down, the challenge from the German Empire brought a period of expansion for Devonport Dockyard, and new British warships were built there on its huge site of wharves, jetties, dry docks, berths, basins, cranes and slipways which sprawled along the east waterfront of the Hamoaze.

On 7 and 8 March 1902, Edward VII and his wife, Queen Alexandra, visited Devonport, and the Queen launched HMS *Queen*, at that time the largest ship ever built for the Royal Navy. In reply to the speech by the Mayor of Devonport, the King said: "It has interested me much to see the vast dockyards, arsenals and barracks of Devonport which are of such importance to the strength and welfare of my naval and military forces, and give employment to so many inhabitants of the town which has grown rapidly around them. I pray heartily that your municipality may continue to grow in efficiency and prosperity."

Edward VII's prayer was already coming to fruition. In 1899, the Government had decided to build a vast new complex at Devonport Dockyard on 114 acres of reclaimed land at Keyham, to the north of the original site. A year after the King's visit, his son, Prince George, also visited Devonport Dockyard in July 1903 with his wife Princess Mary to view the building works and to launch a new battleship, HMS *King Edward VII*.

In June 1904, with Great Britain and Germany both expanding their navies, King Edward visited Germany at the invitation of his nephew, Kaiser Wilhelm, to inspect its fleet. A month later, on 10 July 1904, a squadron of several German battleships and cruisers arrived in Plymouth Sound on a return goodwill visit, watched by thousands of people from the Three Towns who crowded on to Plymouth Hoe and the seafront. The German crews were entertained, with a Mayoral banquet for the officers and picnics and an evening at Aggie Weston's Royal Sailors' Rest in Devonport arranged for the men. This visit did draw some criticism in the national press, and questions were asked in Parliament as to why some German naval officers had been given access to Devonport Dockyard where the major extension works were still under way.

New commanders who did appreciate the German threat were now being promoted to the top of the Royal Navy hierarchy and they were determined to make changes to the culture and practices of the Senior Service. These men included the charismatic John Fisher, appointed as First Sea Lord in 1902.

As part of his radical reforms of the Royal Navy,[8] Admiral Sir John Fisher wanted to develop its warships' firepower and speed, and he introduced a new type of battleship, the dreadnought. This groundbreaking class had an all-big-gun armament of ten 12-inch guns[9] and a fast speed of 21 knots, powered by the new Parsons steam turbine engines.

The launch of the first of these ships, HMS *Dreadnought*, at Portsmouth on 3 October 1906 galvanised an international race for bigger and faster ships between seafaring nations across the world. France, Italy, Japan and, above all, Germany began to develop their own dreadnought-class warships. Such was the British public's support for the building of more and more dreadnoughts that a popular slogan of the time was 'We want eight and we won't wait'. This was despite the great cost of these ships – HMS *Dreadnought* herself cost £1,783,883, equivalent to nearly £190 million at current prices. The introduction of the dreadnought-class also had the effect of making all previous types of warship – the pre-dreadnoughts – obsolete.

Prince George and Princess Mary returned to Devonport on 21 February 1907 to open the Keyham Extension. The project had taken eight years, involved nearly 3,500 men, doubled the size of the existing yard and required the development of a new residential district, Weston Mill, to house the additional workers.

George was an apprentice and engine fitter at Devonport Dockyard from 1901 to 1909, during its decade of expansion and throughout this period of rapid development in ship construction. He was among the yard's workforce reviewed by the King and the Prince of Wales on their visits in 1902 and 1903, and by those German naval officers in 1904.

George took his School Certificate at the dockyard as an apprentice in July 1903, when his conduct was described on the certificate as 'excellent' and his progress as 'fair'. After a six-year apprenticeship at the dockyard, he received his Certificate of Competency and Character on 25 June 1907 when he was twenty. He was now a qualified engine fitter.

George worked on the new warships, including HMS *Temeraire*, one of the new dreadnought-class of battleships launched at Devonport in August 1907. The working conditions in the dry docks where warships were built, refitted and repaired were harsh. It was heavy, hot and dirty work for the teams of fitters in the engine room down in the bowels of the ship, with the constant noise of hammering, welding and riveting, no protective clothing or equipment and little regard in those days for health and safety. Scalding from the super-heated steam in the engines was just one of the occupational hazards for the men, and George suffered a serious scald to his chest which left him with a scar for life.

Admiral Fisher had also pioneered the development of a new type of armoured cruiser, known as a 'battlecruiser' – a class of ships which were lighter, faster and cheaper than the dreadnoughts. The new facility at Devonport enabled the dockyard to build the battlecruiser HMS *Indefatigable*, which was launched in October 1909.

During George's eight years in the dockyard, naval construction was undergoing major changes in the era of Fisher's dreadnought-class battleships and his new battlecruisers. The installation of the larger calibre guns on the turrets, the transition from coal to oil to power the ships and, most important, the new turbine engines and boilers all involved the radical redesign of warships.

The heavier guns and engines affected in particular the level of armour protection on the battlecruisers. In order to achieve a top speed of 25 knots, the tonnage of these ships had to be reduced by their designers, and it was the thickness of the ship's armoured belt that was sacrificed. The battlecruisers' main armoured belt was only 6 inches thick as opposed to the 11-inch belt on battleships. For his new class of cruiser, Fisher claimed that 'speed is the best protection', and that 'hitting is the thing, not armour'.

Speed at sea required good engines. As an engine fitter, George worked on both the older reciprocating triple-expansion steam engines and, after the introduction of the dreadnought-class battleship, the new Parsons steam turbines, as installed in HMS *Temeraire* and HMS *Indefatigable*. Operating the huge, thundering reciprocating engines was difficult and dangerous work, while the new turbines were cleaner, quieter, safer and much more efficient. The turbines did not require as much room as the tall reciprocating engines, so the height of the engine room could be lowered, allowing more space on the ship for armament.

Admiral Sir Reginald Bacon, who had been the first captain of HMS *Dreadnought* and was described by Fisher as 'the cleverest officer in the Navy', wrote:

No greater single step towards efficiency in war was ever made than the introduction of the turbine. Previous to its adoption every day's steaming at high speed meant several days' overhaul of machinery in harbour. All this was changed as if by magic.

These far-sighted admirals, Fisher and Bacon, knew that the quality of its engineering, and its engineers, would be vital to the success of the Royal Navy in the twentieth century.

Recreation

A central part of George's social life in the 1900s was the St John's (Devonport) Recreation Club, which he joined in 1906, aged nineteen. This was an all-male private club, similar to the working men's clubs common in industrial towns, but this one was associated with the church that gave the club its name and where George had attended Sunday School as a boy.

In October 1893, two young men who were Sunday School teachers at this church founded a walking group called the St John's Amateur Pedestrian Association, and they organised walks from Devonport out to Bickleigh Vale on the edge of Dartmoor, or across Plymouth to Plymbridge Woods. The group's activities were extended to boating on the Tamar with the acquisition from Kesslers, a local boatyard, of two small boats called *Emma* and *Arctic* – described as 'old, patched and occasionally leaky'.

The membership grew, and the association was renamed the St John's (Devonport) Recreation Club, with its clubhouse at 58 Chapel Street. The club flag was initially blue with a gold horseshoe, and in 1897 the flag became a white ensign with a blue diamond to commemorate the Queen's Diamond Jubilee that year, the gold horseshoe emblem within the diamond. Reflecting the club's maritime location, its senior elected officer was known as 'The Captain'.

The members, the majority of whom were young men, could play billiards, snooker, whist and draughts at the club, with home and away team fixtures for the billiards league and club tournaments for the other games. The club acquired two rather better boats, *Rambler* and *President*, for river excursions. It amalgamated with a local rugby club in 1909, and in 1910 a cycling club was started for members for an additional annual subscription of sixpence, the same as for the boating club.

But the club was much more than a working men's club providing alcohol, sport and light entertainment. Club members took part in the Annual Church Parade, and, with its President always being the Vicar of St John's, its church associations influenced its educational programme to a great extent. Its members, and their wives, were the first generation to benefit from the compulsory state-funded education for boys and girls introduced by Forster's Elementary Education Act in 1870. The development of such clubs, and other contemporary national movements such as the Workers' Education Association (founded in 1903), the nascent Labour Party and women's suffrage, reflected a greater appetite among working men, and women of all classes, for knowledge and engagement in current affairs.

In 1909, some of the members with journalistic aspirations decided to publish the *Horseshoe Magazine* as the monthly 'unofficial organ' of the club. They typed up and reproduced several copies of the magazine, using one of the stencil duplicator machines patented by David Gestetner in the 1880s. Each issue had a different and beautifully hand-painted cover showing a sailing boat, a Greek goddess, a view from Mount Edgcumbe or a sunrise.

The *Horseshoe Magazine* is a fascinating publication which reflects the social activities of that generation of young men in Edwardian England whose lives were to change so dramatically just five years later. These men, who would be labelled 'working class' or 'lower middle class' according to the traditional socio-economic categorisation of twentieth-century Britain, demonstrated in their writing an articulate level of engagement in current affairs and strikingly high standards of literacy and expression, as well as a rather quirky sense of humour.

In its first edition in September 1909, the editorial states:

TO OUR READERS: it is with great pleasure that we submit this, the first number of our new venture for your perusal.

The 'Horseshoe' is first and foremost to be readable – light topical articles and comments, amusing yet just touched with enough of the graver side to be of value to the Club – we trust that this magazine will link even closer the bonds of good fellowship and friendship between the Members and call forth a strong patriotism for the Club.

Football, Billiard and Sub-Editors have been appointed and are on the lookout for 'copy' – while the Club 'Crank' for whose views we cannot accept any responsibility, will with pointed good humour monthly contribute comments from all quarters. The tame Poet will also rhyme topically as occasion permits.

We anticipate that the Correspondence Column will prove a great source of interest and amusement.

This is an 'Unofficial' organ and we are not therefore bound by convention but to be a power for good work in the Club – to raise interest in current events, and to rally the Members round the old Club is the earliest desire of the whole Staff, including:
Your sincere friend,
THE EDITOR

As part of its educational mission to raise interest in current affairs, the club ran a debating society, and the December 1909 edition of the *Horseshoe* included a report of a mock Parliamentary debate:

With the idea of stimulating the interest of members in debating in general, and politics in particular, the Committee arranged a debate on Free Trade and Tariff Reform.

Individual club members assumed the roles of the Prime Minister, the Leader of the Opposition, the Speaker and the Hon. Members of Parliament for Devonport, Plymouth and Saltash respectively, each giving speeches in a lively debate during which order had to be restored:

…when an Hon. Member called the attention of the Speaker to the condition of the Hon. Member for Plymouth, who appeared to his own supporters to be suffering from a fit of hysteria, and to his opponents, something far worse.

In subsequent years the club held debates on 'Socialism', 'Should profes-sionalism in sport be abolished?' and, in January 1913, 'Conscription'. By then, the club members, mostly servicemen or workmen in the dockyard building battleships, must have been more conscious of the growing men-ace of war.

The club promoted musical programmes, including a 'Smoking Concert' in October 1909 with several songs contributed by member soloists and performances on the piano and concertina. There was also some Shakespearean drama that year: a presentation of the trial scene from *The Merchant of Venice*.

In December 1909, one member, Mr F. Ware, took on the task of organising a Subscription Ball, an initiative not entirely welcomed by some members, who perhaps objected to inviting ladies to their club activities. The venture was a great success, though, and the *Horseshoe* reported a scene, and in a style, reminiscent of Jane Austen:

> Friday December 3rd, was a wet, cold night outside – but, inside the Granby Hall was a scene of mirth and joy. About seventy-five were assembled under the auspices of the Club for a Ball, and should any chance visitor have appeared, he would have beheld an exceedingly pretty scene – the ladies all in light dresses – gentlemen in stately black, the maze of moving figures, a happy ripple of laughter, bright faces beaming, such as one (unless he is a misanthrope) must have gone away with a lighter heart, for nothing in this world lightens a good heart more than seeing young people happy in pretty surroundings.
>
> The Ballroom was tastefully decorated. The Music was bright and popular tunes made hearts, already light, carol out occasionally the entertaining ditties of the day.
>
> Twenty-eight dances appeared on the Programme and all twenty-eight were danced – and all went happy as a marriage bell.
>
> Refreshments, in demand particularly during the intervals, were served in the inside room by volunteer Staff from the Club.
>
> With such trifles 'dancing and eating' – the time flew merrily on and 2 a m was reached before we quite realised it was past midnight. The last Waltz, danced with an energy equal to the first, commenced at 1.50 and finished about 2 – when it seemed strange that six hours had passed since 'the fun began'.
>
> Certainly the whole thing was a great success, and although we deprecate the idea of running too many, yet as an Annual Event at least, the Subscription Ball has, we venture to think, come to stay.

The Club's Annual Dinner remained resolutely an all-male affair, and fortunately George kept his Annual Dinner cards. The first card is for the twelfth Annual Dinner in 1906, the year when George joined. It was held at Sleeman's Restaurant in Old Town Street, Plymouth, also the venue for the 1910 and 1911 dinners. Other annual dinner cards are from 1909 (at the Royal Hotel, Devonport), 1912 (at Day's Restaurant in Devonport) and the last in 1913 when the nineteenth Annual Dinner was on Saturday 18 January at the Criterion Restaurant in Devonport.

The menus for all of these dinners were very lavish affairs, with some five or six courses consisting of soup; fish – boiled cod, oyster sauce, fillets of sole; joints – roast beef, boiled leg of mutton, poultry; sweets; and cheese and celery to finish.

The cards' Toasts Lists name the people proposing toasts, and included ones to the King and Royal Family, the President and Vice-President, the club itself, old members – home and abroad – and the club teams (football and billiards). No 'Toast to the ladies', as none were present.

During or after the meal, some of the members would make music – the Song Lists on the back of the dinner cards list various songs performed, with an accompanist, by gentlemen of the club, including 'Songs (humorous)'. The 1910 dinner card names some of the songs for that evening – 'The Flying Dutchman', 'The Old Campaigner', 'Widdecombe Fair' and 'The Highwayman' – and it also names some of the many performers – Mr W.J. Phillips, Mr H. Whitelock and Mr J. Ronson (who was George's future brother-in-law, Jack, the husband of his sister Ellen, who married him in October 1911).

Dinner entertainment also included a pianoforte selection, a recitation, a gramophone selection (quite an innovation in those early days of recordings) and a banjo selection. The evening's proceedings would always conclude with everyone singing 'Auld Lang Syne'.

In this church-based club, some older members disapproved of the more indulgent social activities, as there was a strong and long-established Puritan tradition in the Three Towns.[10] The social problems and violence caused by alcohol in this naval port with a pub on most street corners had produced an active temperance movement in Devonport, supported by organisations such as the Devon Temperance League and the Royal Naval Temperance Society, which advocated total abstinence from alcohol. The older congregation of St John's, being a 'low' Anglican church, was closely aligned to the non-conformist Methodists and their abhorrence of strong drink, gambling and other such self-indulgent amusements.

The Editor of the *Horseshoe* magazine was keen to generate a lively Correspondence Column in the new journal, and in each edition he included letters from an anonymous member, writing under the pseudonym of 'Purist', who expressed sternly critical opinions as to the prevalence of gambling, smoking and dancing in the club. Any attempt by him to suggest abstinence from alcohol would have been a step too far for the club members. The views of Purist were clearly exaggerated and provocative even for England in the 1900s, and were undoubtedly written by one of the magazine's own staff in order to elicit ostensibly outraged but often witty ripostes from members, which were published in the next issue.

This was Purist on gambling:

> Sir – May I as a member of the Club use your columns to protest... our Rules are emphatic that no gambling may be indulged in on the Club Premises, yet this rule is habitually broken, not only by the common or garden members but by all the prominent officials – I allude of course to the practice of the loser paying for the game on our Billiard Table.

Purist's views on 'Infantile Smoking' were more in accord with those of a century later, but were probably regarded as laughable by the men of 1909:

> Will you allow me to call your attention to another matter which I consider a disgrace to the name of our Club, to wit:– the practice of allowing the pernicious habit of smoking to be indulged in on the Club premises – we cannot but consider the Club is run to a certain extent on money derived from the ruination of the bodies and souls of its younger, and alas some of its older members: I mean on the profits derived from the sale of cigarettes.
>
> Sir, can anyone describe a more pitiable spectacle than that which is frequently to be seen in our Club of young lads (I had almost said boys) sitting in the corner of the Club Room proudly smoking a cigarette and reading sporting news in the Herald, and to add to the pathos thinking how manly they look, whilst all the time the elder members of the Club are inwardly smiling at their asinine affectation.

This letter provoked a response from a correspondent calling himself 'Anti-Cant':

Sir – Your Correspondent 'Purist' has probably joined our Club under a misapprehension – He undoubtedly should be a member of a Kintergarten [sic] School where all the sweet little Cherubs sit sucking their fingers all day long…

I myself am almost a non-smoker, but I recognise that the average young man of 18 or 19 years of age is surely entitled to decide for himself whether the habit is beneficial or otherwise, and personally I think he is much better employed in sitting in the Club, even if he is smoking, than toiling through muddy lanes arm in arm with a person of the opposite sex as I have a shrewd suspicion that your sanctimonious correspondent may be discovered doing.

It were better, Sir, if before endeavouring to remove the mote from his brother's eye, he were to cast it from his own and cease writing what can only be considered slanders about other members of the Club who venture to think for themselves and indulge in smoking in spite of such puritanical humbugs as your correspondent.

The undesirability of consorting with the opposite sex was taken up by Purist in his next letter:

I am sure that anyone who thinks for himself cannot but be dismayed by noticing how insidiously the terrible evil of DANCING is working its way into our Club…Now Sir, it is an undisputed fact that dancing has a great tendency to lead young men just arriving on the verge of manhood into those obvious paths which they should all endeavour to avoid and we as a Club should on no account assist in encouraging them to indulge in the habit. Dancing, taking place in a hot room, with the germs of every known and unknown disease being beaten into the air by the constant stamping, cannot fail to be most unhealthy – Added to this we see young lads of Eighteen years with young girls of the same age starting on their homeward journey at 2 o'clock in the morning, overheated, overfatigued and consequently particularly liable to contract a chill from the keen night air.

This rant from Purist produced in the next issue a letter signed 'Terpsichore'[11] expounding the moral and physical benefits of dancing, together with an attack on 'the character of Purist as he has revealed it to us in his letters':

We find him, I think, a neurotic person, on whom the very mention of the word 'Tobacco' seems to have a terrible effect; a Miser, in that he is afraid to play Billiards because he may have to pay for the game, and again one who appears to be walking the streets at 2 o'clock in the morning that he may spy on those who doubtless call him friend; his knowledge (how and what obtained?) of the ages of the lady friends of his fellow members and the unblushing way in which he makes use of this knowledge: a breach of all the codes of honour. Such, Sir, is the person who is pleased to call himself 'Purist', the self-appointed Censor of the morals of his fellow Club-men. Has he never heard of the saying, so delightfully applicable to himself, 'Unto the pure, all things are pure'.

The entire Purist correspondence, as we have seen, was written by the magazine staff to provide entertaining copy for their new journal, and as a mild satirical spoof of some of the more Puritanical, or Victorian, opinions of their elders in the St John's Church congregation. These letters and the other contributions to the magazine do, however, demonstrate the impressive standard of literacy of both the journalists and their readers, and a fluency of expression that was later to be shown in the letters home that many of these members wrote while on active service in the Great War.

In the autumn of 1909, the club amalgamated with Hope United Football Club, a local rugby club. An earlier proposal at the 1909 AGM to form an Association Football Club had been rejected, as 'soccer' was clearly viewed as an inferior sort of game. The rugby team travelled by train for matches against Falmouth, Camborne, Teignmouth and other towns in South Devon and Cornwall, with more local fixtures, including games with other Devonport church clubs, the Police, the Naval Harlequins and HMS *Lion*.

The October 1909 edition of the *Horseshoe* included a photograph of the rugby team, all fine-looking young men. But the reports of their matches indicate that their record of success was not impressive (they usually lost), and correspondents criticised the players for often failing to turn up (missing the train being a regular issue) and for having insufficient muscle power:

It is generally conceded that the worst fault of the Hope forwards is their lack of weight. Hence the necessity for a Club Dinner.

For the match in February 1910 against the naval mechanics from the training establishment HMS *Indus*:

> Every effort was made to whip up a strong team for the replay [the first match was a draw], but again the spectacle was seen of twelve players of an average weight of 9 stone playing fifteen averaging 13 stone!

The Hope team did well to lose by only 9–8.

The *Horseshoe* carried a variety of feature articles, including an interview in 1910 with an un-named yardie, a worker at the dockyard who had recently completed his six-year apprenticeship, as George had done in 1907. This man had been celebrating his receipt of a 'man's wages' for the first time:

> I went to the Territorials' Ball at St. George's Hall, Stonehouse last week with two or three other ex-apprentices and had a rare time!

The magazine published suggestions for Christmas party games, and there was a report from a member who had visited Philadelphia in the United States over Christmas and New Year on the festivities there. Another writer projected himself forward by fifty years in an article entitled *1959*, a (rather unimaginative) account of how he envisaged the club would be in that far-off year.

In addition to the AGM reports and the publication of Standing Orders for the Management Committee, the magazine's 'Tame Poet' contributed light-hearted but rather tedious rhymes, including one about ice-skating at the local Millbay Rink, and the 'Club Crank' made silly observations in every issue about his fellow members.

Sadly, the *Horseshoe* magazine was published for only six months, from September 1909 to February 1910, after which the editorial staff's energy, ideas and enthusiasm must have failed them, or they ran out of copy and the members' support. But those six issues, bound into 'Volume 1' and kept by George for posterity, reveal a group of likeable, sociable working men of good humour, with a great sense of community spirit and civic responsibility, interested, of course, in sports and games, but also wanting to improve their knowledge of current affairs, music and culture. George himself sought and valued educational opportunities and applied himself to further training and self-improvement throughout his life, and his membership of the club must have promoted his wide-ranging interests and good general knowledge.

By 1913 the club had moved to new premises at 27 St Aubyn Street, Devonport, and George's membership card for the 'Winter syllabus 1913–1914' sets out a programme of fixtures for the general billiard handicap, snooker handicap, cribbage tournament, bezique tournament and the general handicap, (small table). There was also a dance class in the Granby Hall every Thursday (to which presumably women were admitted, provided, of course, that they did not demonstrate suffragist tendencies).

The club had been founded as a Pedestrian Association in 1893, and its group walking activity continued. One weekend when he was twenty-one, George went on a camp with a group of friends from the club to Calstock, a village on the Cornish bank of the river Tamar, and two photographs record their outing. They show several young men clowning around before some white canvas tents, acting up for the camera, making silly faces and posing with a sign at the front which says 'St John's Ramblers' Camp July 1908, Calstock'.

The men in the photographs are in their late teens or early twenties, wearing caps, long-sleeved shirts, waistcoats and braces, and pretending to be in 'Easy Street' according to the sign on the milk churn in the photos. A couple of the lads are playing their banjos, and another is holding his violin. They are smoking pipes, and in one photo a young man in a suit is standing to attention, holding a Union flag.

This is 1908, that relatively carefree Edwardian period of calm before the storm. Most of these young men, including George, would go on either to serve in the Royal Navy's battles at sea or in the trenches during the Great War. How many of them survived?

The Navy

On 21 June 1909 George joined the Royal Navy. He was twenty-two years old, and according to his naval record[12] his occupation prior to enlistment was an 'Engine Fitter and Turner'. His height was 5' 4",[13] he had 'light hair, blue eyes, a fair complexion, and a scar of scald on chest'.

His father had retired from the Royal Navy as a Chief Petty Officer on his fiftieth birthday on 18 February 1908, the normal time of discharge on age grounds. George senior continued working in Devonport Dockyard after his naval discharge as an electrical fitter's labourer to supplement his naval pension, and his younger sons Joseph and Alfred were also working there – Joe as a shipwright and Alf as an apprentice engine fitter.

Why did young George determine on a naval career for himself in 1909? At the age of twenty-two, and after learning a skilled trade as an engine fitter from the age of fourteen through his six-year apprenticeship, he may have been keen, as the eldest Lancaster son, to go to sea like his father. He had grown up imbued with the naval tradition, as evidenced by the photograph of him, aged three, wearing a sailor suit.

In the spring of 1909, George was still living at home with his parents and three younger siblings in the small terraced house in Canterbury Street, with no electricity or hot running water inside and just one outside toilet in the back yard. His father, George, was a stern, unbending man, rather lacking in emotional warmth, his character formed by the loss of his own father at the age of three and an unsettled childhood in Liverpool before he went to sea aged fifteen. His wife, Emma Lancaster, was a woman of limited experience and narrow outlook, quite possibly frustrated with life, and who became more difficult as she grew older.

Their eldest son, George, was clearly a studious young man, receptive to cultural and literary influences, a sensibility probably not shared by his parents. His activities at the Recreation Club and conversations with fellow members had stirred his interest in politics and current affairs, opened up new horizons and developed his ambition to travel and to better himself. George had spent eight years in the dockyard and he did not want to remain a yardie all his life.

A sailor's working conditions on warships were often better than ashore in many factories of the time, where ten- or twelve-hour days were normal, the working routine was monotonous, and unregulated safety standards were low, with frequent industrial accidents.

Naval hours, pay and pensions were also more attractive, shipmates were generally congenial and good at teamworking, and they were able to engage in plenty of sport and exercise. With the British Empire still extending across the globe, 'Join the Navy and see the World' was a real invitation to experience extensive travel overseas. Moreover, in the 1900s more opportunities were opening up for ambitious young men in the Royal Navy, thanks largely to the reforms initiated by the First Sea Lord, Admiral Sir John Fisher, regarded by many as one of the most important leaders ever of the Senior Service.

After a century of unchallenged supremacy since Trafalgar, many admirals in the Royal Navy had become complacent. The risks of a culture of inflexibility and unquestioning obedience from their officers at all times had been epitomised by a naval disaster off the coast of Lebanon in the Mediterranean in 1893, when Admiral Sir George Tryon made a basic blunder in ordering two columns of ships to turn inwards. The resulting collision caused the sinking of his flagship, HMS *Victoria,* and the deaths of 358 men, including Tryon himself.[14]

While attitudes were slow to change, the design and construction of warships had evolved dramatically in the latter half of the nineteenth century. The first iron-hulled and screw-driven steam warship, HMS *Warrior,*[15] was launched in 1860, and the first warship without masts or sails, HMS *Devastation*, was launched in 1871. The guns on the Navy's ships became more and more powerful, the armour plating on their hulls and turrets became thicker. Torpedo boats and mines were being developed in Great Britain and by overseas navies from the mid-nineteenth century, and the use of submarines in the American Civil War in the 1860s heralded the advent of underwater warfare, which was to transform naval strategy in the twentieth century.

Admiral Sir John Arbuthnot Fisher – known as 'Jacky' Fisher – was born in Ceylon (now Sri Lanka), the son of an unsuccessful British tea planter. He had joined the Royal Navy as a thirteen-year-old cadet in 1854 when it was still in the era of wooden warships with sails. As a gunnery instructor and lecturer, he was a pioneer in new technology and tactics, inventing gun-sights to improve accuracy, and writing papers on torpedoes and submarines. He served on ships across the globe and achieved rapid promotion to the rank of captain by the age of thirty-three. He served as a lieutenant on the first HMS *Warrior,* and in 1881 he was appointed the captain of the revolutionary new iron-clad and steam-powered battleship, HMS *Inflexible.*

As First Sea Lord from 1902 and Admiral of the Fleet from 1905, Fisher's wide-ranging but controversial reforms, with their emphasis on economy and efficiency, transformed the highly conservative Victorian Navy into a service ready to meet the threat of the expanding Imperial German Navy – the *Kaiserliche Marine.* Fisher reorganised the distribution of the Royal Navy's fleets, bringing the majority of its ships back from overseas stations across the Empire to home waters, ready for action in the North Sea and the English Channel. He introduced a nucleus crew system for the Reserve Fleet to make its ships ready for war, and scrapped over 150 obsolete warships. He pensioned off many admirals who were resistant to change and promoted, from what became known as the 'Fishpond', those younger officers who supported him, such as John Jellicoe.

Fisher developed the Navy's flotillas of submarines, realising the potential of these boats in naval warfare, unlike some senior officers such as Admiral Sir Arthur Wilson who regarded their use as weapons as 'underhand, unfair and damned un-English.' Fisher also oversaw the transition from coal to oil in the fuelling of warships, not necessarily a popular move as it meant the employment of fewer stokers on board.

Fisher was not troubled by unpopularity and drove through his radical and wide-ranging programme of change in the face of extensive hostility from many senior officers. His determination to implement wholesale reform of the Navy was particularly opposed by the well-known Admiral Lord Charles Beresford, also a Member of Parliament, and this led to a bitter, personal and prolonged feud between the two men which divided the Royal Navy into camps of pro-Fisher reformers and pro-Beresford traditionalists.

Fisher's work culminated in his development of the new classes of battleships and battlecruisers with turbine engines, including the ships which George had worked on when he was an engine fitter in Devonport Dockyard. As previously discussed, the launch of the revolutionary HMS *Dreadnought* in 1906 led to the international naval race in the construction of warships.

Fisher also worked hard to transform the culture of a naval service which had become hidebound by an old-school officer class drawn, as was Beresford, from the nobility and upper classes of society. Many of them, in the absence of active battle service during the long period of peace, had an obsessive concern for rigid discipline and cleanliness and smartness on board ship. It was common for a senior officer to pay very considerable sums out of his own pay for the purchase of good enamel paint for his ship, and to order the crew to spend days painting the vessel: black for the hull, yellow paint on the deck and red markings on the funnels. From 1902, Fisher decreed that all warships should be painted a uniform grey.

Fisher overhauled naval training and examinations and introduced courses in mathematics, science, engineering and electricity for all officer cadets, in addition to the established naval subjects such as navigation, gunnery, signalling and seamanship. In 1903 the former summer residence of Queen Victoria at Osborne House on the Isle of Wight became the Royal Naval College, Osborne, for the training of junior officers. The Royal Naval College at Dartmouth in south Devon was opened in 1905, a shore-based establishment by the River Dart where cadets had previously trained on the moored wooden hulk, HMS *Britannia*.

The social hierarchy of the Royal Navy was also very rigid. Between 1818 and 1902, when Fisher became First Sea Lord, only four men who had started their naval career on the lower deck were promoted to lieutenant rank, in each case for gallantry.[16] In June 1910 the leading service journal, *The Naval and Military Record*, stated that 'We should view with grave apprehension any attempt to officer the fleet at all largely with men of humble birth'. Fisher, whose own family origins were regarded in upper class circles as somewhat dubious, had no such prejudices. He was instead concerned that such exclusive attitudes, and the high fees charged for naval training, were depriving the Royal Navy of a vital pool of talented men. As early as 1902, he wrote 'Let every fit boy have his chance, irrespective of the depth of his parents' purse'. He campaigned to abolish the fees charged at the Osborne and Dartmouth

Naval Colleges for officer training, but although Churchill, as First Lord of the Admiralty[17], largely concurred with Fisher and reduced the fees in 1913, it was not until 1947 that free education for naval cadets was finally introduced.

Two of Fisher's wide-ranging reforms of the Royal Navy may have induced the young George Lancaster to join the service. As sail gave way to steam during Victoria's reign, a culture of snobbery and deference had developed, as the executive 'sailing officers' – officers on the ship's quarter deck, from where the captain had traditionally commanded his sailing vessel – looked down on the engineering officers, whom they regarded as their inferiors and referred to in pejorative terms.

In 1903, Fisher and the First Lord of the Admiralty, the Earl of Selborne, announced a scheme, the Selborne-Fisher Scheme, to amalgamate the executive, or command, branch of the Navy with its engineering branch. Under this, all future officers, including the engineers, would have the same technical training up to the age of twenty-two, and the engineering officers would have the opportunity to achieve a command. The Scheme also introduced the commissioned rank of Chief Artificer Engineer (later re-named Commissioned Engineer). Fisher's recognition of the importance of the engineer's role was a controversial move opposed by many admirals in the Royal Navy, but it must have been encouraging to George as an engine man himself.[18]

Of more relevance to George's own hopes, perhaps, was Fisher's reform that in future warrant officers (a non-commissioned rate) would be able to qualify as commissioned lieutenants, even though this opportunity would not usually be realised until late in a man's career. Ben Wilson in his history of the Royal Navy claims 'It was the victory of middle-class swots over dashing gentlemanly officers'[19]. Nevertheless, the social structure of the Royal Navy remained very rigid and class-conscious, with a wide gulf between the men of the lower deck and their often autocratic officers, trained in Queen Victoria's Navy, who expected unquestioning obedience and maintained a regime of harsh discipline.

In the naval town of Devonport, Admiral Fisher's many far-reaching reforms must have been widely discussed in the pubs and around the kitchen tables by the tight-knit community of men who served in the Navy or who built and repaired its ships. Fisher had improved the conditions of service for the sailors of the lower deck by increasing their pay and pensions, improving their rations and modernising the heating and sanitary arrangement on ships. They had also at last been given cutlery with which to eat their meals, although many men resented having to polish and present their knives and forks each Sunday for inspection, and so gave them back to the ship's paymaster. Generally the morale of the ships' crews, such an essential factor for an effective fighting force, was raised considerably by these reforms, and seamen admired the consideration given to them by their 'Jacky'.[20]

George had started courting his future wife, Ida Horne, by the summer of 1909, and as he was no doubt considering marriage, the Royal Navy probably now offered him more opportunities and a better livelihood than remaining as a manual worker in the dockyard. Throughout his life, George was quite an ambitious man, keen to improve his qualifications and to widen his horizons, and his father, as a retired Chief Petty Officer, would have encouraged his son's ambitions.

George senior and Emma were shortly to leave 8 Canterbury Street and move to 5 Paradise Place, further east in the Stoke Damerel parish of Devonport. This may also have prompted their son George to go to sea rather than move into another small house with his parents and three siblings.

As a skilled engine fitter coming from the dockyard, George was able to join the Navy in June 1909 as an 'ERA' – an Engine Room Artificer. With the transition from sail to steam, and from wooden to iron hulls, this class of rating was introduced in 1868 when a new scheme was instituted by which qualified tradesmen aged between twenty-one and thirty-five years were recruited into the Royal Navy directly from the engineering industry. They were given the rate of a Chief Petty Officer and the title of Engine Room Artificer as a statement of their specialisation.[21] The demand in the Royal Navy for these technical skills increased and in 1903 Fisher introduced a scheme for boys to join the Navy from the Royal Hospital School at Greenwich as 'Boy Artificers'. They were trained for four years, at Chatham on HMS *Tenedos*, on HMS *Fisgard* in Portsmouth or in Devonport on HMS *Indus*, a complex of old wooden hulks moored on the Hamoaze near Torpoint.

As an adult ERA recruited from the dockyard, George's first six weeks were spent at HMS *Vivid II*, the shore training establishment at the Royal Naval Barracks in Devonport.[22] His programme during these six weeks included practical seamanship, field training exercises based on realistic scenarios which might occur in actual battle, and squad drills. He also worked in the machine shop on his specialist skills as a mechanic and engine fitter and turner.

On 10 August 1909, George joined HMS *New Zealand*, a battleship of the Home Fleet, which was recommissioned on that date in Devonport.[23] He served as an ERA on the ship for two years until 31 July 1911, drawing pay, equivalent to a Chief Petty Officer's, of four shillings a day.

The ERAs, known as 'Tiffs' or 'Tiffys' in the Royal Navy, were trained in all the workings of engines, boilers, hydraulic systems and machines, and worked under the Engineer Officer. They were the senior operators responsible for the maintenance and operation of all the parts of a warship's marine engines and its auxiliary machinery, and were regarded by many as 'the elite of the lower deck'.[24] On joining the Navy, a rating received a full set of kit which he had to keep clean and in good repair. As part of his pay, he was given a Kit Upkeep Allowance to cover the cost of buying his uniform from the Naval Clothing Stores. If he wished, a man could pay for better quality or more stylish kit from the Naval Tailors at his own cost. A fully qualified ERA's uniform was that of a Chief Petty Officer, with gold badges and a peaked cap, dark navy blue jacket with brass buttons, a stiff white collar and dark navy tie.

When working with the ship's engines or in other machinery spaces, the ERAs wore blue overalls. Conditions down below in the engine room were, of course, hot and dirty, and in the worst spots the temperature could reach a blistering 130 degrees Fahrenheit. In well-ventilated areas, though, it was usually a tolerable 80–90 degrees, and it was often more comfortable to be in the engine room than exposed up on deck in rough weather or in a very hot or cold climate. As on any large ship, there was also less motion from the sea down below decks than up top.

On board ship, the Royal Navy operated, then as now, a schedule of working known as the 'watch system'. By this, the whole crew, including the engine men, were split into two or three sections, depending on the ship and the number of officers available to be watch keepers. Each section was assigned a work period of four hours at a time. To enable all the men to take their evening meals, one of the watches would be split into two shorter 'dog watches' of two hours each. This also allowed for the rotation of the watch schedule so that crew members were not always on duty during the same hours each day. Under a 'three-section dogged watch' schedule, which allowed men more time off-duty, each crew member would normally work two periods of four hours plus one two-hour dog watch over a twenty-four-hour period. The watch system enabled the effective operation of the ship throughout each day and night while at sea.

In the Royal Navy, teamworking and companionship were fostered by the crew eating and sleeping in groups, according to their rate, of about ten to twenty-five men, which were called 'messes'. ERAs had their own mess on board ship, which might be just a small area curtained off for privacy. The men's kit bags were usually stowed on a large ship in a central store, but in their mess, George and the other ERAs could keep their more personal possessions in ditty boxes (small lockable containers).

They ate their meals in the mess sitting on stools or lockers at a long stowable table covered with lino for a tablecloth. Thanks to Fisher's reforms, the food for the crew was much improved since George's father's day, with more fresh meat and vegetables, and the Daily Standard Naval Rations were prescribed by the *King's Regulations and Admiralty Instructions*. The men had three square meals a day, and a bowl of soup mid-morning.

Meals consisted of basic but filling British fare such as mutton, corned beef, tinned salmon or rabbit, potatoes, bread, dripping and jam, and boiled suet and raisin puddings, with tea or cocoa to drink. If fresh meat was not available, the men would have to eat unpalatable salt pork. The food was prepared by a mess cook for the day. In the ERAs' mess, these cooks were more junior crew, often stokers, who bought the staples of bread, meat, potatoes, sugar and beverages from the ship's stores using the men's standard ration allowance. They could also use each crew member's additional allowance of four pence a day to buy extras requested by the mess, such as bacon, cheese or tinned fruit. The cook prepared the ingredients, took the meal to the ship's galley to be heated in the ovens, served it in the mess and then cleared up.

The traditional daily rum ration for petty officers (who included the ERAs) was neat rum, about a fifth of a bottle, while the issue each noon to the rest of the lower deck men was 'grog', diluted three parts water to one part rum. At Christmas and on special dates, such as Trafalgar Day on 21 October, there would be an extra rum ration to 'splice the main brace', and on a man's birthday his messmates would often give him their ration. Rum was hoarded and bartered by some crew members who, against regulations, used it as a currency to obtain goods or favours in return.

At night, or if he were off duty during the day, George would, like all sailors, sleep in his hammock, which he slung above the table in the ERAs' mess area. On waking, the men would lash up their hammocks and stow them away in lockers, where they could be reached in an emergency for damage control purposes. On any ship several hundred men worked and lived together in very cramped and stuffy conditions, sleeping in hammocks in close proximity to each other, only 18 inches apart. There was no privacy. Sanitary facilities in the 'heads', the ship's lavatories, were limited, and most of the men smoked, so the smells and the atmosphere below deck would not have been pleasant with no air conditioning in those days. Hot water was always available, though, and the messes were warm places to eat and sleep when the ship was in a cold climate, and ventilated through ducts and shafts. The armoured scuttles (portholes) on warships also gave some air and light, but they would need to be closed in action with a steel deadlight covering them as protection against enemy shells.

The Navy taught men to be self-sufficient. When not on duty, the crew had to wash and mend their own clothes, shoes and kit. Every man had to do his own laundry, a laborious process involving a bucket of hot water, a bar of soap and a scrubbing brush. George could at least dry his clothes in the engine room. On most ships there were sailors, often married men, who set themselves up as 'firms' of two or three to launder and press clothes, repair shoes or, with a sewing machine, do tailoring jobs on uniforms, all for a small fee. These enterprising crew members were often able to earn a couple of hundred pounds from such private activities in the course of a ship's tour, enough to buy a house at home.

In their moments of leisure, the crew would relax by playing cards (but no gambling), write regular letters home, or, as George would have liked to do, read a book. The men had plenty of opportunities for exercise and sport, and for organised recreation there would be boxing competitions, or the ship's small boats could be used in 'pulling' or rowing races between teams of sailors. There would be occasional concert parties, especially if there was a Royal Marines' band on board or some string players, with perhaps even a dance, the men having to partner each other. However, boredom was a very prevalent feeling at sea when off-duty.

Every Sunday, Church Parade was compulsory for the whole ship's company, but most of the men would be regular churchgoers in any event, as was George.

While flogging and birching had been abolished, the men were still liable to a range of summary punishments for minor offences such as poor performance of duties, smoking on duty or failure to maintain kit. Official penalties known as '10As' would be handed out by the Officer of the Day or Divisional Officer, and these ranged from stoppage of rum or leave to regular reporting or two hours' extra work in the evening. Some senior ratings might impose on more junior offenders an unofficial and demeaning punishment known as 'keeping the flies off the paintwork', which involved being made to stand for hours facing a bulkhead on the exposed upper decks in all weathers. More serious offences such as insolence, dereliction of duty or theft would result in being confined to the ship's cells for up to fourteen days.

The American historian Christopher McKee collated accounts from eighty Royal Navy ratings who served between 1900 and 1945 in his book *Sober Men and True*, which gives a graphic insight into their tough, often monotonous, frequently dangerous lives, and the spirit of true camaraderie that life at sea engendered.[25]

Depending on the location of the ships, short leave was given for an afternoon or evening ashore, or long leave of up to fourteen days if the ship was in port and being refitted. The traditional image of the Navy on shore leave is of the heavy-drinking, libidinous sailors swaying from pub to pub and looking for women in the bars and brothels of a port's red light district, such as Union Street in Plymouth.

The ratings' accounts in McKee's book confirm that this was a fair representation of their shipmates' activities on leave, as it no doubt still is of sailors across the world. But that is not the whole story. When on long leave in the British Isles in a port away from home, a sailor was allowed one or two railway warrants a year so he could travel back to visit his family, and most took advantage of this. In foreign ports, some of the crew on a run ashore would attend church, visit museums or go on trips to see the local sights, and George's diaries and letters home later in his career confirm that he used his leave overseas for these activities.

Although George had worked for eight years in the tough conditions of the dockyard, going to sea and adapting to the rigid routines, traditions and discipline of the Royal Navy was a challenge for any young man, and particularly so for this twenty-two-year-old who by nature was quiet and reserved. He could, however, cope with such challenges, and on his naval record each December from 1909 to 1917 the annual reports on his character were consistently the standard expected norm of 'VG'.

On 6 May 1910 Edward VII died and George V succeeded to the throne. The new King was immediately thrown into a major constitutional crisis, one of the most serious of the century, which presaged the changes to British society that were to take place in his country over the next fifty years.

The Liberal Government under Prime Minister Asquith had introduced old-age pensions in 1908, a radical step. In 1909 David Lloyd George, the charismatic Chancellor of the Exchequer, had introduced the 'People's Budget' to raise additional revenue to fund old-age pensions and sickness insurance for poorer people, as well as the costs of new warships in the arms race with Germany. This heavy expenditure was to be paid for by increases in income tax and new surtaxes on the rich and their landed estates. The House of Lords rejected the Finance Bill that would implement the proposals, the first refusal of a money bill by the Lords since the seventeenth century. The Lords regarded this budget, and its new social welfare measures, as an instrument of class war; an attempt to redistribute wealth that would cause, according to Lord Rosebery, a 'social and political revolution'.

The rejection forced a General Election in January 1910, when the Liberals retained sufficient seats and the support of Labour and Irish Nationalist MPs to pass the bill, to which this time the Lords assented. The Liberals were now determined to restrict permanently the power of the House of Lords to block money bills, as the power to govern was entirely dependent on these being passed.

The new King was controversially drawn into the crisis when Asquith asked him to create enough Liberal peers to outvote the usual Conservative majority in the House of Lords, an act that would undermine the sovereign's traditional impartiality. After prolonged and difficult political discussions between the Prime Minister and George V and his advisers, and a second General Election, the Parliament Act of 1911 was passed without the King having to create Liberal peers. It removed forever the power of the Lords to veto finance bills and established the constitutional superiority of elected Members of Parliament over the inherited titles and wealth of the 'Upper House'.

A week after the accession of the new monarch, George Lancaster sent a card, dated 15 May 1910, from HMS *New Zealand* while moored at Portland. It was addressed to Ida – Miss I. Horne, 48 Marlborough Street, Devonport, Devon – and it said:

> *Dear Ida*
> *I came across this postcard. I thought I would send it on to you to give you some idea of the appearance of Spanish towns. We leave Spithead on the 23rd.*
> *George*

Spithead is a stretch of water in the Solent off the Hampshire coast of southern England, known for the Royal Navy fleet reviews, such as the Coronation Fleet Review for the new King which took place in June 1911. But the postcard is a view of the port of Vigo in Galicia, northwest Spain. George's message indicates that he has already been travelling with the Navy to overseas ports. This is the first card from George's lifetime collection of picture postcards and letters that he sent home from his overseas travels over the next quarter of a century.

After leaving HMS *New Zealand* on 31 July 1911, George returned to Devonport to the shore base HMS *Vivid II*, where he remained for the next two years as an ERA working on the maintenance and repair of engines and other machinery on warships. Serving here in his home port enabled him to continue his courtship of Ida, and they finally married on 1 June 1912 at the Church of St John in Devonport.

Ida Spriddle Horne was a Devonport girl whose father's family had come from the village of Maker just across the Tamar in Cornwall; a family with a centuries-long association with the sea.

Ida

Rame Head, in the Parish of Maker with Rame, is a promontory on the coast of southeast Cornwall[26] jutting out into the English Channel, where on fine days there are wonderful views along the edge of England to the east and west. Horses graze on the grassy slope that sweeps down before rising again to the head and the small ancient chapel of St Michael on the edge of the cliff.

The churchyard of the Parish Church of St Germanus at Rame contains a number of graves of the Spriddle family, who had lived at Rame for many centuries, their menfolk earning their livelihood from the sea as mariners or fishermen who sold their catches of pilchards to the Plymouth fish merchants. A family tree dating back to 1590 records a John Spriddell who had married in that year and had sons called John and Pascal.

Smuggling also flourished in this area, with small boats bringing in goods from cross-Channel traders and other merchant ships arriving from across the globe. The two villages of Kingsand and Cawsand were the main centre of smuggling in the West Country in the eighteenth and early nineteenth centuries. Contraband cargoes, particularly kegs of brandy, were regularly landed there and taken from the beach through secret caverns and tunnels to evade the Revenue Service. There were many local incidents of violent, sometimes fatal, skirmishes with the customs officers before the smuggling trade in Cornwall was suppressed by 1850.

The churchyard at Rame includes a headstone with an anchor motif commemorating two brothers who both died at sea in the service of Queen Victoria's Royal Navy:

In affectionate remembrance of THOMAS SPRIDDLE
seaman on board HMS *EURIDICE* who was drowned by her foundering
March 24th 1878 aged 20 years.
also RICHARD SPRIDDLE

brother of the above seaman on board of HMS *WASP* who was drowned
by her foundering off Tory Island September 22nd 1884 aged 29 years.
And the sea shall give up her dead.

The adjacent village of Maker is at Mount Edgcumbe in Cornwall and can be reached from Plymouth by the ferry over the Hamoaze to Cremyll. There is a lovely walk from the ferry quay through Mount Edgcumbe Park over to Kingsand and Cawsand, and then back up to the Parish Church of St Mary and St Julian in Maker, where more Spriddle family graves lie in the churchyard. Their headstones sometimes spell 'Spriddle' in the alternative form 'Spriddell'.

SACRED to the memory of HENRY SPRIDDELL
who departed this life January 8th 1857 aged 62 years.
also 3 children of the above who died in their infancy.
also HENRY his son who departed this life November 5th 1866 aged 43 years.
also SUSANNA wife of the above who departed this life
2nd March 1870 aged 75 years.
'Blessed are the dead which die in the Lord.'
Also Sarah Horne daughter of the above who died April 28th 1904.

The last-named Sarah Horne was born Sarah Spriddle in 1827 at Kingsand, the daughter of Henry, a ship's pilot, and his wife Susanna (*née* Lobb), whom had he had married in 1816 in the parish of Stoke Damerel in Plymouth.

Sarah grew up in Maker, and family legend was that she regularly rowed across the River Tamar from Cremyll to Richmond Wharf at Mount Wise on the Devonport side to sell pilchards in the town.

Sarah Spriddle was from tough seafaring stock, and she needed to be tough throughout her life. On 5 October 1859, aged thirty-two, she married a sailor called David George Horne, who was thirty-seven and a boatswain from Devonport, then serving on HMS *Royal Adelaide*. At the time of her marriage Sarah had left her home in Maker, and was living across the water in Mutton Cove when she and David Horne married in the Parish Church of St Mary in Devonport. Sadly the marriage was short-lived, as David died less than a year later, aged thirty-eight, in the Naval Hospital in Devonport on 21 August 1860, cause of death unknown.

Sarah was pregnant when her husband died, and on 13 March 1861 she gave birth to a son, whom she named David John, who was baptised later that year on 13 October. The 1861 census records that the twenty-eight-year-old widow Sarah, the head of the household, and her baby son were living at 3 Morice Square, Morice Town, Stoke Damerel, which was in the north part of the town of Devonport. But by the 1871 census Sarah, still the household head, was back living in Mutton Cove with ten-year-old David, a 'scholar' – that is, a pupil at a local school.

Young David Horne became a mariner himself, and he and his mother remained resident at Mutton Cove until the 1900s, part of a small community living and working at the busy little harbour there, west of Richmond Wharf and the commercial dock at Mount Wise. The Customs House and bonding warehouses were sited at Mutton Cove, and ferries, steamers and cargo ships called in there. David was one of many watermen working on the boats that took sailors and supplies out to the large ships moored in the Hamoaze or the Sound, or on the ferry service from the Cove over to Cremyll on the Cornish side of the Tamar estuary.

In addition to some local shops, there were coal, coke, potato and salt merchants and a corn miller at Mutton Cove, together with the business of Sibleys' Wagonettes. Sibleys' well-known horse-drawn carts and carriages transported goods from the harbour and warehouses to shops and Devonport Market. They also took passengers off the boats into town, and local people out to Dartmoor and to events such as the annual Tavistock Goosey Fair.

David drank at the Waterman's Arms tavern at Mutton Cove and for recreation would row on the river with his mates or go swimming at the baths for men and boys only at Mount Wise known as 'Pikeys'[27]. He would also take part in the annual Devonport Regatta, a popular event for the townsfolk.

In 2015 Mutton Cove still has a small working harbour, and it is a beautiful and rather peaceful waterfront location, with wonderful views across the Hamoaze to Cremyll and Mount Edgcumbe, and to the southeast the Royal William Victualling Yard (named after King William IV) and Plymouth Sound. At the edge of the Cove the 'King Billy' figurehead is still fixed at the front of the old covered ship-yard, just over the dockyard wall, commemorating the earlier monarch, King William III, who founded the Royal Dockyard.

Sarah Horne never remarried and David remained her only child. He did not have to stray far to find a wife. In 1885 he married Mary Ann Wilkey (or 'Wilkie'), who was literally the girl next door – David and his mother were living at 12b Mutton Cove and the Wilkey family were next door at Number 10.

David was twenty-four and Mary was eighteen. She too was from a seafaring family, and, although born in Devonport, at the time of the 1871 census, when she was four years old, she was living in Dartmouth with her mother Mary Jane and baby brother Thomas while her father was away at sea. By the 1881 census, aged fourteen she was back living in Devonport with both her parents and ten-year-old Thomas at 10 Mutton Cove. Her father, also called Thomas, although only forty-one, was a 'Naval Pensioner' according to the census record, and young Mary herself was already working as a 'Tailor's Apprentice'.

David and Mary married in 1885, and Ida Spriddle Horne (or Horn),[28] born on 22 December 1886, was the first of their four children: three girls and a boy. Ida was baptised in the Wesleyan Methodist Church in Ker Street, Devonport, on 9 January 1887. By 1891, David and Mary had two daughters: Ida, who was now four, and Ethel aged two, and they were still living with his mother Sarah at 12b Mutton Cove. Sarah is referred to as the 'Head' of the household in the census record, so she was still clearly the matriarch.

On Ida's ninth birthday in December 1895, Sarah gave her eldest grandchild a family photograph album, in which she inscribed at the front: *Ida Horne given to her by her grandmother on her 9th birthday with best wishes – SH.*

The album is a heavy volume with brown leather binding and a metal clasp which would have been connected to a lock, now missing. There are several family portraits inside, most of them taken by professional photographers in Plymouth or Devonport, of very serious and worthy-looking gentlemen and women, sadly unnamed, and some of young children, probably photos of the Horne and Spriddle families. They include an attractive little girl standing on a park bench with a basketful of flowers, wearing an embroidered tunic dress, a large wide-brimmed straw hat and leather boots. Is this the young Ida?

Another photo is of a rather scary gentleman with a beard standing cross-legged by a pot pedestal, one hand on his waist, another at his side, with a black Labrador dog holding a large stick in its mouth and gazing up at him. There are photos of mothers with babies; of old ladies wearing lace bonnets; stern elderly men, one with an Isambard Kingdom Brunel-like top hat on a table by his side; serious young men and middle-aged matrons: a whole unknown family of the late Victorian era, preserved by the camera.

The 1901 census records the Horne family as David Horne aged forty, who is its 'Head', his wife Mary, who is thirty-six, and their daughters, Ida aged fourteen, Ethel aged twelve, Lily aged ten, and a son, David Thomas Henry, who was three. Ida's grandmother Sarah, described as the 'Mother', is also listed in the census record as living at the same address, aged seventy-four and still probably the real head of the household.

Ida had a friend called Maggie who sent her postcards from Truro and Exeter cathedrals. Maggie clearly had a fervent religious faith, as on 8 April 1904 she gave Ida a copy of Thomas a Kèmpis's *Imitation of Christ* – quite an intense read for a seventeen-year-old. This may have been a gift to help Ida prepare for her confirmation on 24 November 1904 when the Vicar of St.John's gave her a copy of the *Holy Communion – Preparation and Companion* as a memento of the occasion.

Sarah Horne died in April 1904, aged seventy-seven, and was buried in the churchyard at her birthplace of Maker, in the grave of her parents Henry and Susanna Spriddle.

The funeral cards spell her name as 'Horn' without the 'e', and one states: *In loving memory of our dear mother Sarah Horn who fell asleep April 28th 1904. Interred in Maker Church May 3rd.*

An accompanying card, also black-lined, has a picture of snowdrops on the front and the words 'Until the day breaks', and on the back the quotation 'Rock of Ages, cleft for me, Let me hide myself in Thee.'

By 1911 David Horne had become a master mariner, and he and his wife Mary (usually known as Polly) had left Mutton Cove. After living for a short while at 48 Marlborough Street in central Devonport, they and their four children moved back to 54 James Street, just up the road from the cove. By then Ida was twenty-four and working for the Plymouth Co-operative Society as a clerk. Her two younger sisters, Ethel and Lily, had followed their mother's trade and were working as tailoresses, and thirteen-year-old David was still a schoolboy.

In such a small community, George Lancaster and Ida Horne

certainly knew each other from their youth. Their childhood homes in Canterbury Street and Mutton Cove were only a few hundred yards away from each other. They had both gone to the infants' school in Mount Street, and attended the Sunday School at St John's Church, Devonport, at the same time.

In December 1900, both aged thirteen they were each awarded a book prize at this Sunday School from the Exeter Diocesan Sunday School Association. Ida received a black-bound Holy Bible with her Certificate of Merit for passing the Association's Annual Examination pasted in the front. George also received a book prize for passing the same exam, as evidenced by the certificate pasted in the front, decorated with an episcopal mitre and shield surrounded by the words 'Exeter Diocesan Religious Instruction'. Their religious faith remained, and George regularly attended church services while away overseas in later life.

One family issue that George and Ida had in common was that both their paternal grandfathers had died young, and their own fathers had been raised from the age of two or three by widowed mothers.

By the time he sent the postcard from HMS *New Zealand* to her in May 1910, George and Ida were possibly engaged, or at least 'walking out' together. Their friendship developed into an engagement at some stage over the next two years, and by the spring of 1912 they were planning their wedding.

Those first few months of 1912 brought two historical events that were subsequently impressed on British folk-memory and featured in the tales told to most English schoolchildren for much of the twentieth century. Both events had a significant connection with Plymouth.

Robert Falcon Scott was born at a house called 'Outlands' in the Stoke Damerel area of Devonport in 1868, the son of a local brewer and magistrate. A Royal Navy officer and explorer, he led the expedition to the Antarctic which reached the South Pole in January 1912, only to find that the team of the Norwegian explorer Roald Amundsen had beaten them to it a month earlier to become the first men to the Pole. Scott and his four comrades all died on the return journey in March 1912.

In 1925 the Scott Memorial in Mount Wise Park at Devonport was unveiled in the presence of the explorer's son, Peter Scott, and it still stands there, the bronze figure of the explorer standing before a large winged angel and looking out to Plymouth Sound. The memorial was re-dedicated on 23 March 2012 by the Bishop of Plymouth at a ceremony to mark the centenary of the team's expedition.

Less than a month after Scott's death, the British liner RMS *Titanic* hit an iceberg on her maiden voyage to the United States on 15 April 1912, and sank with the loss of 1,517 lives, including three crew members and four passengers from Plymouth.

The *Titanic* had sailed from Southampton, but had not called in at Plymouth on her passage out into the Atlantic – her last port of call was Queenstown in southern Ireland. After the ship's sinking, the liner *Lapland* arrived in Cawsand Bay, just outside Plymouth Sound, on 28 April, carrying 167 survivors of the *Titanic*'s crew. Despite protests by the Seamen's Union, they were required by the Government's Board of Trade to disembark with a police guard at Millbay Docks (which had been closed to press reporters and the public) and were detained to give evidence to the Receiver of Wrecks in Plymouth. A special train then took the crew survivors back to their home port of Southampton.

The *Titanic* disaster was a great shock to all in Great Britain, and particularly to its maritime communities in ports such as Plymouth, where thousands of passengers embarked and disembarked on ocean-going liners in the years prior to the Great War. In 1906 alone, 546 liners had called in at Plymouth. Had the *Titanic* not hit the iceberg, she too would have made Plymouth a regular port of call.

On 1 June 1912, George Samuel Lancaster married Ida Spriddle Horne at their church of St John the Baptist in Duke Street, Devonport. On the marriage certificate George is described as an 'Engine Room Artificer' and Ida is described as a 'Spinster'. A cake card from the wedding ceremony is addressed to a Miss Cole, who remained a friend of Ida until the 1960s.

Formal portrait photographs of David and Polly Horne, Ethel, Lily and young David were taken at about the time of Ida's marriage, perhaps as a gift from her parents to their eldest daughter. David and Polly are a rather striking, jolly-looking couple, their three dark-haired children in more brooding, serious poses.

George and Ida were both twenty-five, and as newlyweds they moved into their own new home at 14 Beresford Street, Ford Hill, Devonport, which George had purchased from the builder, and where they would stay for twenty-seven years until 1939.

Politics and Change

George and Ida celebrated their first wedding anniversary at 14 Beresford Street on 1 June 1913. One month later George was posted to his new ship, the Devonport-based armoured cruiser HMS *Warrior*.

For naval wives like Ida, marriage to a sailor meant enduring long periods of separation while their husbands were away at sea, often on tours of duty lasting over two years at a time. Ida was expecting her first baby by the time George joined *Warrior* on 1 July 1913, and as his ship had been transferred that year from the Home Fleet to the Mediterranean Fleet, he sailed off to Gibraltar and she was left to cope on her own.

Ida did have the companionship of her sister-in-law Ellen Ronson, also a naval wife, who gave birth to her first child, Miriam, on 1 September 1913 and so was able to give some advice and reassurance about the process of childbirth. Ida also regularly saw her mother-in-law Emma who, after seven pregnancies, no doubt held definite views on how to cope. The role of women in this community, where most of their menfolk served in the armed forces or worked in the dockyard or allied trades, was the traditional and passive one, framed by maintaining the home, providing the meals, having babies and raising a family, all in the absence of their husbands in the case of naval and military wives.

Yet even in this far southwest corner of England, national politics were making an impact on these women's self-perception. Plymouth directly experienced the activities of Emmeline Pankhurst's Suffragette Movement, which was campaigning for women to have the right to vote in political elections. On 3 April 1913, Mrs Pankhurst made a court appearance in London after being arrested for militant protests. On the same day, Winston Churchill, then the First Lord of the Admiralty, was due to arrive by yacht in Plymouth Sound to inspect the Fleet.

In Plymouth local Suffragettes took action that day. They cut telephone lines at Lipson and wrote graffiti in white paint on Smeaton's Tower, the lighthouse on Plymouth Hoe and one of the town's most prominent buildings, 'No security till you give women votes, no matter how big the Navy'. On the nearby central Hoe shelter they scrawled 'To Churchill – no rest for Government while they torture women' – a reference to the gruesome force-feeding of imprisoned Suffragettes who were on hunger strike.

Later that month on 19 April, another group of Suffragettes planted a home-made bomb at the foot of Smeaton's Tower, with a note saying 'Votes for women, death in ten minutes'. The sea-wind and rain blew out the lighted wick and the bomb failed to explode.

The militant activities of Mrs Pankhurst's Women's Social and Political Union continued throughout 1913 across the country, including arson attacks on the homes of Churchill and Lloyd George. On 4 December 1913, Mrs Pankhurst arrived on the liner *Majestic* in Plymouth Sound after sailing back from America, where she had been on a fundraising trip for her cause. Police from Plymouth boarded the ship and arrested her, took her by motor boat to a secure naval facility at Bull Point on the River Tamar, and from there by car to Exeter Prison. An Australian newspaper, which covered events across the globe, reported the following day:

> A section of the militant suffragettes had engaged a tug to pursue the police but the tug was forbidden to approach the Majestic, and the police used the battleships in the vicinity to hide their proceedings from the suffragettes' tug. Suffragettes from all parts of the United Kingdom had congregated at Plymouth Docks. Five thousand in number, together with Mrs Drummond and her bodyguard, waited at the dock gates, singing the Marseillaise, blissfully ignorant that the police had stopped the Majestic. They were greatly exasperated when they found they had been deluded by the police.[29]

On 15 December 1913 the Suffragettes set fire to a woodshed at Richmond Walk on the waterfront at Devonport just along from Mount Wise – a minor arson attack, but indicative of their anger at the recent arrest of their leader.

The Suffragettes' militant national campaign continued during 1914, but once war started it was halted. The absence of men, who were fighting at sea or in the trenches, led to the employment of women for the first time in many factories and on the land. Local women were employed in munitions factories and other manufacturing industries, and many became manual workers in several departments of Devonport Dockyard, such as the Electrical Engineers' Department. The Women's Land Army was formed in 1916 and women laboured on farms throughout Devon to maintain food supplies. The Women's Army Auxiliary Corps recruited women to work as drivers and mechanics as well as cooks and waitresses for the army.

Women in Plymouth joined the nursing service during the Great War, working in the Royal Naval and General Military Hospitals at Stonehouse, where they cared for men who had come back injured from the front. Some nurses went to France to work in the front line hospitals there.

It was in recognition of this work that women of thirty and over were given the right to vote by the Representation of the People Act 1918 if they owned a house or were married to someone who did.[30] Ida was able to vote for the first time in the General Election on 14 December 1918.

At a by-election in November 1919 it was the constituency of Plymouth Sutton that elected Nancy, Lady Astor as the first woman Member of Parliament to take her seat in the House of Commons. She was the American-born wife of the previous Member, William Waldorf Astor, who had to vacate the seat when he succeeded to the peerage and became Lord Astor.[31] Nancy Astor represented Plymouth Sutton for twenty-five years.

Back in Devonport in 1913, the Suffragette movement was not the only controversial political campaign under way.

Since 1872 the population of the conurbation of the Three Towns of Devonport, East Stonehouse and Plymouth had nearly doubled. Plymouth, with some 113,300 people, had expanded greatly, while the growth of Devonport, with 84,370, was restricted by the waters of the Hamoaze on the south and west sides, and to the east by Plymouth and East Stonehouse, the smallest town with a population of 13,750.

Part of Devonport's problem was that most of the freehold land within the town was owned by the Lord of the Manor, Lord St Levan, head of the St Aubyn family, whose estate rented out properties – houses, shops and factories – on a long lease subject to an annual ground rent.

Even much of the dockyard was leased by the Admiralty from the St Aubyn Estate. This form of ownership inhibited investment in building repairs and improvements, and new developments.

Devonport became one of the most overcrowded towns in England in the late nineteenth century and much of its housing was squalid, dilapidated and insanitary. In 1897 Henry Whitfield, the editor of the *Devonport Independent* newspaper, produced a pamphlet called *The Curse of Devonport*, of which he sold 12,000 copies in a single day. He wrote:

> Proceeding systematically through the borough slums, I could not fail to be impressed with those recurring views of ruined and collapsed houses which a casual visitor from a volcanic country might be excused for regarding as the evidence of a nineteenth century earthquake. Whilst Plymouth, indeed, still has its overcrowding evils and is trying to cure them, the Manorial System of Devonport results in structural decay and public indifference.

In 1899 Devonport extended its urban boundaries by obtaining an Order of Parliament to annexe the Parish of St Budeaux, despite the opposition of that formerly rural community to becoming part of the town.

The need to house the growing workforce at the dockyard led the St Aubyn Estate, probably at the instigation of the Admiralty, to develop a large new housing estate in 1910 on the eastern boundary of Devonport. On Ford Hill in the parish of Stoke Damerel a number of streets of terraced houses were built, plots being sold off in batches to speculative builders who constructed the houses in accordance with the standard design of the St Aubyn Manor architect.[32] The builders then sold them on to the new residents, subject to an annual ground rent payable to the St Aubyn Estate.

One of these new streets was Beresford Street, named after Admiral Lord Charles Beresford, and it was here that George and Ida moved into their new home at number 14 when they married in 1912. George had bought No.14 as a new house from the builder of numbers 11–14, a Mr Northcott. The purchase of their own home, some distance away from the old Devonport and in a new area nearer to the more prosperous Plymouth, probably represented a good move up the social scale at that time.

Twice in the nineteenth century and again in 1902 Plymouth's leaders had proposed that the Three Towns should amalgamate, but the suggestion was opposed by the Devonport Corporation. However, by 1913 issues other than overcrowded housing were giving impetus to this proposal.

The growing tensions between the European powers and the expansionist ambitions of Germany focused the minds of the Government and its military planners on the logistics of dealing with three different sets of authorities. Local ballots in 1913 had confirmed considerable support for the amalgamation proposal in Plymouth and East Stonehouse, but less so in Devonport. This led to a Local Government Board enquiry which was held in Plymouth Guildhall in January 1914. One of the witnesses was the Officer-in-Command of South West Coastal Defences, Major-General Penton, who said:

> In peacetime the organisation of the Three Towns into three distinct bodies does not affect us much... In wartime it is an entirely different question. You would have the fortress commander having to go to three different bodies... In fact if I was fortress commander here in wartime I should have to go to three chief civil magistrates and say 'One of you must represent the civil community...'

Three months after the enquiry, a Provisional Order was made which united the towns. The decision was opposed by Devonport Corporation, which took the matter to a House of Commons committee. That committee upheld the amalgamation decision on 1 July 1914, but the corporation still tried to block the passing of the Parliamentary Bill, although unsuccessfully. The bill was passed in the Commons on 21 July 1914, and despite further lobbying of the House of Lords by Devonport, it received the Royal Assent on 10 August – a week after the declaration of war by Great Britain against Germany.

The Three Towns were now merged into Plymouth under the control of a single council, with a population of some 214,000. This was a significant stage in the long-term decline of Devonport throughout the twentieth century and its change in status to become a suburb of Plymouth, which became a city in 1928.

On 24 February 1914 Ida had her first child, a daughter who was also given the name of Ida. The baby was born into a country shortly to undergo the massive shock of industrialised total warfare. The impact of two world wars would bring an unravelling of traditional social, economic and political structures, and consequential changes to the rigid class divisions that had prevailed in the Victorian and Edwardian eras. The new values and expectations of the British people would resonate throughout the twentieth century.

In Devonport, some idea of the community that was to be lost in that process is given in an account written in 1978 by Marjorie Laxton, who was eight years old in 1914. She lived with her mother in rented rooms in George Street, near Mount Wise. Her baby brother had died at the age of six months, and her father was away at sea. Marjorie described the pre-war town of her childhood:

> Devonport was a thriving town with everything there anyone could wish for...I remember Pembroke Street, many pubs, many poor families, also good business people like Viggers Dairy, Alfords the Grocers and Mrs Broom's cook shop where beef and pork were cut from the cooked joints on the counter. Joining James Street was the Pembroke Street Post Office, a hive of industry where the servicemen and fishermen would come from ashore at Mutton Cove and then call into the office to send a postcard home before spending their money liberally in the many pubs on their way to Aggie Weston's Home.
>
> I remember the old cabby, Mr Maunder, who used to stand with his horse and cab outside Cumberland Gardens. The Royal Hotel was down towards the Dockyard end and I remember Lord and Lady Jackson arriving here in their carriage just before hundreds of dockyardies swarmed out from the yard at 5 p.m., many on bikes, the others rushing to catch the trams to Stoke, Millbay and Plymouth.
>
> I can recall Blagdon's boatyard at Richmond Walk, where men could hire a boat for an hour or two to go fishing, then bring the fish ashore to sell and often the fish were still flapping about in the basket. Every week a man used to come around with his pony and cart selling salt, which would be cut as required. Mother would buy a large block for 1d. I remember the organ grinder with his barrel organ and the little monkey on top; also the rag man who gave children a balloon or packet of sherbet in exchange for old clothes. These things

I clearly remember, the annual service review held in the Brickfields, a colourful spectacle with the bright uniforms, decorated horses, bands playing, stalls selling paper hats, Union Jacks, toy bugles, ice cream carts where ½d. would buy a generous cornet. A day with a carnival atmosphere everybody enjoyed.

When I was eight years of age my mother was taken ill and the 1914 war broke out on 4th August. I well remember the soldiers running through the streets calling out "War declared, war declared", which proved a very sharp experience for me, but from then on my memories would fill a book.[33]

Mediterranean, 1914

To the Sailors of the First Squadron of the English Cruisers, homage of the Rapallo Town Council, 5th–9th March 1914.

This is the stamp on the back of George's postcard from Rapallo, a port in the northwest region of Italy known as Liguria. On the front is a panorama of the town.

George had left Devonport for the Mediterranean some time before the birth of his daughter Ida on 24 February 1914. By then he had already served for eight months as an Engine Room Artificer (ERA) on HMS *Warrior*, one of four armoured cruisers in the Royal Navy's First Cruiser Squadron – the 'First CS'. The ships of the First CS were its flagship HMS *Defence*, HMS *Duke of Edinburgh*, HMS *Black Prince* and *Warrior* itself.

HMS *Warrior* was the second naval ship of that name. Its predecessor, the first *Warrior* launched in 1860, was a revolutionary ship for the Royal Navy, being its first steam iron-hulled ship. George's HMS *Warrior* was a *Warrior*-class armoured cruiser of 13,550 tons, built and launched at Pembroke Dock in November 1905 and commissioned in December 1906.[34] It had a top speed of 23 knots and a mixed armament of six 9.2-inch and four 7.5-inch guns.

George was a member of a peacetime crew of 712 men, and as an Engine Room Artificer he worked on the ship's steam engines, which were twin 4-cylinder reciprocating engines rather than the newer steam turbines installed in the more modern warships.

In this spring of 1914 the First CS was on what appears to have been a goodwill visit to seaport towns on the Italian coast. These 'flying the flag' visits by the Royal Navy were an important part of British diplomacy, and the British Government was keen to ensure that the Kingdom of Italy, with its important strategic position on the Mediterranean and Adriatic, supported Britain in any confrontation between the European powers. Although a member of the Triple Alliance with Germany and Austria-Hungary, Italy was open to other alliances and had its own ambitions to establish a colonial empire. In 1911 Italy had taken advantage of Ottoman Turkey's weakness by invading and occupying Libya.

In Rapallo, from where George sent his card to Ida in March 1914, the local dignitaries clearly gave the British ships of the First CS a good welcome. Another of George's postcards shows local people and a horse and carriage in the Piazza Cavour in Livorno, known in English as Leghorn, a seaport in Tuscany, also in the northwest of Italy, south of Rapallo. While at Livorno George took a trip to nearby Pisa, and when the squadron sailed south and arrived at Naples, he was able to visit Pompeii – he brought back cards from both excursions.

Two months later *Warrior* had sailed around the toe and heel of Italy and up the eastern Italian coast through the Adriatic to the city of Fiume.

Fiume – 7th May 1914

Dear Ida
I came ashore here this afternoon. I spent a pleasant time. It is one of the best places I have visited so far.
With love George

Fiume is now a city called Rijeka in Croatia at the top of the Adriatic Sea. In 1914 it was an independent city-state within the two empires of the Austro-Hungarian Empire. George's postcard, with a *Magyar Posta* stamp, is a photograph of the dock at Fiume with some ships moored at the harbour, and gentlemen in formal dress and hats walking up and down the quayside, discussing the business of the day.

After leaving Fiume, the First Cruiser Squadron's goodwill tour of Italy continued and they docked in Venice. George bought several black and white and coloured postcard views of the canals, gondolas and palaces, and on 11 May he posted one of them, a view of St Mark's Square, to Ida:

Dear Ida
I came ashore to see Venice this afternoon, it is a delightful spot and I only wish you could come and see it. We spent most of the afternoon in the Ducal Palace on the right of the picture – then we didn't see as much as we might – George xxx

The postmark on this card reads *XI Esposizione Internationale d'Arte, Venezia, Aprile-Ottobre 1914*. But the time for annual international art exhibitions was coming to an end.

Fiume, the independent city-state within the Habsburgs' Austro-Hungarian Empire that George had liked so much in May 1914, was some 200 miles northwest of the principal capital of Bosnia, a place that only seven weeks later became synonymous with the flashpoint for the Great War – Sarajevo.

The Balkans had been an unstable geo-political region for decades, beset by the challenges of nationalist movements and the aggressive ambition of the kingdoms of Serbia, Bulgaria, Montenegro and Greece to expand their territories into lands subject to the imperial rule of both the Habsburgs and Ottoman Turkey. In 1911 Italy's invasion of Ottoman Libya encouraged these four Balkan League states to attack Ottoman territories in Albania, Macedonia and Thrace in the First Balkan War in 1912. Their successful annexation of Ottoman lands led to the Second Balkan War in 1913 when the Balkan League kingdoms fought each other over the spoils of the first war.

The Austro-Hungarian Habsburg Empire had formally annexed the province of Bosnia in 1908 after occupying it since 1878. Bosnia had a large population of Serbs, and the Habsburg annexation provoked those activist nationalist groups who wished to reclaim the lost South Slav lands of Greater Serbia. On 28 June 1914 the Archduke Franz Ferdinand, heir to the Habsburg imperial throne, was visiting Sarajevo when he and his wife Sophie were assassinated by a young Bosnian Serb, Gavrilo Princip, a member of the secret Black Hand militant society.

These murders gave Austria-Hungary the excuse that it had been looking for to serve an ultimatum on Serbia to capitulate to a series of harsh demands, which would mean its effective subjugation to the Habsburg Empire. Austria-Hungary expected Serbia to reject them, and yet the Serbs accepted nearly all these terms except for two which would have allowed the Austro-Hungarian Government to intervene in Serbia's affairs and infringe its sovereignty. This was sufficient excuse for Austria-Hungary to mobilise its army and declare war on Serbia on 28 July 1914, which triggered the agreements in the chain of international treaties and ententes that had been made over the previous decades between the European nation states.

Russia supported Serbia, its fellow Slav nation, and Tsar Nicholas mobilised his army on 31 July against Austria-Hungary. The German Empire, led by the belligerent Kaiser Wilhelm, sided with its Triple Alliance ally Austria-Hungary and declared war on Russia on 1 August. France had an understanding with Russia and Britain – the Triple Entente – that if any of them were attacked they would be under a moral obligation to support each other as allies.

The whole of Europe stood on the threshold of war. British politicians had long recognised the threat of German aggression. However, the attention of Asquith's Liberal Government that summer was on the continuing attempts to introduce Irish Home Rule. The Protestant majority in the six counties of Ulster in the north of Ireland was bitterly opposed to Home Rule, as were many throughout the United Kingdom. Asquith suggested a compromise whereby Ulster would be excluded from the Home Rule legislation, but this was too controversial and there was a real risk of civil war between Ulster Volunteer militias and Irish nationalists. As the politicians at Westminster, and the British public and press, were focusing on the crisis in Ireland, the sudden escalation of events in eastern Europe took them all by surprise.

Sarajevo proved to be the trigger for a conflict for which the European nations had been preparing for well over a decade. In terms of sea power, the challenge of the German Navy was to the global maritime dominance of the Royal Navy, which had been maintained since Nelson's victory at Trafalgar in 1805.

After the outbreak of war with Russia, the Germans, long concerned about being encircled by enemy states, declared war on France, and marched through neutral Belgium on 3 August with the intention of defeating France before attacking Russia. The European powers, including Britain, had guaranteed Belgium's neutrality under the 1839 Treaty of London, and once Germany invaded Belgium, the British Government served an ultimatum on Germany requiring it to respect Belgian neutrality. Germany failed to respond by the deadline of 11 p.m. on 4 August 1914, whereupon Britain declared war on Germany.

Germany's invasion of Belgium also represented a real threat to the Royal Navy and to British commerce, as the Germans now controlled a vital stretch of the Belgian coast which would allow them to use the ports there as bases from which to challenge the free passage of British warships and merchant ships through the sea lanes of the North Sea and the English Channel.

By late July 1914 George was still in the Mediterranean on HMS *Warrior*, in port at Alexandria in Egypt along with a number of other Royal Navy ships, including her sister ship *Black Prince* and the battle-cruisers *Inflexible* and *Indefatigable*. *Warrior* was about to proceed to her base in Malta when she received new orders – with the rest of the First Cruiser Squadron, she was to sail back to the Adriatic.

In the week before war was declared there had been a flurry of signals between the Admiralty in London and the Mediterranean Fleet's station in Malta. The Commander-in-Chief of the Mediterranean Fleet was Admiral Sir Berkeley Milne, who had been appointed as the Commander-in-Chief Mediterranean in April 1912 by the First Lord of the Admiralty, Winston Churchill. Milne was not a highly regarded officer and was nicknamed 'Arky Barky'. He was a dapper man who had spent many years on the Royal Yacht, cultivating the affection of various members of the Royal Family. Churchill's appointment of Milne to such a very senior post provoked an angry response from Admiral Sir John Fisher, who wrote, in his characteristically florid style, to Churchill:

> You are aware that Sir Berkeley Milne is unfitted to be the Senior Admiral afloat as you have now made him… I can't believe that you foresee all the consequences! The results would be IRREPARABLE, IRREMEDIABLE, ETERNAL!

As war became more likely, on 30 July Winston Churchill sent Milne the following signal:

> Your first task should be to aid the French transportation of their African Army by covering and if possible bringing to action individual fast German ships, particularly Goeben, who may interfere with that transportation.

The British Navy was to assist France in transporting its troops across the western Mediterranean from the French colony of Algeria to Marseilles.

The second part of Churchill's signal to Milne of 30 July went on:

> Do not at this stage be brought to action against superior forces, except in combination with the French, as part of a general battle. The speed of your squadron is sufficient to enable you to choose your moment… you must husband your strength at the outset.

The ambiguity of this signal and the vagueness of the term 'superior forces' were to prove crucial to the activity of the First CS, including HMS *Warrior*, in the first week of the war.

On 3 August Admiral Milne received a further signal from the Admiralty, again prepared by Churchill:

> Watch on mouth of Adriatic should be maintained, but Goeben is your objective. Follow her and shadow her wherever she goes and be ready to act on declaration of war, which appears probable and imminent. Goeben must be shadowed by two battlecruisers. Approaches to Adriatic must be watched by cruisers and destroyers. Remain near Malta yourself.

The German battlecruiser *Goeben* was regarded as the most powerful warship in the Mediterranean, with ten 11-inch guns and a reputed speed of 27 knots, representing a considerable threat to the Royal Navy's ships. *Goeben* had been undergoing a refit in the Austro-Hungarian dockyard at Pola in the northern Adriatic, and when the war began she did not want to be trapped in the Adriatic. Curtailing her refit, *Goeben* sailed south with another German ship, a light cruiser called *Breslau*, heading for the open seas of the Mediterranean.

The commander of *Goeben* was Rear Admiral Wilhelm Souchon, a very able and respected officer. After bombarding the French ports in North Africa on 4 August, Souchon turned his ship back towards the east and headed for Messina in Sicily to re-coal – a battlecruiser could use some 350 tons of coal in a day's sailing. Italy, although it had been in the Triple Alliance with Germany and Austria-Hungary, had declared its neutrality and only permitted Souchon twenty-four hours to refuel his ship in the Italian port, failing which it would be interned by Italy.[35] At Messina Souchon succeeded in loading 2,000 tons of coal on to his ship by the back-breaking efforts of all of his crew. He then sailed on down through the Straits of Messina.

Admiral Milne had made a fundamental mistake in not sending a sufficient force to block the southern exit of the Straits in order to trap *Goeben*, so enabling the German warship to escape into the open sea, shadowed only by the British light cruiser HMS *Gloucester*. Instead Milne kept his three battlecruisers, *Inflexible*, *Indefatigable* and *Indomitable*, in the western Mediterranean, patrolling between Sicily and Tunisia. He was keeping rigidly to the order in the Admiralty signal of 30 July to protect the French troop transports from North Africa, without focusing on the Admiralty instruction to maintain *Goeben* as his objective 'wherever she goes' and to deploy two of his battlecruisers to shadow her.

Gloucester's signals confirmed that on 6 August *Goeben*, accompanied by *Breslau*, was now sailing east through the Ionian Sea towards Greece.

When war broke out Milne had sent the First Cruiser Squadron, including George's ship HMS *Warrior*, with a destroyer flotilla to the Straits of Otranto between the heel of Italy and the Greek island of Corfu. The squadron's role was to watch the entrance to the Adriatic, as ordered by Admiralty signals on 3 August and again on 5 August, 'for double purpose of preventing Austrians emerging unobserved and preventing Germans entering'. This British force was under the command of Rear Admiral Ernest Troubridge, who sailed in HMS *Defence*, the flagship of the First Cruiser Squadron. Troubridge was a highly respected officer and second-in-command in the Mediterranean to Milne.

On 6 August the First Cruiser Squadron was waiting off the western coast of Greece near the islands of Cephalonia and Santa Maura. HMS *Gloucester* was following *Goeben* and *Breslau* at this stage and sending clear signals to both Milne and Troubridge of *Goeben*'s location.

The Admiralty's and Milne's fleet dispositions were based on the expectation that *Goeben* would either head for the Straits of Gibraltar to escape into the Atlantic or try to sail back into the Adriatic. During the night of 6/7 August, Troubridge was sailing north after receiving signals which indicated that *Goeben* was aiming to enter the Adriatic. He had also heard the Austrian fleet might be coming south, possibly to meet up with *Goeben*.

In fact, *Goeben* was sailing eastwards for Turkey. On 4 August Rear Admiral Souchon had received a signal from Berlin telling him that Germany had made a then secret alliance on 2 August with Turkey and that he was to proceed to Constantinople.

By 12.30 a.m. on the night of 6/7 August Troubridge had turned south again, following signals from HMS *Gloucester* confirming that *Goeben* was heading east towards Cape Matapan on the southern tip of Greece.

The next few hours of 7 August were to prove crucial for the fate of *Goeben*, the reputation of the Royal Navy, the careers of Troubridge and Milne, and the survival of the First CS, including George and the other crewmen on HMS *Warrior*.

At 2.45 a.m. on 7 August, as they pursued the German ships, Captain Fawcet Wray of HMS *Defence* said to Troubridge, "Are you going to fight, Sir?"

Troubridge answered, "Yes. I know it is wrong, but I cannot have the name of the whole of the Mediterranean Squadron stink." Troubridge then dictated this signal to his First Cruiser Squadron:

> I am endeavouring to cross the bows of Goeben by 6 a.m. and intend to engage her if possible. Be prepared to form on a line of bearing turning into line ahead as required. If we have not cut her off I may retire behind Zante [a nearby Greek island] to avoid long range action.

However, forty-five minutes later Troubridge and Fawcet Wray had a further conversation. Fawcet Wray said, "I don't like it, Sir."

Troubridge replied, "Neither do I, but why?"

Fawcet Wray, who was a gunnery expert, pointed out that *Goeben* had much more powerful guns with a range of 24,000 yards (over thirteen miles), while the range of the guns of Troubridge's ships was only 16,000 yards. *Goeben's* shells would hit the First CS's cruisers without them being able to return successful fire.

"It seems to me it is likely to be the suicide of your squadron," said Fawcet Wray.

Troubridge said, "I can't turn away now, think of my pride", to which Fawcet Wray replied, "Does your pride count in a thing like this?"

Troubridge was torn between his instinct to engage with the enemy warship *Goeben*, his prime objective, and the Admiralty order of 30 July not to engage with superior forces. He consulted his navigator to see if the First CS could close in on *Goeben* so that the enemy ship was within range of the British guns, but the navigator said no.

At 3.55 a.m. Rear Admiral Troubridge changed his mind and altered course, a decision which Wray approved, telling Troubridge, "Admiral, that was the bravest thing you have ever done in your life."

"I think he was in tears," said Fawcet Wray later of his Admiral.

Just after 4 a.m. Troubridge sent a further signal to Milne:

Being only able to meet Goeben outside the range of our guns and inside hers I have abandoned the chase with my squadron, request instructions for light cruisers. Goeben evidently going to Eastern Mediterranean. I had hoped to have met her before daylight.

Rear Admiral Troubridge was not only giving up his plan to engage *Goeben* across her bows but was abandoning the chase altogether. Fawcet Wray subsequently claimed that this decision had horrified him, saying he had only expected Troubridge to change course.

Milne replied to Troubridge's signal:

Why did you not continue to cut off Goeben? She was only going 17 knots and so important to bring her to action?

Troubridge answered:

With visibility at the time I could have been sighted from 20–25 miles away and could never have got nearer unless Goeben wished to bring me to action which she could have done under circumstances most advantageous to her. I could never have brought her to action... I was too late to intercept her when she altered course to the southward. In view of the immense importance of victory or defeat at such an early stage of a war I would have considered a great imprudence to place squadron in such a position to be picked off at leisure while unable to effectively reply. The decision is not the easiest of the two to make I am well aware.

Goeben and *Breslau* sailed on to Constantinople (now Istanbul) where Rear Admiral Souchon handed his ships over to the Turkish Government and they were formally, if not actually, received into the Ottoman fleet. In fact, their German crews stayed on board, and although as a token demonstration of the change of flag they exchanged their German naval caps for Turkish fezzes, they remained under Souchon's command.

For several years before the war the Kaiser's diplomats and generals had made extensive overtures towards the Turkish Government, and Germany cultivated the Young Turks' Nationalist Reform Party, which in 1908 had led a revolution against the absolutist rule of the Ottoman Sultan and established a new Constitutional Government. The German military mission sent to Constantinople in 1913, led by General Liman von Sanders, was very influential over the Young Turks' leader Enver Pasha, who became Turkey's Minister of War, and this relationship paid off with the alliance concluded between Germany and Turkey on 2 August 1914.

The Turks had been infuriated by Britain's impounding two days earlier, on 31 July, of two powerful dreadnought battleships constructed in England at the Armstrong Vickers shipyards at Newcastle upon Tyne. These ships had been ordered by Turkey and paid for by public subscription from the Turkish people. Churchill, the First Lord of the Admiralty, feared that they might fall into German hands and seized both ships at Newcastle just before they were due to be handed over to the Turks. This provocation pushed Turkey further into the German camp, and on 2 August Germany and Turkey signed a formal but secret alliance, which was sealed the following week by the arrival in Constantinople of *Goeben* and *Breslau*.

The failure to intercept these two German warships had wide ramifications which could not have been foreseen by Troubridge. Its alliance with Germany still secret, Turkey held back from joining the conflict on Germany's side in the first months of the war. But in late October 1914 Souchon sailed his two ships into the Black Sea, and on his orders *Goeben* and *Breslau* bombarded the Russian ports of Odessa, Sevastopol and Novorossisk. Souchon took this action without the authority of the Turkish Government even though these two warships were by then nominally part of the Ottoman Navy. As a result of this aggression, four days later Russia declared war on Turkey, which then entered the conflict on the side of Germany and Austria-Hungary, the Central Powers, on 31 October 1914.

The consequences of Turkey's entry and the creation of this new theatre of war were huge for the direction of the Great War. Britain and France also declared war on Turkey, and as a result the Allies had to fight the Ottoman Empire on a broad front in the Middle East, in Egypt, Palestine, Syria and Mesopotamia, for the next four years. Most controversially, the Allies became embroiled in the bloody and disastrous Dardanelles campaign against Turkey on the Turkish Gallipoli peninsula throughout 1915.

At the outset of the Great War, Troubridge's decision not to engage the *Goeben* in battle was soon regarded as a strategic disaster for the Royal Navy, which significantly damaged its reputation and morale. A court of enquiry was held which led to Troubridge's subsequent court martial in November 1914. The charge was that Troubridge did '…from negligence or through other default forbear to pursue the chase of His Imperial Majesty's German ship *Goeben*, being an enemy then flying'.

The issues before the court were complex, the evidence technical, but the key issue was Churchill's signal to the Mediterranean fleet of 30 July not to engage with superior forces. This had been instrumental in Troubridge's decision not to engage the enemy. The court held that he was justified in considering that *Goeben* was a superior force, and he was acquitted.

Troubridge's acquittal was a controversial decision as many even thought he should have been charged with cowardice – a capital offence. The Admiralty – and Churchill – shared much of the responsibility for the disastrous outcome with their ambiguous and sometimes incorrect signals. Admiral Milne sought to blame Troubridge entirely for the debacle, but Milne himself had failed to manage the operation effectively, in particular by missing the opportunity of engaging with *Goeben* in the Straits of Messina and for not sending at least one of his battlecruisers to support the First CS in time. Captain Fawcet Wray was shunned by his fellow officers and blamed by Troubridge for encouraging him to change his decision to attack *Goeben*.

Troubridge never again had a command at sea, but he served with distinction as head of a British Naval Mission in Serbia from 1915 and received a British knighthood for his services there in 1919. Milne, who was not court martialled, was left on half pay for the rest of the war without any further command.

But were *Goeben* and *Breslau* a superior force to the First Cruiser Squadron?

The view of several senior naval officers, then and since, was that the four armoured cruisers of Troubridge's squadron constituted a strong force that, acting together, could have been deployed to disable, even sink, *Goeben.*

Admiral Sydney Fremantle, who had been the prosecutor at Troubridge's court martial, later wrote:

> Troubridge might well have expected to lose one or two of his ships, but he might also have expected to do Goeben such damage as would make it possible for Milne with the battlecruisers to come up and finish her off.[36]

One of those ships that might have been lost was HMS *Warrior.* Troubridge's decision, however misjudged, meant that *Warrior* and George Lancaster were spared a sea battle in the first week of the Great War which might have sunk them both.

Just nine days after the *Goeben* episode, *Warrior* was involved on 16 August 1914 in another naval engagement in the Adriatic – the Battle of Antivari, off the coastal town of Antivari[37] in Montenegro.

Austria-Hungary was by now at war with Montenegro and the Austro-Hungarian Navy was blockading the Montenegrin coast. An Allied force of fifteen French battleships and cruisers and five destroyer squadrons, supported by a small English fleet comprising HMS *Defence,* HMS *Warrior* and three destroyer flotillas, went into the Adriatic in an attempt to draw out the rest of the Austro-Hungarian fleet to meet them in battle. At this stage Troubridge was still in command of the First Cruiser Squadron, and his ships, including *Warrior,* combined with the French light cruisers to sweep up the Albanian coast to try and drive the enemy ships towards the main French fleet.

The Austrians would not be drawn out of the safety of their port, and the Allied force was able to attack only two ships of the Austro-Hungarian Navy, the light cruiser SMS *Zenta* and the destroyer SMS *Ulan,* which had been bombarding Antivari. The French ships sank the *Zenta,* which lost 173 of its men and suffered over fifty wounded, and the *Ulan* escaped. There were no Allied casualties.

One of HMS *Warrior's* crew, Stoker Philip Brady, wrote in 1972 to a naval researcher that the Allied force 'engaged an Austrian cruiser, which we sank. She fought most splendidly against the famous French ships although she was only a small boat. Her men lined on deck as she went down, cheering'.[38]

This colourful account in a letter of a seventy-eight-year-old man written fifty-eight years after the event may not have been entirely accurate, but gives a flavour of the action.

The Battle of Antivari is a mere footnote in accounts of the Great War, if that – one respected book on the naval battles of the First World War does not even mention it. Yet the failure of its fleet to engage the Allied Forces in August 1914 was a symptom of the decline of the Austro-Hungarian Empire, which finally collapsed at the end of the war in 1918. All the ships of the Austro-Hungarian Navy then passed to the newly created state of the Slovenes, the Croats and the Serbs as neither Austria nor Hungary had any coastline or ports after the Great War.

This action was also a rare instance of a joint action of the French and British fleets in the Mediterranean during the Great War. After Antivari, Troubridge was ordered to take most of his squadron of cruisers to blockade the Dardanelles, but HMS *Warrior* was left in the Adriatic with two light cruisers, *Weymouth* and *Dublin*, under the command of the French Admiral.

However, within a few days the Admiralty ordered *Warrior* to Port Said, where she arrived on 21 August, in order to escort two captured German merchant ships to Alexandria. George's ship was instructed to remain in Egypt to defend the Suez Canal against any threatened attack from enemy forces and to intercept other enemy merchant ships taking refuge in the Canal.

The Suez Canal was built by the Universal Suez Ship Canal Company, which was controlled by the Egyptians and French. After it opened in 1869, it transformed the movement of naval and merchant ships around the world. Debt forced the Egyptian Government to sell its shares in the Canal Company to the British Government, but, under an 1888 international convention, the canal was open to ships of all nations to use, subject to the payment of dues.

If the Turkish army, based in the adjacent Ottoman territory of Palestine, supported by German forces and ships such as the German-manned *Goeben*, had succeeded in taking over the Suez Canal, merchant shipping from countries east of Suez destined for Great Britain and the other Allied countries could have been blocked and a lifeline to Europe would have been severed. In particular the increasingly vital supply of oil for the Allies from the Persian oilfields could have been stopped.

Such enemy occupation of the canal would also have halted the passage via Suez of all military shipping to and from the British dominions, colonies and ports in India, Ceylon, Singapore, Hong Kong, Australia and New Zealand, including the troopships bringing forces from all those territories of the British Empire to fight on the Western Front and in other fields of conflict such as the Dardanelles. Instead these ships would have had to take the lengthy diversion to Europe around the Cape of Good Hope.

Such was the strategic and commercial importance of the Suez Canal to Great Britain that, soon after the outbreak of the war, it sent British and Indian troops to defend the canal. As part of that operation, and to safeguard the passage of troopships through the canal, HMS *Warrior* remained in Egypt, sailing between Alexandria and Port Said on guard duty for nearly three months from late August until November 1914, where, under the command of Captain George H. Borrett, it served as the senior officer's ship in Egyptian waters at that time. Meanwhile her sister ships *Black Prince* and *Duke of Edinburgh* were on patrol in the Red Sea.

Despite the importance of defending Suez, Sir Julian Corbett, in his official history of naval operations during the Great War written in the 1920s, criticised the wasteful use of 'these three fine ships' on such 'minor services…notwithstanding the critical situation in South American waters'.[39]

During those months in Egypt, *Warrior*'s crew was occasionally able to take shore leave and explore the ancient sights of that country. The wonderfully named Able Seaman Alfred Theophilus Swain, a policeman's son from Nunney in Somerset, went with another sailor from *Warrior* to visit the Pyramids at Giza. There was a British military camp near the Pyramids during the war so there were plenty of servicemen in the vicinity. As holidaymakers still do, Alfred and his shipmate did the full tourism jolly of hiring a camel each, and they had a photo taken of themselves in front of the ancient Sphinx of Giza and the Great Pyramid. Each sailor sits astride a camel, wearing their rating's uniforms with naval straw boaters on their heads, the animals held steady on leads by their robed Arab guides who stand on each side. Alfred kept a large framed print of this photograph for the rest of his life back home in Nunney.[40]

No such photograph of George exists, sadly, but while stationed in Egypt on *Warrior* in late 1914 he too was able to take some shore leave and he visited the Pyramids and the Sphinx, and added postcards of them to his collection.

The Ottoman Empire of Turkey formally entered the war on the side of Germany on 28 October 1914. In the first week of November 1914 *Warrior* was ordered to leave Alexandria to sail towards the Egyptian city of El Arish on the Mediterranean coast of the Sinai Peninsula and to stop, by shelling, any enemy Turkish troops based in Palestine from advancing along the coast road there.

But by now the Admiralty itself had decided it should use its First Cruiser Squadron ships to better effect, and in mid-November *Warrior* and *Black Prince* were ordered to proceed to Gibraltar. They were relieved from their guard duties at Suez at first by French ships, and later by older light cruisers from the Royal Navy's Irish Station.

The British Government declared Egypt to be a protectorate in December 1914. Turkey controlled Palestine, which was adjacent to Egypt, and to defend Egypt from an attack from this neighbouring territory Britain continued building up its military presence there, so that by January 1915 it had some 70,000 troops in the Canal Zone. After some minor Turkish raids in late 1914, in February 1915 Turkey launched a major attack on the Suez Canal with the ultimate objective of causing an Islamic revolt in Egypt. British and Indian forces successfully resisted the Turkish army, which suffered the loss of some 1,500 of its soldiers.

According to Stoker Brady:

[HMS *Warrior*] left for Malta on November 14th 1914 and after getting some leave in Malta and repairing the ship in dock we again sailed for Gibraltar, spending four days there. At Gibraltar we were ordered to prepare for South America and get in provision but that order was cancelled so we went to 'Scapa Flow', the great Naval base in the North Sea.

The order at Gibraltar had been for HMS *Warrior* to join a squadron of British and French ships to search for German warships off the African coast, and *Warrior* did in fact sail down to Sierra Leone in West Africa in late November.[41] The intention was for this new West Coastal African Squadron to search for the German fleet of Admiral von Spee operating in the Atlantic and to protect Britain's colonies in West Africa. Von Spee had inflicted a crushing defeat on the Royal Navy at the Battle of Coronel on 1 November 1914, but following that battle the survivors were able to supply intelligence as to the location of the German ships, which led to the British defeat of von Spee at the Battle of the Falkland Islands on 8 December 1914.

After this victory the West African Squadron was disbanded, and later that December HMS *Warrior* was transferred from the Mediterranean Fleet to the Grand Fleet[42] based at Scapa Flow, the huge natural harbour in the Orkney Islands off northern Scotland. The First Cruiser Squadron was then re-formed that month under the command of Rear Admiral Sir Robert Keith Arbuthnot.

HMS *Warrior*'s home port was Devonport, and she may have called in there on her passage to Scapa Flow for a few days to allow George and the other crew some leave to be reunited with their families. George had not seen Ida since leaving for the goodwill visits to Italy in the peace of early 1914, and this was the first time he had seen his baby daughter Ida, now aged ten months.

North Sea, 1915–1916

HMS Warrior, 25th May 1916

My Darling Wife,
I received your ever welcome letter of the 20th and am glad to find that
it left you and the baby quite well as this also leaves me. The weather still
continues pretty good up here and it is much milder than it was now that
it is light up on deck of an evening up until 10 o'clock or so we are able to
get more exercise on deck walking up and down and other ways.

(Letter from George to Ida.)

After the failure to engage the German ships *Goeben* and *Breslau* in the
Mediterranean, the first few months of the Great War brought mixed
fortunes for the Royal Navy.

The first significant naval action took place at the Battle of Heligoland
Bight on 28 August 1914 when a British force of cruisers and destroyers,
with some submarines, attacked enemy patrols near the German coast
and sank three cruisers and a destroyer with the loss of 1,200 German
crew killed, wounded or missing.

The boost in national confidence from this victory did not last long.
On 22 September 1914 a German submarine, the U9, torpedoed three
old British cruisers – the *Aboukir*, the *Cressy* and the Devonport ship
Hogue – which had been patrolling without a destroyer escort off the
Dutch coast. The British suffered the loss of 1,489 sailors, including
many young naval cadets and 750 of HMS *Aboukir*'s crew of 800.

As their casualties in the trenches and at sea mounted and the
British public heard news of actual or alleged atrocities committed by
German soldiers against civilians in Belgium, a wave of anti-German
feeling, even hysteria, swept Great Britain. In October 1914 the First
Sea Lord, Prince Louis Battenberg, was forced to resign because of his
perceived German connections, and Admiral Sir John Fisher, now aged
seventy-three, was recalled in his place.

On 27 October 1914 a new 'super-dreadnought' battleship, HMS *Audacious*, was sunk off the Irish coast when it struck a German mine. All its crew were rescued apart from one petty officer hit by a piece of armour plating. The loss of this modern battleship was considered such a blow to British naval prestige that it was kept a secret, and no official announcement was made as to its sinking until after the end of the war in 1918.

Meanwhile in the Pacific Ocean, the East Asiatic Squadron under Vice Admiral Count von Spee had been intercepting British merchant ships carrying goods to Australia, New Zealand and India. The Admiralty ordered the South Atlantic Cruiser Squadron under the command of Rear Admiral Sir Christopher ('Kit') Cradock to sail from the Falkland Islands to engage von Spee's squadron. Cradock's ships were four inferior cruisers accompanied by an obsolescent pre-dreadnought battleship *Canopus*, and his crews were mainly inexperienced reservists.

The Admiralty vetoed Cradock's request for the armoured cruiser HMS *Defence* as a reinforcement, signalling by telegraph to the Rear Admiral that with the support of *Canopus* he had a 'sufficient force'. The Admiralty had misread the situation and did not realise that as Cradock's squadron approached von Spee's ships he had left *Canopus*, too slow and in need of engine repairs, some 250 miles behind to guard coaling ships.

Cradock knew full well that his chances of success against the Germans' far superior forces were low, but he was a courageous commander who had been ordered by the Admiralty to search for and engage the enemy. He was determined to fight, and his actions were influenced by the Navy's recent debacle with the *Goeben*. It was the week of Troubridge's court martial, and before he sailed from the Falklands Cradock had sent a letter to an old friend in which he wrote 'I will take care not to suffer the fate of poor Troubridge'.

On 1 November 1914 – All Saints' Day – Cradock's four cruisers met the five more modern, and better armed and armoured, German cruisers off the coast of central Chile near the port of Coronel. Admiral von Spee's fleet inflicted an overwhelming defeat on the British, whose two old armoured cruisers, the *Good Hope* and the *Monmouth*, were sunk. While the Germans lost no men, Cradock and the entire crew of both British ships died, a total of 1,654 men. The Battle of Coronel was the first time the Royal Navy had suffered a defeat for over a century since the Napoleonic Wars.

One sailor who died on HMS *Monmouth* was a forty-two-year-old Chief Engine Room Artificer called James Ronson, the father of George's brother-in-law Jack Ronson. George's sister Ellen Lancaster had married Jack Ronson in October 1911, and the death of her father-in-law, the grandfather of her one-year-old baby daughter Miriam, was a huge shock to the Ronson and Lancaster families in the first months of the war. James left a widow, Jane, the mother of their nine children, and she too died the following year in September 1915, leaving them orphaned. James Ronson's name is commemorated on the Naval War Memorial on Plymouth Hoe.

The Royal Navy's demoralising defeat at Coronel was soon avenged on 8 December 1914 at the Battle of the Falkland Islands when two Devonport-based battlecruisers, the *Inflexible* and the *Invincible*, were sent under the command of Admiral Sturdee to Port Stanley in the Falklands, where they engaged with von Spee's ships and sank his armoured cruisers *Scharnhorst* and *Gneisenau*. Some 2,200 Germans drowned, including Admiral von Spee and his two sons. German sailors were attacked by albatrosses as they struggled to survive in the freezing waters, and HMS *Inflexible* was able to rescue some of the enemy crewmen.

On 3 November 1914 Great Britain experienced its first attack on British soil in some 250 years when German warships shelled the Norfolk port of Great Yarmouth, although there were no casualties on that occasion. An even greater shock to the British civilian population came the following month when German ships attacked Hartlepool, Whitby and Scarborough in northeast England on 16 December 1914. One hundred and thirty-seven British people were killed in these three towns, mainly civilians and including several children. There were nearly 600 more injured.

The British made return raids on the German coast in the same month, including an aerial raid on the naval installations and the Zeppelin airship sheds at the port of Cuxhaven on the Elbe on Christmas Day 1914, supported by the ships of the Harwich Force.

After its return from the Mediterranean in December 1914, George's ship HMS *Warrior* was assigned with the First Cruiser Squadron to the British Grand Fleet, which was by then based at Scapa Flow in the Orkney Islands.

The historic ports of Devonport, Portsmouth and Chatham in the south of England had been developed to wage war against Britain's traditional enemy, France. The rising threat of Imperial Germany had led to the building of new naval ports on the north-eastern coast of the British Isles, Rosyth in the Firth of Forth, Invergordon in the Cromarty Firth, and Scapa Flow.

At the start of the war, Scapa Flow had been vulnerable to German U-boat attacks. After vigorous lobbying by the Grand Fleet's Commander-in-Chief, Admiral Sir John Jellicoe, by the end of 1914 Scapa was protected by anti-submarine booms, nets and mines, artillery guns and searchlights, and by the sinking of old merchant ships at the eastern entrances to the harbour's inner waters.

The strategic roles of the Royal Navy at Scapa Flow and at its other bases in Scotland, and down the eastern coast of the British mainland to the English Channel, were many and various.

The Grand Fleet was comprised of some thirty-five to forty modern battleships and battlecruisers – the capital ships – plus several destroyers, cruisers and submarines, and two seaplane carriers. It was intended to maintain, in size and number of ships, the long-held supremacy of Great Britain at sea and to be prepared for 'The Day' – *Der Tag* – of the anticipated battle with Germany's expanding fleet.

The defence of Great Britain itself from raids, even landings, by German ships was another vital function of Jellicoe's Grand Fleet in the North Sea, and in this role its very size acted as a deterrent to large-scale attacks by the enemy on the British mainland. In this it was supported along the east coast of England by the Harwich Force of cruisers, destroyers and submarines in Essex, and by other such patrol flotillas based at Dover and in the rivers Humber and Tyne.

The ships of the Channel Fleet also performed the essential job of protecting the troopships which transported over five million British and Empire troops to and from the trenches on the Western Front in France and Flanders throughout the four years of the war.

In 1912 Vice Admiral Sir David Beatty, then Churchill's naval secretary at the Admiralty, had clarified how the geography of Great Britain would determine the main strategy of the British fleet throughout the war:

> The British Isles form a great breakwater across German waters thereby limiting the passage of vessels to the outer seas to two exits, the one on the South, narrow, easily blocked and contained, and the other on the

North of such a width (155 miles) that with the forces at our disposal it could be easily commanded so as to preclude the possibility of the passing of any hostile force without our knowledge and without being brought to action by a superior force.

The role of Jellicoe's Grand Fleet was to block the German High Seas Fleet's northern passage out of the North Sea through the 200-mile stretch of water between the Orkneys and Norway. In combination with the Channel Fleet's blockade of the twenty-mile-wide Straits of Dover across the English Channel, this meant that Germany's battleships were bottled up in the North Sea and unable to sail out into the Atlantic and beyond to attack British merchant shipping, or to pose a threat to the British Empire's sea routes to her colonies across the globe.

This policy of 'distant blockade' of both north and south exits from the North Sea was adopted in preference to one of 'close blockade' of German ports by British warships positioned near the mainland of Germany which would put them at risk from the enemy's minefields, submarines and coastal gun batteries. In conjunction with a distant blockade, the Royal Navy could carry out regular sweeps of the North Sea to intercept the German *Kaiserliche Marine* as well as merchant ships taking goods to Germany.

The shipping of supplies directly to Germany in German merchant ships ceased soon after the outbreak of the war, but cargoes were still reaching Germany via neutral shipping and neutral countries. Jellicoe's Grand Fleet, and in particular its Northern Patrol of the Tenth Cruiser Squadron, enforced the blockade of merchant shipping bound for ports in the Netherlands and Scandinavia, from where supplies could be transported on to Germany.

This Northern Blockade was a British naval operation that continued throughout the Great War to restrict the supply of materials and food to Germany. The Northern Patrol consisted of twenty-four armed merchant cruisers, converted passenger and cargo ships which watched the 450-mile stretch of sea between the north of Scotland and Iceland as well as the 150-mile stretch between Iceland and Greenland. Some of these former cargo ships had carried fruit imports before the war, and so the Tenth Cruiser Squadron became known as the 'Banana Fleet'.

The cruisers sailed in line about twenty miles apart from each other, so blockade runners trying to pass between them could be seen and intercepted by one or both British ships. In what was a potentially dangerous operation, a Royal Navy boarding party would go in a small open boat over to the cargo ship, often in heavy seas. The British officer in command of the party, wearing a sword and carrying a revolver, inspected the cargo. If he found contraband goods the cargo ship was escorted to a British port and the goods seized.

Neutral countries such as Norway, the Netherlands and especially the United States complained loudly about the Royal Navy's interception of their commerce and removal of allegedly offending cargo, and indeed the British blockade was not in compliance with international treaty agreements. As early as 29 September 1914 Prime Minister Asquith reported: 'The Americans are making themselves disagreeable about the seizure and detention of cargoes sent in their ships…but we cannot allow the Germans to be provided for.'

On 30 March 1915 the US Government protested to the British:

…the methods of blockade which are now being used are clearly obnoxious to the well-recognized rights of neutral nations on the high seas.

The British would not alter their blockade policy. The Northern Patrol intercepted an average of 286 merchant ships each month between March 1915 and December 1916, as well as a monthly average of 150 fishing and coastal vessels. This blockade proved to be a key element in the Allies' ultimate victory in 1918.

In 1915 the Admiralty also started using special service ships, later known as 'Q-ships', as decoys. These were usually small tramp steamers disguised as merchant vessels but carrying Royal Navy officers, merchant crewmen and marines armed with guns and depth charges, and in later years torpedo tubes. They plied the trade routes of the Atlantic, English Channel and North Sea with the aim of enticing German submarines (U-boats) to the surface where the Q-ships could attack them. The Q-ships received much publicity after the war, but, as Arthur Marder pointed out, they only sank eleven U-boats during the war, some 7 per cent of the total number of the 145 German submarines sunk by the British, whereas twenty-seven Q-ships were sunk.[43]

After the disasters of the first months of the war in 1914, relieved only by the British victories at the battles of Heligoland Bight in August and the Falklands in December, the year 1915 commenced with the British success at the Battle of Dogger Bank in the North Sea. On 24 January Sir David Beatty's battlecruiser squadrons, led by his flagship HMS *Lion,* sank the German armoured cruiser *Blücher* with the loss of nearly 1,000 German crew.

HMS *Warrior*, as one of eight armoured cruisers attached to the Grand Fleet, was based at Scapa Flow from December 1914. Its published log book[44] for the year from April 1915 to April 1916 records that *Warrior* was putting to sea for sweeps searching for enemy ships in the northern waters of the North Sea. She also reported sightings of merchant ships apparently destined for Germany so that they could be inspected and if necessary blocked by the ships of the Northern Patrol.

The sheltered waters of Scapa enabled the ships of the Grand Fleet to engage in regular gunnery and torpedo practice out of range of German submarines. *Warrior* participated in these exercises, and also sailed regularly between Scapa Flow and the Fleet's other base in the Cromarty Firth, which was some 130 miles away down the Scottish coast, just north of Inverness.

In the main, *Warrior's* log book for 1915–16 focuses on matters of naval routine, and while it refers briefly to its sea patrols through the northernmost waters of the British Isles, it records little of the ship's wartime naval operations and does not give any sense of the threats from the enemy's ships and U-boats.

The log book does mention George V's two-day visit to Scapa Flow in July 1915.[45] On 7 July the King, a former naval officer himself, sailed into the harbour with his son Prince Albert,[46] a serving officer, on the destroyer HMS *Oak*, to be met by the Commander-in-Chief Admiral Sir John Jellicoe.

The King recorded the visit in his diary:

I then inspected the fleet by steaming between the lines. Each ship cheered as we passed, splendid sight, but it was cold and overcast with NE breeze which was a pity.

Going ashore at Longhope, George V inspected the crews of destroyers and trawlers, and the officers and men of the base's dockyard and stores. The following day, 8 July, the King, accompanied by Jellicoe and several other Admirals, boarded the flagships of the Grand Fleet, including HMS *Defence* of the First Cruiser Squadron. The log book of HMS *Warrior* states that 85 per cent of its crew embarked on HMS *Defence* to be inspected by the King, George Lancaster probably being among them.

That evening the King wrote in his diary as he left on HMS *Oak*:

> On board each flagship all the officers and men, not only of the flagships, but of their respective divisions, marched past me on the quarter deck. Everything was beautifully arranged, I must have seen close on 20,000 men. I also walked round some of the ships when there was time. Got back to Longhope at 6.30, a distinctly long but interesting day. The spirit of the fleet is splendid. Dined aboard Iron Duke with Commander-in-Chief at 8.30. 26 at dinner, including 11 Admirals.
>
> It was a great success in every way, I saw over 35,000 men in two days and the spirit of officers and men is splendid.

In August 1915 *Warrior* sailed from Scapa around the far north of the British Isles, passing the Dunnet Head Lighthouse (the most northerly part of the Scottish mainland), the aptly named Cape Wrath and down past the Isle of Lewis in the Outer Hebrides, past Islay and the Mull of Kintyre and into the Irish Sea. She was heading for the port of Birkenhead in the northwest of England where she spent a fortnight, probably for a refit or repairs at the Cammell Laird shipyard. George's ship then returned in late August to Scapa Flow where she was based for the rest of the year, with occasional voyages down to Cromarty and back.

Apart from enforcing the Northern Blockade, in 1915 much of the Grand Fleet had a relatively uneventful year in the North Sea. The main naval operations during that year were taking place in the eastern Mediterranean where the Royal Navy's role was to support the Allies' military landings on the Gallipoli Peninsula in the controversial Dardanelles Campaign from February 1915 to January 1916. The failures at Gallipoli caused a bitter falling out between Churchill, the First Lord of the Admiralty, who had planned the campaign, and the First Sea Lord Admiral Fisher, and led to the resignation of both men in 1915.

HMS *Warrior* was based at Scapa Flow for most of the winter of 1915–16, and life for the ships' crews in this remote inaccessible base was uncomfortable. In the winter months in the Orkneys daylight ended at 3.30 or 4 p.m., and the men endured bitter cold and sweeping gales. At sea for two days over Christmas 1915, HMS *Warrior's* log book records that many items of equipment were washed overboard in the heavy seas.

HMS *Warrior* and the other armoured cruisers in the First CS, like the majority of naval ships in the Great War, were still fuelled by Welsh coal, not oil. A cruiser could use 350 tons of coal in a day's steaming, much more at a higher rate of knots in battle conditions. All of its crew and all the officers, except the captain and those on duty, regularly had to undertake the exhausting and dirty process of loading the coal on to their ship from the quayside when in port, or from colliers, ships carrying bulk cargoes of coal, which came alongside. A cruiser took a load of 2,500–3,000 tons of coal, and with a loading rate of 300–400 tons an hour, coaling would take the men a whole day, and was often undertaken as a competitive race with other ships being coaled.

On the collier or quay, the men, all wearing old clothes, with Vaseline in their nostrils, shovelled the coal into two-hundredweight bags which were hoisted in batches of ten by a derrick on to the cruiser, and then tipped down iron chutes fitted by the stokers from the upper deck down through several decks to the coal bunkers in the ship's hold. Big tubs of lime juice might be available on the decks to refresh the men as they laboured, but that drink would soon be tainted by coal dust.

After eight or ten hours of this, all the men and the whole ship were covered with layers of filthy black soot, so once the coaling was complete the next job for the crew was to wash down the vessel, clean themselves up and change back into their proper uniform. At least in Scapa the cold, wet climate made the whole coaling process a little more bearable than it was for crews in the Mediterranean or the tropics.

As well as coaling of the ship, while on duty in harbour the men had to polish and paint the vessel. Regular musters in divisions for inspection, and physical drills, were part of the daily routine; punishments were meted out to offenders, and sick crew members were discharged to the hospital ship. Canteen facilities were primitive, and the only drinks bar for the men at Scapa was in a hut with a trestle table and two or three large beer barrels.

Many servicemen were sent items from home by churches and voluntary organisations to supply some comforts. For example, the

Church of St Thomas the Martyr in Bristol sent the sailors parcels, each containing two tins of Wills' Gold Flake cigarettes; two tins of Wills' Capstan Navy Cut Tobacco; one large cake; two packets of Fry's Milk Chocolate; one woollen comforter; one pair of socks; two pairs of boot laces, and a letter of moral support from the congregation.

The Grand Fleet's Commander-in-Chief, Admiral Jellicoe, a respected and well-liked leader, was concerned for the welfare of his sailors and encouraged various forms of recreation at Scapa Flow. There was a golf course for the officers, a football pitch for all ranks, and for the men boxing was popular. The crews also organised their own recreational activities, including shooting, fishing and walking, boating picnics, regattas, amateur dramatics, lectures and educational classes. Gambling was widespread even though it was banned, and ships' dances were popular despite the absence of women partners.

But generally life for the men at Scapa was tedious and boring, as indicated in this letter home from one rating:

Dear Mum,
I cannot tell you where I am. I don't know where I am. But where I am
there is miles and miles of bugger all.
Love Ted [47]

The monotonous routine was exceptionally frustrating for a naval force trained for a major battle with the German High Seas Fleet, raring to go into combat with the enemy, but instead hearing daily of the war experiences of the British Army in the trenches of France and Flanders. For George and the crew on HMS *Warrior* the frustrations of life were not improved by the harsh regime which the Commander of the First Cruiser Squadron, Rear Admiral Sir Robert Arbuthnot, imposed on the crews of his four armoured cruisers at Scapa Flow. They were not 'happy ships'.

Arbuthnot was a man of high Christian standards, but also a strict disciplinarian, obsessed with physical fitness, a boxer and a keen motorcyclist.[48] He has been described by one naval historian as 'in a colloquial if not a clinical sense, insane…as a tyrant, bully and physical-training fanatic, Arbuthnot was loathed'.[49] Even his good friend Ernle Chatfield, then the respected captain of HMS *Lion*, admitted that Arbuthnot was 'difficult to serve'.

Arbuthnot's rigid and intimidating management of his officers, which also stifled the initiative of his First CS captains, apparently created problems at a senior level. In September 1915 Admiral Jellicoe wrote to the First Sea Lord Sir Henry Jackson:

> *There is trouble in the 1*st *Cruiser Squadron. I put Burney on to investigate for the day. Arbuthnot is one of the finest fellows in the world but somehow can't run a squadron. His ideals are too high and he can't leave people alone.*

After receiving Burney's report, Jellicoe again wrote to the First Sea Lord suggesting that the First Cruiser Squadron be broken up. He added:

> *All is now well in the Warrior, but I find today that Arbuthnot is still – although to a much lesser extent – centralising the work too much to himself. He does not seem able to understand the objections to this & therefore, in spite of his many fine qualities, I think it as well that the change should be made.*

However, the First Cruiser Squadron remained intact under Arbuthnot's command, with fateful consequences.

In early February 1916, *Warrior* sailed to Cromarty and remained based there for the next month. In an entry in March 1916 the log book simply records that on 1 March the ship 'retrieved the body of D. Owens AB [Able Seaman] of HMS *Natal*', and on 6 March it 'retrieved the body of AB Hartle [Hartley] late of HMS *Natal*'.

HMS *Natal* was another *Warrior*-class armoured cruiser of the Second Cruiser Squadron. On 30 December 1915 it was moored off Invergordon in the Cromarty Firth, some twenty miles north of Inverness. Its Captain had invited some wives and children of the officers on board HMS *Natal* to watch a film as part of the Christmas festivities. While the crew and their guests were watching the film, an explosion occurred and the whole ship blew up.

The number of casualties was initially hushed up, but it was subsequently confirmed that a total of 421 people were killed, including the visiting women and children. The official enquiry found that the explosion had been caused not by enemy fire, but internally by cordite stored on HMS *Natal* which had been accidentally ignited, perhaps just by a spark.

HMS *Warrior* picked up these two dead crew members from HMS *Natal* over two months after the tragedy, but very few of the bodies of those killed were ever recovered. In the midst of war little publicity was given to the event. This was not the first such catastrophic internal explosion of a warship. On 26 November 1914 the pre-dreadnought battleship HMS *Bulwark* had also blown up near Sheerness owing to cordite charges being stored too near a boiler room and overheating, causing the death of 738 men. The poor storage of cordite was to cause the further terrible loss of many more British lives during the war.

Warrior returned from Cromarty to Scapa on 9 March, staying there for another six weeks, with a couple of voyages back to Cromarty. On 19 April *Warrior* sailed around northern Scotland again, past Cape Wrath and the Hebrides and down to the Mersey, this time berthing in Liverpool for a week before crossing over the Mersey to Birkenhead for three days of repairs. It was here that the published log book's record ended on 30 April 1916.

In May *Warrior* returned via the Hebrides and Cape Wrath to Scapa Flow, and by the end of that month it was moored back in the Cromarty Firth. On 25 May, George wrote a letter to his wife Ida from his ship:

HMS *Warrior*, 25th May 1916

My Darling Wife,

I received your ever welcome letter of the 20th and am glad to find that it left you and the baby quite well as this also leaves me. The weather still continues pretty good up here and it is much milder than it was now that it is light up on deck of an evening up until 10 o'clock or so we are able to get more exercise on deck walking up and down and other ways.

I am very glad to know that the baby is getting on so well as you say and I have no doubt she can talk much better now than even when I was home. I am pleased to know she has not forgotten me and at times talks about me to you. I was amazed to read what she said when she saw the photos of Nell and Mi.[50]

I read in the Independent about a court-martial on Stanley Beer and he has been sentenced to six months' detention. I feel rather sorry he should hold such ridiculous views especially as his people must have scraped

*a good deal to give him an education like he had. They must be terribly
worried about it and if he gets the full measure of the Military Detention
Punishment such as I have been told it is, it will either kill him or
cure him…*

George signs off 'Your Ever Loving Husband', but sadly his signature
and the last part of the letter has been torn away and are lost. Nor do
we know of what specific offence Stanley Beer was guilty – it appears he
may have held views regarded in war-time as seditious.

By the early summer of 1916 the Royal Navy's Grand Fleet and the
German Navy's High Seas Fleet were still operating in expectation of
what had been termed *Der Tag* – The Day – when these two huge naval
forces would at last engage in a major battle at sea to determine their
competing claims to global maritime supremacy.

Just a week after George's letter to Ida, his ship HMS *Warrior* was
involved in the Battle of Jutland on 31 May 1916.

The Battle of Jutland

Jutland was more than the largest naval engagement of the First World War – the military historian Sir John Keegan wrote that this battle 'was to be the biggest and the last purely surface encounter of main fleets in naval history'.[51]

The British Grand Fleet that sailed under the command of Admiral Sir John Jellicoe, along with the Battlecruiser Fleet under Rear Admiral Sir David Beatty, comprised twenty-eight dreadnought-class battleships, nine battlecruisers, eight armoured cruisers, twenty-six light cruisers, seventy-eight destroyers, one seaplane carrier and a minesweeper – a total of 151 ships carrying some 60,000 men. The Royal Navy by a considerable margin outnumbered the German High Seas Fleet under the command of Admiral Reinhard Scheer, which had sixteen dreadnought battleships, six pre-dreadnoughts, five battlecruisers, eleven light cruisers and sixty-one destroyers – a total of ninety-nine ships with 45,000 men.[52] Both sides had submarines at sea as well, but none of these took any part in the battle.

Admiral Scheer had taken over command of the High Seas Fleet in February 1916 and immediately adopted a more offensive strategy than his predecessors. That spring he sent out several naval sorties, including bombardments by his ships of Hull, Lowestoft and Yarmouth, to try to lure out part of the British fleet so that his High Seas Fleet and U-boats could attack them. Even if he could not achieve an outright victory, Scheer's aim was to cause sufficient damage to a segment of Jellicoe's Grand Fleet to equalise the respective strengths of the British and German navies, so ending Great Britain's century-long global maritime supremacy.

In the early hours of 31 May 1916 Vice Admiral Hipper's battlecruisers of his Scouting Group, followed by Scheer's Battle Squadrons, sailed from the Jade Bight outside the German naval base at Wilhelmshaven and north towards the Skagerrak, the area of sea off the coast of the Danish region called Jutland. Scheer's objective was to threaten British merchant ships and so draw out a few of Jellicoe's battleships to where they would be vulnerable to attack by the Germans.

Scheer was unaware that the British already knew something of his plans and had decided to lay their own trap for him by sending the whole Grand Fleet to meet him. The Admiralty's intelligence unit in London was based in 'Room 40', and the Germans did not know that Room 40 was able to decode their signals after the Allies had obtained German signal books from destroyed or captured ships at the beginning of the war. The British had picked up messages that the Germans were commencing a major naval operation, and by midday on 30 May Room 40 had deciphered information that the German High Seas Fleet was putting to sea the next day. The Admiralty had notified the Commander-in-Chief, Jellicoe, of these plans at noon on 30 May, and its signals at 5.40 p.m. later that afternoon were the orders to Jellicoe to take the Grand Fleet to sea in preparation for battle.

The first shells at Jutland were fired at approximately 2.30 p.m. on the afternoon of 31 May, and the fighting continued for the rest of that day and through the night. Naval historians usually divide what was a complex action into five phases – Beatty's Battlecruiser Fleet's 'run to the south' towards the High Seas Fleet; its 'run to the north' to draw the German ships towards Jellicoe's Grand Fleet; two clashes between the British and German dreadnoughts resulting in the German turn away from the heavier British firepower, followed by Jellicoe's own turn away in the face of the German destroyers' torpedo threat; and the night action on 31 May/1 June, involving torpedo attacks from both sides by destroyers and torpedo boats, during which Scheer's High Seas Fleet escaped to safety.

By the conclusion of the battle the British had lost 112,000 tons of warships, which were three of Beatty's battlecruisers, three armoured cruisers and eight destroyers. Of its total crew strength of 60,000, some 6,094 men had died, 674 were wounded and 177 sailors had been picked up from the sea and taken as prisoners of war by German ships – a casualty rate of 8.84 per cent. The German losses were lighter – they had lost 62,000 tons of warships, being a battlecruiser, a pre-dreadnought battleship, four light cruisers and five destroyers. Out of a total crew strength of 45,000, 2,551 German sailors were killed with 507 wounded, a casualty rate of 6.79 per cent.

At the time, the outcome of the battle was a great blow to the morale of the British public, who had grown up with such great expectations of its Navy. Kaiser Wilhelm and the German press immediately hailed their 'Victory of the Skagerrak'. In the days after the battle there was considerable despondency in Great Britain, not helped by the Admiralty's delayed and weak statement which underestimated the German casualties.

Within weeks a 'Jutland Controversy' developed, with naval officers, politicians and journalists debating its strategy, tactics and outcome. In their own post-war accounts, Admiral Jellicoe and Vice Admiral Beatty criticised each other, and in assessing the decisions and omissions of these two naval commanders, many commentators took partisan and often unseemly 'pro-Jellicoe' or 'pro-Beatty' stances. In the century since, the intense debate over Jutland has endured in the many historical studies of the battle.

Even before battle was joined, grossly incompetent handling of Room 40's intelligence by an Admiralty official in London meant that Jellicoe was informed that at 12.45 p.m. on 31 May Scheer was still in port at Wilhelmshaven, whereas the German Admiral had already sailed into the North Sea. As a result of the Admiralty error, Jellicoe slowed his fleet's progress, thinking he had more time before encountering the enemy, and thereby lost the opportunity of a vital two hours or so of action in daylight. The Grand Fleet did not arrive in the battle area to join Beatty's forces until the late afternoon of 31 May, and Jellicoe had already decided to avoid a night action by his capital ships as his crews were not well-trained for this, and at night his dreadnoughts would be at greater risk from German destroyers.

Once he discovered the Admiralty's signal was incorrect, Jellicoe was not prepared to rely on its subsequent valid and vital intelligence information, which might have changed the course of the battle to his advantage.

At the outset of the war, Jellicoe, a centralist planner who did not like to delegate, had produced lengthy and meticulous Grand Fleet Battle Orders in preparation for a major encounter with the German High Seas Fleet. Jellicoe was a cautious commander, whose Battle Orders were criticised after Jutland for being too defensive in dealing with the risk of torpedoes, mines or submarines. They were also over-prescriptive, and as the fighting progressed they no longer applied. In the appalling visibility and the confusion of battle, with communication between ships difficult, if not impossible, the British squadron commanders and flotilla captains had to exercise their independent judgement and use their initiative, something they were not used to doing.

Yet Jellicoe was very effective in the deployment of his Grand Fleet at Jutland, twice 'crossing the T' of the German ships' line of battle, a difficult but very advantageous naval manoeuvre. He was criticised for his order to the Grand Fleet to turn away from the enemy later on as darkness fell, but he had planned this in advance in his orders as a manoeuvre, not a retreat, to reduce the risk of major underwater damage to his battleships from the torpedoes of German destroyer flotillas. Jellicoe believed his duty was to maintain his Grand Fleet as the superior maritime force and as a deterrent to the enemy, and not to jeopardise that position, particularly at night, by exposing his ships to attack by torpedoes.

In this strategy he was successful, and Admiral Scheer failed in his attempt to isolate and destroy a group of Jellicoe's battleships in order to reduce the Grand Fleet's strength and numbers to parity with his High Seas Fleet. In fact the German celebrations of their alleged victory overlooked the facts that Scheer had fallen into a British trap when he sailed into the whole of the Grand Fleet, which he had never intended to do; that the German Commander-in-Chief had turned away to escape the British attack before recklessly turning back towards Jellicoe's dreadnoughts, thereby again placing the German ships in a very exposed position; and that to save his High Seas Fleet from likely destruction, Scheer had finally fled to shelter behind the German minefields near Horns Reef off the Jutland coast, before making a run for home to the Jade Bight.

It was Rear Admiral David Beatty who was seen as the dashing and gallant hero of Jutland by much of the British public. He had demonstrated his Nelsonian offensive spirit when his battlecruisers successfully enticed the German High Seas Fleet directly into the trap of Jellicoe's Grand Fleet in the 'run to the north'. Beatty's supporters blamed Jellicoe for failing to follow up on the Battlecruiser Fleet's achievement by twice turning away at crucial stages instead of taking the offensive against the enemy. But Beatty, regarded by many as arrogant and impetuous, made serious mistakes at Jutland. His signals were haphazard, and he and other commanders did not keep Jellicoe informed as to their fleet movements or pass on vital intelligence, wrongly assuming that the Commander-in-Chief could see whatever they saw.

Most damaging was Beatty's failure to liaise with Vice Admiral Hugh Evan-Thomas, the commander of the four super-dreadnoughts of the Fifth Battle Squadron which had sailed from Rosyth with Beatty's battlecruisers. A lack of advance communication between these two commanders, poor flag signalling by Beatty's incompetent signals officer, and a complete lack of initiative by Evan-Thomas resulted in his Fifth Battle Squadron twice steaming away in the wrong direction. As a result his super-dreadnoughts, the most powerful ships in the world, were too far off to support Beatty at crucial stages in the battle, particularly when Beatty's battlecruisers encountered those of Admiral Hipper's Scouting Group which shelled the British ships with terrible consequences. Evan-Thomas's squadron could have made a decisive contribution to the battle's outcome if Beatty had effectively concentrated his forces from the start. Beatty also damaged his own reputation after the war when, as the First Sea Lord, he ignobly used his position to try to influence an official report on Jutland so that criticisms of his own role were removed and the contribution of his Battlecruiser Fleet was enhanced.

The signals procedure of Beatty's Battlecruiser Fleet was inefficient, but the fog and funnel smoke at Jutland created the conditions of very poor visibility for flag signalling by all the ships, which caused confusion and communication errors. The Royal Navy was still relying heavily on signalling at sea by flags, as many officers were concerned that the relatively new wireless telegraphy gave away their ships' positions, or that it would be subject to enemy jamming or interception. It was common procedure to confirm flag signals in Morse code by flashing lamps or searchlights, but it was often difficult to do this in the heat of battle.

Another crucial factor at Jutland was that the Germans' gunnery, with superior range-finding optics, was more accurate over longer distances than the Royal Navy's, and the standard of gunnery of Beatty's Battlecruiser Fleet was inadequate. German shells were better at piercing the armour of British ships, while unreliable British shells, if striking at oblique angles, shattered on impact without penetrating the better armoured and more robustly constructed enemy ships. After Jutland it was discovered that the explosive charges on British shells were often faulty and that there were serious defects in their design.

Once the German shells had hit British ships and set them on fire, the poor storage on board of explosive cordite charges caused several of them, including the flagship of George's squadron, to blow up completely. Flashes of high-velocity flame penetrated from the gun turrets down to the magazines where the ammunition was stored, and the warships exploded with the loss of virtually all their crews. The Germans' ships were not affected in the same way, as following an explosion on the *Seydlitz* at the Battle of Dogger Bank in 1915, the Germans had adopted effective anti-flash arrangements on their warships.[53]

Three of the ships that suffered this fate were Beatty's battlecruisers *Indefatigable*,[54] *Queen Mary* and *Invincible*. A total of 3,309 men were killed on those three ships alone, casualties largely caused by their own explosives after being hit by German shells. As he watched these disasters at Jutland, Beatty uttered his famous remark 'There seems to be something wrong with our bloody ships today'.[55]

Beatty was right in that, as Jutland demonstrated the flaws in Admiral Fisher's concept of the heavily-armed but fast class of cruiser which he had developed in 1907. In order to carry eight large 12-inch calibre guns and still achieve speeds of up to 25 knots, the designers of the new battlecruisers had to sacrifice armour, and their thin armour plating made those ships tragically vulnerable to shelling in battle.

Yet despite the stark imbalance in the British and German losses and the indecisive outcome, the Battle of Jutland is generally held to have been a strategic victory for Great Britain, despite the Kaiser's claims to the contrary. On the day after the battle, the Royal Navy still had twenty-four dreadnought battleships ready for action, while the German *Kaiserliche Marine* had only ten such ships which could put to sea. The British retained control of the North Sea and the waters beyond.

Winston Churchill said of Jellicoe that he 'was the only man on either side who could lose the war in an afternoon'. Even if it did not appear he had won the battle on the afternoon of Jutland, Jellicoe did not lose the war that day, as he would have done if Admiral Scheer had succeeded in crippling a major part of the Royal Navy's fleet. If that disaster had occurred, Germany would have been able to break the British blockade of their own ships and ports, attack Allied merchant shipping, block vital shipments to Britain and cut off supplies to British armies in France and elsewhere overseas. The High Seas Fleet would have been able to sail out into the world's oceans to assert its maritime supremacy. Great Britain might even have been invaded.

Instead, after Jutland, the German High Seas Fleet engaged with the Royal Navy on only one further occasion during the Great War, in the inconclusive Second Battle of Heligoland Bight on 17 November 1917. That apart, for the remainder of the war the German ships were confined to their ports and emerged again on only three other occasions, in August and October 1916 and in April 1918, for sorties of no effect. On this last occasion the German Admiral Hipper turned his ships back home following a malfunction on SMS *Moltke* which caused it to break essential radio silence.

An American journalist wrote of the fighting at Jutland that 'The German Fleet has assaulted its jailor but it is still in jail'.

Germany thereafter turned to unrestricted submarine warfare, which did prove to be a very significant challenge to British merchant ships in 1917–18 and a real danger to Great Britain herself. However, the Royal Navy maintained it superiority and kept the sea lanes to Britain open so that food and supplies could reach its population.

For those wishing to know more detail of the Battle of Jutland, an excellent and very readable account is *Jutland 1916: Death in the Grey Wastes*[56] by Nigel Steel and Peter Hart, which studies the background to the battle and gives a detailed account of the action and aftermath. This book is also especially good in focusing on the experiences of the officers and men of all rates on the ships involved, both in the British Grand Fleet and in the German High Seas Fleet.

In an era when men did not tend to tell even close relatives of their appalling war experiences, George Lancaster left no record of his service at Jutland. However, the importance to historians of obtaining a set of first-hand accounts of the battle was fortunately appreciated early on, and in addition to the contemporary accounts and records of interviews with servicemen taken soon after the event, a book called *The Fighting at Jutland: The Personal Experiences of Forty-Five Officers and Men of the British Fleet* was published in 1921. One of the officers interviewed was Captain Vincent Molteno of HMS *Warrior*.[57]

In 1972 a valuable archive of letters and accounts was compiled by an English researcher called Robert Church, who was preparing a book on Jutland. He placed newspaper advertisements throughout the country asking to be contacted by men who had fought at Jutland, and he received dozens of letters and replies to his questionnaire from former

British sailors, by then in their seventies and eighties, whose memories of the battle remained sharp and poignant. Church never completed his book, but his collection of responses now forms a valuable archive on Jutland and is held in the Imperial War Museum in London.

The historian Peter Liddle also undertook considerable research into service in the Royal Navy during the Great War, and the Liddle Collection includes many first-hand accounts from men who served at Jutland.[58]

In their book Nigel Steel and Peter Hart (both research staff members at the Imperial War Museum) quote these testimonies of the sailors themselves to provide extraordinarily readable and graphic stories of the conditions endured during and after the fighting. Much of the following account of George's ship HMS *Warrior* at the Battle of Jutland is taken directly from these personal stories of its crew, both officers and men.[59]

Jutland – Warrior's Fight

On Tuesday 30 May 1916, just a few days after George's letter to his wife, HMS *Warrior* was moored in the Cromarty Firth in northeast Scotland, along with the other ships of the First Cruiser Squadron, on a break from its duty of patrolling the North Sea.

It was a calm summer's day, and according to Reuben Poole, a signalman on *Warrior*, a few of the officers had gone ashore to Invergordon on leave, including the Squadron's commander, Rear Admiral Sir Robert Arbuthnot, a keen sportsman who was playing tennis that afternoon. Surgeon Lieutenant Charles Leake, one of HMS *Warrior's* medical officers, said it 'was a routine change of a few days at Invergordon – weather propitious, so made most of shore leave'.

Shortly before the men's tea-time, at about 6 p.m., there was a flurry of signals, and orders went out for all crew to return to their ships and to prepare to sail. That afternoon Jellicoe had received the Admiralty's message that its Room 40 intelligence unit in London had read the German signals confirming that Scheer's High Seas Fleet was about to leave port early the following day. Jellicoe's ships were to leave their harbours before any of the Germans had set sail.

Stoker Philip Brady on HMS *Warrior* remembered that evening:

> It was on Tuesday night and the weather was very calm and everything quiet when we were having a short rest in Harbour and a few of our ships' company were ashore in Cromarty indulging in a few pints of beer when a signal came through raise steam and report when ready. As soon as this signal was made all men were recalled from shore and all got to work to prepare ship for sea. All is ready and steam raised we reported ready for sea, this would be about 9 o'clock at night. At half past 9 another signal came through for its 'weigh anchor' which all the ships in Harbour did. Then we got under way taking our place in the line on leaving Harbour, little thinking…what dramatic circumstances we were going to go through in the next 48 hours.

At about 9 p.m. on the night of 30 May, Jellicoe sailed the Grand Fleet from its base at Scapa Flow in the Orkney Islands. The Second Battle Squadron, comprising the flagship HMS *King George V* and seven other battleships under the command of Vice Admiral Jerram, was moored further south in Scotland, in the Cromarty Firth alongside Arbuthnot's First Cruiser Squadron. At about 9.30 p.m. this Battle Squadron set sail, accompanied by the four armoured cruisers of the First CS, being the flagship HMS *Defence*, HMS *Warrior* (George's ship), HMS *Duke of Edinburgh* and HMS *Black Prince*. With them were some ships of the Eleventh Destroyer Flotilla.

Meanwhile Rear Admiral David Beatty was taking his Battlecruiser Fleet, accompanied by the Fifth Battle Squadron of four modern battleships under the command of Rear Admiral Hugh Evan-Thomas, from Rosyth in the Firth of Forth out under the Forth Rail Bridge into the North Sea.

Jellicoe's fleet met Jerram's battleships and Arbuthnot's armoured cruisers in the North Sea, and then they all proceeded to some 100 miles south-west of the coast of Norway and north-west of the Jutland region of Denmark, where the waters of the Skagerrak meet the North Sea. There they would be joined by Beatty's Battlecruiser Fleet and the Fifth Battle Squadron.

This huge fleet of battleships and battlecruisers, with an array of powerful 15-inch and 10-inch guns,[60] was escorted by its protective screen of light cruisers and destroyers, and led by the armoured cruisers whose role was to act as a forward screen and to scout ahead of the main fleet on reconnaissance.

By May 1916 these armoured cruisers of the First CS were over ten years old (HMS *Warrior* had been launched in 1905). They were widely regarded as obsolescent, being slow with a top speed of only 23 knots, and under-gunned with their six 9.2-inch and four 7.5-inch guns.

Even more crucially, these ships were under-armoured. They were still fuelled by coal, and the need to carry heavy stocks of coal for long voyages to far corners of the British Empire required the weight of the ship itself to be reduced. This was achieved at the expense of the cruisers' armour plating. HMS *Warrior* and her sister ships in the First CS were armoured with a 3- to 6-inch thick metal belt at the waterline, with deck armour protection of between 1½ inches and only ¾ inch. This was not thick enough to provide sufficient protection against the penetrating 11-inch shells from bigger and more accurate enemy guns. Yet despite their age and deficiencies in armour and speed, the First CS ships were deployed as a vanguard several miles ahead of the main British Fleet.

Stoker Philip Brady:

> All went well Tuesday night waking up next morning Wednesday, the fatal day, May 31st. It was a very clear morning and a very calm sea, steaming along at about 15 knots up and down the North Sea, trying to find any enemy craft about. Turn on watch at the guns and others down below in the stoke hold and engine room. Others writing and reading, sleeping etc. waiting for the turns to come to relieve the other men on watch, everything as usual when a ship is at sea. The reader must understand there are a number of ships together, you are not by yourself. Every ship must keep its proper place in the line when we are at sea not one yard 'ahead' or 'astern' which plays a prominent place in action.

As *Warrior* sailed into the North Sea, the whole ship's company, whether on or off duty, were no doubt hoping they were about to engage in the long-awaited battle with the enemy, even though it threatened them with appalling injuries or death. Every crew member knew what role he had to perform. The men working in the engine room were not able to hear or see what was happening up on deck or beyond, but their Engineer Commander would have drilled them thoroughly in their exercises preparing for war, and they were ready to contribute to the ship's fighting efficiency. Once they heard the order for 'Action Stations' and *Warrior's* guns started firing, every man in the engine room knew what he needed to do to help keep the engines running, maintain power and keep the ship afloat.

When on their watch, George and the other engineers on duty were below deck, well below the vessel's waterline, in very hot, dirty, noisy and claustrophobic conditions. They worked in the two cramped engine rooms, at risk from burns and scalding, surrounded by a packed metal mass of vibrating pipes, rods, shafts, cranks and condensers, pumping cylinders, thudding pistons and the other dangerous machinery of triple-expansion reciprocating steam engines.

Sweating in temperatures of up to 130 degrees Fahrenheit, they choked on coal dust as they worked alongside teams of stokers shovelling the coal into the roaring furnaces of the boilers, others heaving more stocks of it from the bunkers, as the ship pitched and rolled through the seas. The officers on the bridge passed down the voice pipe the Captain's orders for more speed to the Engineer Commander, the ERAs worked on the engines to boost the steam pressure, and the stokers redoubled their efforts to fire up the boilers. When an ERA was not on duty in the engine room, he was assigned other active duties, such as working on machinery elsewhere in the ship, fire-watching or being prepared for damage control. He snatched such sleep as he could when off duty.

At 3.30 p.m. on the afternoon of 31 May, HMS *Warrior*, with its crew of over 800, was steaming ahead of the Grand Fleet with the rest of the First CS, which was performing its role as a cruiser screen and advance reconnaissance on the starboard wing of the main fleet. Signalman Reuben Poole recalled that the men on his watch section were sent for an early tea.

Stoker Brady continued:

All went well as I have said before, until half past 3 in the afternoon when a signal came through, 'Beatty's fleet sighted. The German High Sea fleet is engaging them off the Jutland coast, make full speed and try and cut them off from retreating back to their base'. So we started full speed for the scene of action, Defence leading as she was flagship to us. At twenty minutes to six p.m. we sighted the two Fleets in action. Then the Captain gave orders to sound Action Stations on the bugle as every man has a job allotted out to him in action. At fifteen minutes to six our ship fired the first angry shot.

Rear Admiral Sir Robert Arbuthnot, the First CS's Commander, was on the squadron flagship HMS *Defence*. As the Grand Fleet engaged with the German High Seas Fleet, the position assigned to Arbuthnot's First CS by Jellicoe's detailed Grand Fleet Battle Orders should have been for the four armoured cruisers to move to the rear of the battle line. But instead of manoeuvring his armoured cruisers down the disengaged wing of the British Grand Fleet to its rear, Arbuthnot had decided to move his flagship HMS *Defence* and two of his other cruisers

111

into the engaged space between the two opposing fleets. Arbuthnot was clearly determined that his squadron would engage with the enemy as soon as possible, and he commanded his ships to set off towards the German light cruiser *Wiesbaden,* which had already been disabled and immobilised by the guns of HMS *Indomitable.*

Steel and Hart write:

> The obsolescent cruisers had been acting as a screen and now found themselves in the dangerous waters between the Grand Fleet and the High Seas Fleet. Arbuthnot pulled the Defence and the Warrior together with the Duke of Edinburgh trailing slightly behind, and seems to have set off towards the sound of the guns, heading direct for the Wiesbaden. This put them on a collision course with the Lion and the Battlecruiser Fleet.[61]

HMS *Lion,* the flagship of Rear Admiral Sir Robert Beatty, had just begun to engage the enemy as well. A collision between HMS *Defence* and HMS *Lion* was very narrowly avoided:

> At that exciting moment I saw the First Cruiser Squadron leading from port to starboard across my back bows. It was clear that unless I altered course drastically I should collide with one of his ships, so I jammed the line's helm over and swung her under the stern of their second cruiser which only cleared us by a cable's length. By forcing the Battlecruiser Squadron off its course in the low visibility, which was then only 5 miles, Arbuthnot caused us to lose sight of the enemy fleet and he himself took the place of the Battlecruisers as their targets.
>
> *Flag Captain Chatfield, HMS* Lion, *First Battlecruiser Squadron*

Some insight into Arbuthnot's thinking is given by the following account:

> Admiral Arbuthnot had made it abundantly clear in a series of addresses to the ship's companies of the vessels under his command that when he encountered the enemy he would close to the rather meagre range of our guns and engage remorselessly. In the action he put his precepts into practice, but the old ships of the First Cruiser Squadron were no match for the German Battlecruisers.

Lieutenant Leslie Hollis, HMS *Duke of Edinburgh*, First Cruiser Squadron.

After narrowly missing Beatty's battlecruisers, the *Defence* and the *Warrior* began to shell the German ship *Wiesbaden* with their 9.2-inch guns. As Signalman Poole of the *Warrior* later related, they were 'belting away at the crippled *Wiesbaden*'. However, while Arbuthnot's First CS ships were blasting the *Wiesbaden*, the German battlecruisers could clearly see the *Defence* and the *Warrior*.

> When I first saw them I felt they were doomed. They were steaming at their utmost speed between the lines, endeavouring to get clear round us, i.e. round the end of the Grand Fleet, smoking very heavily, being continually straddled and frequently hit. They were soon on fire in several places, but they still continued to fire to the very last.
>
> *Lieutenant Patrick Brind, HMS* Malaya

The Commander of the *Derfflinger* wrote:

> In the misty grey light the colours of the German and English ships were difficult to distinguish. The Cruiser was not very far away from us. She had four funnels and two masts, like our Rostock. "She is certainly English," Lieutenant Hauser shouted.
>
> "May I fire?"
>
> "Yes, fire away!"
>
> I was now certain she was an English ship, the secondary arma-ment was trained on the new target. Hauser gave the order, then just as he was about to give the order something terrific happened. The English ship which I had meanwhile identified as an old Eng-lish Army Cruiser broke in half with a tremendous explosion. Black smoke and debris shot into the air, flames enveloped the whole ship and then she sank before our eyes. There was nothing but a gigantic smoke cloud to mark the place where just before a proud ship had been fighting.
>
> *Commander Georg von Hase,* Derfflinger

The German ship *Lutzow* had hit and destroyed the *Defence* before the *Derfflinger* had a chance to open fire.

The explosion was seen from the destroyer HMS *Maenad*:

Poor fellows, I had only had such a cheery lunch with them all a few days ago. She never had a chance. As the fleets closed so rapidly that she couldn't get out of the way, though tried to do so. She went up in a huge sheet of flames 1,000 feet high, and of the vestige remained 5 minutes after but falling bits of iron which fell all around us. No one could have known, they died instantaneously.[62]

Commander John Champion, HMS Maenad *Twelfth Flotilla*

HMS *Defence* had a crew of 903 and there were no survivors from the explosion. Arbuthnot was killed with his men.

Many senior officers were unable to explain Arbuthnot's impetuous actions that day. Admiral Sir Frederick Hamilton described them as 'a mad rush for the enemy, the reason for which it is so difficult to understand'.

Vice Admiral Sir Rosslyn Wemyss wrote:

It is difficult to understand what Robert Arbuthnot and all those cruisers were doing – Poor Robert – anyway I expect he died perfectly happy in a blaze of glory and gallantry.

Steel and Hart carefully assess the possible reasons why Arbuthnot charged at the *Wiesbaden,* but they conclude that:

Whatever the reason, he led his squadron on, getting closer to the Wiesbaden and blasting away at his stationary prey, as if only he and they existed on the high seas. No thought of his smoke obfuscating the view of the all-important battlecruisers and dreadnoughts. No thought of what might lie ahead cloaked in the poor visibility. No thought, really, at all, at least as far as now can be judged.[63]

In partial defence of Arbuthnot, he belonged to a generation of senior naval officers who had seen little or no active service during their careers until the start of the Great War. There had been no great sea battle since Trafalgar in 1805, and for most of the officers this was their first real experience of naval warfare. Like the impetuous Beatty, Arbuthnot badly wanted to have a go at the enemy to prove his fighting qualities and lead his men into battle, even to be another Nelson. That was also what the British public wanted their Admirals to do. But Arbuthnot was operating the obsolescent cruisers of his squadron in conditions where his visibility was blighted by smoke and mist so he would not have known how close he was to the German battlecruisers. Determined to fight, he embarked on what he saw as a Nelsonian course of action: to attack an enemy ship, the *Wiesbaden,* and engage it in battle.

That said, the faults in Arbuthnot's authoritarian style of command, his rigidity of thought and intimidation of his officers clearly identified by his superiors in 1915, largely contributed to the loss of his flagship and his entire crew. His decisions also contributed to the fate of George's ship *Warrior.*

On Arbuthnot's orders HMS *Warrior* had been following HMS *Defence.* At about 6.20 p.m. the German ship *Derfflinger* aimed at *Warrior* and bombarded the British cruiser with over fifteen direct hits from heavy 12-inch shells and six hits from secondary 5.9-inch guns.

> I stopped to have another look and saw one of our four funnelled cruisers being heavily shelled. Splashes were all around her and one salvo straddled her quarter deck, with one or two shots this side. At the same time as the splashes arose a tall column of smoke, 200–300 feet high, rose from her quarter deck, the smoke being lit up by the flame inside it in a very pretty way. She went on, however, and immediately afterwards was again straddled but I didn't notice any hits. There was a good deal of smoke about and I didn't see what damage had been done by the explosion.
>
> *Lieutenant Patrick Lawder, HMS* Benbow, *Fourth Division, Fourth Battle Squadron*

Stoker Brady on HMS *Warrior*:

> We will now go back to the time of sighting the enemy. Our Admiral being eager to engage the enemy ran us right into the thick of it. Here we found ourselves engaging six German Battlecruisers, our flagship the Defence was blown up within 5 minutes time with the Admiral aboard, that left us to take our own course. Our ten big guns firing all the time, we stuck to them sinking one Battlecruiser, one Light Cruiser and a Destroyer.

One of the German shells hit the aft end of the starboard engine room of HMS *Warrior* at the waterline, so that all the engine room was flooded. William Davis, a Leading Seaman on the *Warrior*, wrote:

> All the German gunfire was very accurate, all falling on the upper decks – the salvo which hit us found our Engine Room and boiler room were struck so all the manual pumps were manned but we could not stem the inflow of water.

Warrior did not have the turbine engines of the more modern battlecruisers, but instead had the old reciprocating engines. At the top of these were huge cylinders, whose pistons operated crank shafts, which drove the propellers, mounted in crank pits at the bottom of the engine room. If those engines were damaged or dislodged by enemy shells they could crush the engine room men, causing death or horrific injury.

There are two separate and very vivid accounts from the Engineer Officers of *Warrior* of their experiences that night of 31 May/1 June in the ship's two engine rooms as the waters rose within them. We do not know definitely whether George Lancaster was with either of these officers as they tried to make their way up to the deck. But as an Engine Room Artificer on *Warrior*, his job was to work under the orders of the Engineer Officers and to operate the warship's engines and boilers. We know from their Captain's report that the engine crew of *Warrior* stayed at their stations and tried to pump out the water and keep the ship moving. It is likely that George experienced something very similar to what his two Engineer Officers later described.

Henry Kitching was the Engineer Commander on *Warrior* and was in the starboard engine room when the German shells hit the ship:

> I heard a tremendous explosion at the aft end, a heavy jar went through the whole fabric, and most of the lights went out. Immediately afterwards there was a heavy roar of water and steam and my impression was that we had been torpedoed. Several men came running forward from that end, one of them with blood streaming down his face. In that moment I realised fully what cold drawn funk is like. But I had to make a decision, and advancing towards the aft end, I tried to gauge the extent of the damage. The engine still went on running, which

seemed to show that the cylinders had not been hit, but in the dim uncertain light I perceived what appeared to be Niagara at the aft end of the engine room, though whether the sheet of water was rising up from below or pouring down from above I couldn't be sure at the time. Anyhow a blast of steam on my face warned me that I hadn't long to think about it, and I soon made up my mind that no pumps could deal with the quantity of water that was coming in, and that the only thing to do was to get the men out as quickly as possible.

Kitching goes on to give a vivid account of their escape from the dark, complex warren of corridors and gangways in the bowels of the ship.

At first the men didn't know what to do, as the ladders at the aft end were inaccessible, but I shouted to them to go up the mid-ship ladder and hustled all towards it in front of me. As soon as it appeared they had all gone up, I followed them myself, but by that time all the lights had gone out and it was pitch dark. When I got to the top knowing it was hopeless to go aft, I turned forward and felt my way by the handrails along the platform at the tops of the cylinders towards the doors at the fore-end which communicated with the port engine room and with the mess deck. When I got there however a stoker told me that we could not get through there as the mess deck was on fire and when I tried to do so I was met by a rush of thick smoke and blinding fumes that drove me back. At this moment with this in front and the roar of steam behind me I felt like a trapped rat, for there seemed no possibility of lifting the heavy armour hatches overhead, and a spasm of sheer terror came over me; which is when I realised that the man was calling my attention to a glimmer of light above, and the next minute I found myself climbing out through a torn rent in the deck.

Engineer Commander Henry Kitching, HMS Warrior,
First Cruiser Squadron

His junior officer Engineer Lieutenant Geoffrey Morgan was in the port engine room of HMS *Warrior*, and he gave the following verbal account of his experiences at Jutland to his commanding officer who made a permanent record of the interview:

The shell which drove the Senior Engineer Officer and his crew out of the starboard engine room came through both engine rooms and burst mid-line, leaving most of its gas in the port engine room where I was. I was knocked down by the concussion, but got up and tried to see what could be done. I found it impossible to escape by any of the ladders, and as we were getting choked by the fumes and the steam we attempted to open the mid-line door to the starboard engine room. There we discovered that water was coming over the floor plates, that the crank pits were full up and the cranks were swishing around in the middle of it. Initially, I hadn't realised we were making water fast until a cold feeling around the ankles woke me up to the true state of affairs.

I tried to put the pumps on, not realising the full extent of the damage at first. I soon found it hopeless. My next thought was to ease the engines and shut off the steam, as I feared further accidents, but by this time, the water was breast high over the floor plates and I decided the only thing to do was to clear out. But by this time, the ladders were inaccessible as the floor plates were dislodged and there was every chance of being drawn into the swirl of the racing cranks. We climbed up over pipes and condensers, holding hands to prevent the swirling water carrying us away. Unfortunately, on two occasions, the chain of men was broken with the result that several men were somehow jammed and drowned. The remainder climbed from one vantage point to another as the water rose until they reached the upper gratings, but by this time it was quite dark, and having no purchase anywhere they could not dislodge the gratings overhead and found themselves doomed to certain death. Not only were they expecting to be drowned, but escaping steam almost suffocated them and they kept splashing the oily water over their faces to keep them from being peeled. Some men had wrapped scarves round their heads to protect themselves, and all kept as much of their bodies as they could in the water. The surprising thing was that the engines went on working until the water was halfway up the cylinders, and only stopped then because the boilers were shut off.

And this agony of terror went on for nearly two and a half hours in pitch darkness and apparent hopelessness before some of us were rescued. There was one man, a Petty Officer, who absolutely refused to recognise the horror of the situation and kept talking and cheering us up to the very end. At the start there were about 8 of us, but one by one men kept dropping off and getting lost and drowned in the water, until at last there were only 3 of us left. I owe my life to that Petty Officer, I lost my hold on him and found myself being drawn down into the machinery but he never lost his grip on me and somehow kept me up.

It began to occur to me that the ship had been abandoned, until we heard the click of a valve. Then a noticeably cold stream of water came in, which we stirred up as much as possible and from this we got the idea that the ship must be under way in tow and that began to encourage us. At long last we heard some order being piped round the ship and we began to shout together – shouts which someone thankfully heard and we were rescued.

Engineer Lieutenant Geoffrey Morgan, HMS Warrior

A signalman on the ship gave this account:

From my sheltered action stations I was ordered to go up aloft to clear some halyards which were fouled. Just as I was about to climb the rigging a shell whistled overhead, shattering some super structure. My mission was abandoned. I was near a hatchway to the boiler room; a burst main steam pipe caused some injured stokers to come from below scalded by steam. With the noise of guns, explosions and the knowledge that the ship was crippled and likely to sink, I prayed.

Signalman Reuben Poole, HMS Warrior

On the mess deck, stoker David Williams had been told to try and repair damage.

A shell came through the upper deck and killed 3 of my mates working with me – another mate had his leg blown off. After that the firing was so heavy that we could not move around like we should have done. I got hit myself. The Sick Berth Steward tried to bandage me and as he did another shell came and blew off his two middle fingers – they fell on my leg so I picked them up and gave them back to him as he did not feel what had happened. The only thing he could do now was to tie my trousers over my thigh with my cap ribbon.

Stoker First Class David Williams, HMS Warrior

One of the medical officers on board was Surgeon-Lieutenant Charles Leake:

> News was brought to me by a messenger of a fearful explosion aft: the aft's dressing station had been wiped out and no one knew if there were any survivors. Hearing this, and as wounded were being reported, I resolved to try to do my best to get there. It was impossible to get aft owing to gas fumes, except by way of the upper deck, so I took a risk which a Medical Officer is not supposed to take, as circumstances were exceptional. On arriving aft and whilst attending to the wounded, much to my surprise Surgeon MacDonald appears, somewhat shaken, but none the worse for his experience. His Sick Bay Steward had had his left hand shattered as a result of the explosion and many people were killed near that spot – about 40 or more by one shell alone. We set to work and rendered first aid and gave morphia to the wounded as fast as we could. Meanwhile the forward dressing station was becoming untenable owing to gas fumes and fumes from burning paintwork so it was deemed advisable to evacuate the position.
>
> *Surgeon Lieutenant Charles Leake, HMS* Warrior

In the meantime the Engineer Commander Henry Kitching was trying to put out the fires:

> I then endeavoured to collect my scattered wits with a view to putting out the fire, but I found that I had the greatest difficulty in getting my brain to work at all. I have heard other fellows say that they have been seized with this temporary mental paralysis, which seems to last for ages, but really lasts for moments only. On such occasions when it is difficult to originate anything, evolutions rehearsed at drill work automatically, and at this moment I found my subordinates readier than myself in carrying out measures that I had myself devised.
>
> *Engineer Commander Henry Kitching, HMS* Warrior

Another man had been in the ship's cells:

> One of our crew members was under punishment and was in the cells when we went into action. He was immediately released as

the first salvos hit us driving great holes in Warrior. If you had seen this man going into action pulling hosepipes along the decks to tackle the fire with great speed, pushing anyone in his way aside – it was very humorous and brave.

Signalman William Robertson, HMS Warrior

A Royal Marine called J.C. Jones was manning a telephone in the 9.2-inch gun turret on the ship, and he gave the following contemporary account to his family soon after the battle, as related by Peter Liddle:[64]

Our Captain of the gun was ever cool and all the gun crew, as if from inspiration, the same.

As news of the annihilation of their sister cruiser (*Defence*) was given, it was in the Marine Captain's 'very quiet voice'. Their turret was filled with smoke and fumes as their gun continued in action.

Then that voice again "Put your gas masks on men". The turret was struck a glancing blow as it traversed.

Once outside they saw the turret had been opened as if by a 'tin opener'.

The order 'fire stations' was given, dead and dying had to be ignored to secure the ship against a magazine explosion of uncontrollable fire.

HMS *Warrior* had fought on, exchanging fire with a combined line of German dreadnoughts for a considerable time. While able to manoeuvre somewhat to minimise the damage, *Warrior* was suffering large fires, extensive flooding and many casualties on deck and below. Captain Vincent Molteno steered *Warrior* away from the German guns, but the ship was still within their range and could have exploded like her sister ship, HMS *Defence*. She was saved from that fate by the involuntary intervention of the dreadnought battleship, HMS *Warspite*.

The Fifth Battle Squadron was following Beatty's battlecruisers and was about to fall into line astern of the Grand Fleet when one of its battleships, HMS *Warspite*, was hit by a German shell which disabled its steering mechanism. This resulted in *Warspite* unintentionally turning two full circles around the floundering HMS *Warrior*, which was thereby spared from further enemy fire as the German ships decided to concentrate their guns instead on the more valuable prize of the modern and powerful *Warspite*, enabling *Warrior* to escape from the action.

Warspite survived, but as it was severely damaged and disabled, it was ordered to leave the battle and sail back to Rosyth. Its turning circles had saved *Warrior* from being blown up – but *Warrior* was badly damaged, and at risk of sinking in the North Sea with its crew still on board.

Warrior's Fight – Aftermath

It's a small photo – a snapshot taken from one ship, a converted ferry, which has come alongside a much larger armoured cruiser on which a group of men are standing. A scene of sailors waiting in rows, part of a lifeboat, a funnel, a ship's gun. The men's faces betray none of the horror of the circumstances, or their fear – there is no panic. At that very moment many of their fellow crew members are dead or dying on that ship, from shellfire, drowning, flash and fire burns, scalding by steam, crushed bodies, suffocation, loss of blood, shock. The men are waiting in turn before leaping from their crippled warship across to the safety of the ferry, their rescuer.

The photo's caption is: 'Jutland: HMS *Engadine* alongside the stricken *Warrior*, taking aboard her crew.'[65]

The Captain of *Warrior* recorded the damage his ship had sustained in the battle:

> We had been hit at least 15 times by heavy projectiles – 11" or 12" – and about 6 times by smaller shells. Fires were raging so badly aft that it was impossible to get access to the engine room. The whole main deck was full of flame, smoke and gas from enemy shells; the upper deck was torn to pieces and every boat was damaged beyond repair. Masts still stood and so did the funnels, although the rigging had been shot away and there were many holes in both masts and funnels. The most serious damage was that caused by an 11" or 12" projectile which struck us on the waterline on the port side, passed through the aft reserve coal bunker, across the upper part of the port engine room and burst as it went through the middle line bulkhead, leaving most of its gas in the port engine room, whilst several large fragments of it were deflected downwards and tore a large hole in the double [bottom] at the aft end of the starboard engine room.
>
> *Captain Vincent Molteno, HMS* Warrior

From the Captain to one of the most junior ratings on board – this account was given by John William Thompson, a Boy First Class:

I served in the fore control on beaming indicators. There were six or seven people in that control. That was including the Gunnery Officer by the name of Robert Hornends, Lieutenant or Lieutenant Commander.

I saw HMS Defence blow up ahead of us. She was a sheet of flame one minute and gone the next.

Our Captain turned sharply to starboard and as we turned a salvo of shells fell where we turned from. There were about six German ships firing at us. We seemed to be in the middle of the two fleets so we were not very comfortable.

We were at this time getting pretty well knocked about. As far as I know at this time we were still firing all guns, as this time our ships seemed to be having the worst of it, especially the Battlecruisers. I saw two of them go down and one, I am certain, was the Queen Mary. Our destroyers took a hammering but as they went past us they all cheered. By this time the Warrior had had it. We were a sitting duck for everybody and they were doing their best to sink us and they would have done if some of the big ships of the Grand Fleet had not turned up. One in particular, HMS Warspite she saved us. She took the salvo of shells that was meant for us, she suffered some considerable damage but got back to Port.

Surgeon Lieutenant Charles Leake was still doing his best to deal with the severe casualties on board:

As soon as the action ceased, medical and stretcher parties busied themselves looking for and collecting the wounded from isolated parts of the ship. The sick bay was left almost intact and so cases were moved there and the adjoining part of the mess deck was cleared for the reception of the wounded. The wounded were collected and temporarily made comfortable, dressings being quickly applied and tourniquets seen to which had been put on previously. As most of the wounded were suffering from severe shock one tried to combat this. The wet clothes were taken off and they were put into dry bed gear and wrapped up, given warm drinks and morphia. Fortunately one galley fire was uninjured after the action. Everyone worked with a will and by about 8.30 the wounded were fairly comfortable and we could have a look around and decide what to do. During this time several cases succumbed to their injuries. In all we had 80 or so killed or died of wounds soon after the action. Having sorted out the wounded as far as possible it was obvious that something more must be done. The wounds were very ragged as caused by pieces of metal. Compound fractures were common and limbs had been torn off. Of the survivors the majority had wounds of lower extremities. Several had limbs smashed to pulp and had embedded pieces of clothing and metal which needed removal. We commandeered the bathroom near the sick bay for a theatre and prepared it as quickly and as best as we could. We had plenty of instruments and water, but our stores were not too abundant, as the ship had been badly knocked about, and in spite of our precautions and scattering the stowage of gear, we were still short-handed. The only antiseptic we had was carbolic acid and a little perchloride. We had enough cyanide gauze and wool however. The lighting of the theatre was the main disadvantage and obstacle. We had only candle lamps available and these gave very little illumination for critical operations. But, one has to make what one has do. We boiled our instruments and set to work. No gloves were served out. These would have been invaluable as in a short time one's hands became fearfully sore owing to the antiseptic solutions. The Fleet Surgeon operated, assisted by myself, and Doctor MacDonald gave the anaesthetic. We commenced at 9.30 and went on until about five the next morning when one had to cease owing to the fearful tossing the ship received in the heavy seas. All sorts of wounds were dealt with and several amputations were done. Plain circular, no flaps. Needless to say several men were beyond all hope of recovery and others had died whilst waiting their turn – plainly from shock.

Royal Marine Jones continued his personal account:[66]

We went down below to bring up our dead and wounded, to strengthen our bulkhead doors, to plug the holes in our ship's side with blankets and hammocks. Some of us were ordered to our anti-submarine guns.

We carried on bringing our mates up from down below and laid them out on deck, the dead to be buried overboard.

Captain and Officers moved amongst us helping and cheering us. We managed to eat some sandwiches and drink a little cocoa – it passed a little time away. We had a bad list, the water was washing our upper deck and the wounded continued to moan.

Jones decided to try and retrieve his money and family photos from his locker.

I made my way over wreckage of all description, slipping on blood covered decks, but gradually worked my way down below.

He found his ditty box containing his belongings, but was unable to open it, and as he struggled with the lock he was submerged by the incoming water. He surfaced, left the box and escaped back to the top deck.

HMS *Warrior* was by now to the west of the battle and was trying to sail back to a home port, but was clearly foundering as water flooded the engines rooms and rose through the ship. Then she was seen by another British ship whose signaller later wrote:

…another cruiser was sighted steaming towards us on our starboard bow. Steam and smoke were pouring from her, the flames were seen coming from the stern ports. We made her out to be British and when near enough we signalled 'Can we be of any assistance?' and received a reply 'Stand by me'. Her name was Warrior, she informed us that both engine rooms were full of steam and she couldn't stop. We turned and came up on her port quarter. She had a bad list and had been holed on the water line. Her W/T had gone and she was on fire aft. She began blowing off steam and signalled that they were trying to shut off steam. When eventually this was done, she signalled, 'Stand by to tow me' and we lowered our motor boat and after a long toilsome business with tow ropes, the first of which parted, we got a steel hawser aboard and took her in tow at 20.40 hours but experienced great difficulty in getting her on the move.

Signaller H.Y. Ganderton, HMS Engadine, *Battlecruiser Fleet*

Stoker Brady:

> By that time our own ship the Warrior was in a pitiful state, a big list to starboard, engine room blown up and other shell holes in us, we began to sink. Still we kept doggedly on until the Warspite seeing our state came and covered us until we backed out of the line, then the Warspite took our place in the line, this would be about 7 o'clock pm. We had just enough power left in the engines to take us out of the danger zone. There the engines finished and we were at the mercy of anything tossing about until we sighted the sea plane ship the Engadine which played a prominent part in that battle, we signalled to her to stand by us so she came to our assistance, taking us in tow until next morning Thursday 1st June until about 6 o'clock am.

HMS *Engadine* had originally been a cross-channel Folkestone to Boulogne ferry of the South Eastern and Chatham Railway Company that had been converted to a seaplane tender to carry four Short 184 seaplanes.[67] *Engadine* had no flight deck and so lowered the aircraft by crane into the sea for take-off, and recovered them from the sea after they had landed. It was only 316 feet long and 41 feet in the beam, while *Warrior* was a much bigger and heavier ship of some 500 feet in length and 73 feet in the beam.

Despite this difference in size HMS *Engadine* took *Warrior* in tow as the night set in.

> I will never forget the first pull of the wire. Keep in mind that Engadine displaced about 1,400 tonnes and the Warrior was 14,900 – with the water in her she was probably 19,000 so the very first time all that happened there was a colossal shower of sparks and she stopped dead.
>
> *Flight Lieutenant Graham Donald, Royal Naval Air Service,*
> *HMS* Engadine

At last the *Engadine* was able to get the *Warrior* slowly moving away from the battle, but they remained very vulnerable to any German submarines or warships. Signalman Poole recalled:

In the darkness of the mess deck I saw a torch light, the surgeon was searching a pile of dead bodies, looking for life – about 30 bodies of a stoker fire party. All of them had been killed by a heavy calibre shell. Down below decks, tired seamen struggling with the hand pumps to keep the ship afloat. Holes were plugged and bulkheads shored up, but the struggle all night was in vain as the water in the ship was rising and it was a question of how long Warrior could stay afloat.

Meanwhile on the *Engadine*:

It was a terrific strain on our small ship, as we struggled on against a rising sea and she shook and trembled as her revolution indicator was pushed up from 12 to 19 knots. All through the night we struggled on, making only 8.2 knots through the water. Unfortunately the weather began to get worse, the sea became rough. Fire could still be seen coming from Warrior's stern ports and even newspapers were blown out with the draught of the fire, as the ship slowly heaved to the swell. Steel hawsers were at breaking strain, stern plates and bollards nearly wrenched and torn from their seating by the tugging of the heavy cruiser astern as she rose and sank on the heaving waves, threatening every moment to engulf her altogether. Her gallant crew, weary and battle worn, worked hard at the pumps all night long to keep her afloat.

Signaller H.Y. Ganderton, HMS Engadine

On *Warrior* the crew began to bring the wounded sailors up on deck:

They carried me to the middle mess deck and while I was lying there the Padre came and asked me for my home address and if I had any mates aboard from my home town. While I was there the ship was sinking and they carried me from the mess deck up to the bows of the ship. The crew kept on working the pumps to keep her afloat.

Stoker First Class David Williams

By extraordinary efforts *Engadine* had managed to tow the damaged armoured cruiser some seventy miles overnight, but at a rate of some three knots this had taken ten hours, and the two ships were still in a dangerous area where they could be attacked by German submarines or destroyers. Young John Thompson continued:

By now the action had gone away from us and there we laid. We could not move as we had no engines and we were on fire. We had no boats left so we were making rafts out of mess tables and stools. The party were bringing the dead up, sewing them in canvas and the Padre was doing the funeral service. The morale of the ship's company was terrific. No one complained, considering that we were sinking, and to make matters worse the weather got very rough. Everybody was wet through because we could not get below, we could not even get a drink or anything to eat. We were just waiting for the order to abandon ship.

It became clear that the crew of the *Warrior* would indeed have to abandon their ship.

I was on the bridge during the early morning watch and at about 7 a.m. I heard the Engineer Commander report to Captain Molteno that the after main bulk head had burst and that the ship would soon sink. This was confirmed by the Ship's Commander. On the Captain's orders I personally made a signal to the Engadine by semaphore hand flags from the port side of the bridge, 'Come along side, am sinking'.

Signalman Reuben Poole, HMS Warrior

Coming alongside in the rough seas was a challenge for *Engadine*, but as a former cross-channel steamer she had a thick rubbing strake surrounding her that enabled her to go alongside jetties, and this acted as a buffer between the two ships:

Already heavy seas were sweeping across the decks amid ships, and it was plain that it was a question of moments only when she would make the final plunge. There were 700 men on board of whom many were wounded and what had to be done must be done quickly. But would it be quick enough? Boats were out of the question and in any case it was unlikely that any of the Warrior's boats were undamaged.

The tow ropes and hawsers were hurriedly cast off, and we steamed around in a circle to bring us astern and on her port quarter. The first attempt to go alongside failed owing to the heavy seas now running and we began to have the terrible fear that we should be too late. A second attempt was made. Our Captain, seemingly unperturbed, with supreme skill and judgement gauged it exactly; and although at one moment high on the crest of a huge wave it seemed that we must crash downright upon her decks now already awash, yet we managed to run right alongside, and grappled on with steel hawsers and stout hemp ropes. Men were ordered to stand by with axes to cut them through should the Warrior founder before they could be cast off. The two ships were grinding together horribly. With a crash part of the stout rubbing chock, which ran nearly the whole length of the ship near the water line and served as a fender, was splintered by some projecting piece of armour on the other ship's side. At any moment the thin plating itself might be stove in by the pounding blows that shook the whole vessel to her very keel.

Signaller H.Y. Ganderton, HMS Engadine

After much difficult manoeuvring Engadine's captain brought his ship along Warrior's starboard side, and the crew of the sinking ship were ordered to muster in divisions on deck.

With vicious bumping the two ships were made fast. Captain Molteno had given the orders 'Close all water tight doors, batten down all hatches, prepare to abandon ship'. As my work was finished on the bridge I was sent down to join the crew for 'Abandon Ship'! I nipped down the hatchway to the mess deck for a few personal items and in the light from the hatchway I saw a worn out sailor, oblivious to the danger, fast asleep in a hammock netting. I gave him a good shaking, saying "Come on, mate, abandon ship, she'll be sinking any minute now!" I hope that seaman heeded my warning. If not he would be battened down. The souvenirs I brought down from the bridge were one White Ensign, one Union Jack, my pair of hand semaphore flags and binoculars. From the canteen I salvaged one large carton of Player's cigarettes and one large carton of Fry's Cream bars. Yeoman Parsons asked me to try and save his sewing machine as he had to stay on the bridge with the Captain – I ignored his request!

Signalman Reuben Poole, HMS Warrior

Leading Stoker Samuel Roberts wrote:[68]

> At the time of battle I was stationed in galley giving messages through the voice tube to lower conning tower which was in bottom of ship. I was there until told to abandon ship. But I did go to engine room to see if all hands heard to abandon ship. But as I stepped from ladder to one deck I stepped on body and guess the others never had much chance in engine room. I got to engine room door and all you could see was drowned bodies all washed up against the gratings, it was a terrible sight. The engine room was flooded where the ship was sinking. When I went up to abandon ship all you could see was your own shipmates, lying around deck dying and dead. We had to jump on to the aircraft carrier [*Engadine*]. I was very lucky as the leading stoker who relieved me from engine room couple of days before was one in engine room. I get very choked now when I hear about the battle. It was a terrible sight.

William Robertson, another Signalman, said:

> As darkness fell we were all engaged in trying to keep Warrior afloat by hand pumping which was a strenuous job indeed. My duties during the dark hours were keeping a look out and also taking my turn at hand pumping, endeavouring to keep this great ship afloat, but it was all in vain. By daylight our decks were well awash and it was too dangerous for the Engadine to continue towing us so orders were given to abandon ship (Signalmen to report on the Bridge for special duties regarding secret and confidential books etc.). Signalmen and officers were last to leave the ship. Those of us in the water were expertly got out by great work by Engadine crew.
>
> *Signalman William Robertson,* HMS Warrior

As confirmed by Royal Marine Jones in Peter Liddle's book, some of the fit men abandoned ship by jumping off *Warrior* and swimming to jettisoned floating material from which they were picked up by lifeboats from HMS *Engadine*.

Over on the *Engadine*:

It wasn't a very easy job so everyone had to lend a hand making odd wires fast to try and hold her tight to the Warrior's side; put down fenders as best we could. It is not the sort of thing an aircraft carrier or a warship is really equipped for doing at sea as a rule. But the really nasty moment was just as we were getting ready, the Warrior gave a nasty sort of shudder – it just looked as if she was going to sink. It was unmistakable. Apart from pulling us with her, just for a moment there was a slight look on all these chaps' faces – and keep in mind they have had an awful hammering, the scuppers were running with blood and casualties. There might have been a panic. The Captain just signalled the bugler. He blew the still – just a toot of the still – every man Jack stood to attention and then they carried on in a very orderly manner.

Flight Lieutenant Graham Donald, Royal Naval Air Service,
HMS Engadine

Leading Seaman William Davis in his account to Robert Church stressed that there had been 'No panic – smooth embarkment of survivors to HMS *Engadine*, but we were told that German destroyers were after us'.

That there was no panic is certainly borne out by the photograph taken from *Engadine* of the men patiently waiting on the *Warrior's* deck to make the leap across the gap to the rescuing ship.

Warrior's crew were fallen in by divisions on her deck, in perfect order, awaiting further command. Because of the large number of men to be taken off it was decided to get all the able-bodied over first and send them below, thus leaving the deck free for handling the wounded. Then, at the word of command, the able-bodied – though very weary and battle-grimed – leapt over the short space to find an uncertain foothold upon our decks helped by our own men.

Signaller H.Y. Ganderton, HMS Engadine

The operation abandon ship was carried out as smoothly and calmly as a Sunday morning divisional muster. When my turn came to abandon ship my goods and relics were thrown onto the deck of our rescue ship. Then as the ship rose with the waves, I grabbed at the Engadine's taffrails and rolled inboard. What a relief! I felt as though I could go below and sleep for a week.

Signalman Reuben Poole, HMS Warrior

Our Officers and men lined Engadine's side and grabbed each man as he came across. The two ships were working heavily, the noise of rending steel was terrific and only orders shouted in one's ear could be heard. Davits were sheared off from their supports, Engadine was holed in several places, though not badly, and the fenders, mostly bundles of hazel wood sticks wired together, quickly went to pieces.

Flight Lieutenant Frederick Rutland, Royal Naval Air Service,
HMS Engadine

Next the wounded had to be transferred over, some of them on stretchers:

As the ships lurched towards each other the stretchers containing the wounded were quickly and tenderly handed across the gulf to willing hands. The sea down below, like some savage beast imprisoned in a cage, madly leapt at them with foaming jaws. One poor fellow was being passed across when the ship gave a sudden lurch and for a moment those who were handing the stretcher on which he lay lost their hold on it and with a cry of pity and despair from the helpless onlookers he slipped from the stretcher and fell down into the seething waters below. Instantly several men sprang forward and would have gone over the side after their mess mate had not the Captain of the Warrior ordered them back.

"It is madness to go down there," he cried. Indeed the terrible sound of rending timber and buckling plates proclaimed all too loudly that no human could hope to escape being crushed to death in those relentless steel jaws.

Signaller H.Y. Ganderton, HMS Engadine

Lieutenant Rutland of the *Engadine* took a different view:

The last stretcher was being passed when a wounded man slipped out of it and fell into the sea between the two ships. At that time two Officers and the Captain of the Warrior were crossing to the Engadine, near where I was standing. Several Officers and men jumped on the netting or bulwarks as though to go down after him, but the Captain shouted that no one was to go over the side. It was in fact impossible for the poor fellow had fallen through the gap between Engadine's rubbing-strake and Warrior as the two ships drew apart, before taking another charge at each other. He had fetched up on a bundle of hazel wood sticks, the remains of a fender, and for the moment these supported him. But it seemed that it would only be a matter of seconds before he fell through them. So I decided that nothing could be done and went on helping the wounded, of whom there were nearly a hundred to be placed in shelter.

Flight Lieutenant Frederick Rutland, Royal Naval Air Service,
HMS Engadine

However Rutland looked again at the situation:

Then I saw a group of men looking over the side near where the wounded man had gone overboard; I ran forward and saw that, though still between the ships, he had drifted far enough ahead to be rescued without any real risk. So I grabbed a rope with a bowline in it in which two men had been trying to lasso him, told them and others to hang on to the end, went down the rope, swam to the man, brought him to the rope, put myself into the bowline and, holding him in my arms, ordered those on deck to heave away. There was one tricky moment when we were nearly up to the deck and I saw the steel hawser from Warrior's bows cutting across my rope. Had the hawser parted at the wrong moment it could have cut us both in two. Had it merely carried away our rope, it would have meant another swim. Because I have always had the habit of talking to myself in moments like this, many people heard me say to the unconscious man, "Sorry me lad, I'm afraid we've got another dip coming." But old Hancock, the Captain of the Engadine in peace time and now serving in her as Lieutenant R.N.R., saw what was happening and rammed the engines ahead, thus taking the strain off the hawser. Two minutes later we were aboard, the hawser had parted and the ship swung clear with Warrior sinking fast.

After all, the poor fellow died of his wounds. He had been very seriously wounded and it was apparently known that he had only a short time to live. As for myself I had never been in danger, except from the steel hawser, for I had weighed up the situation in a second before going over the side and reckoned that, so long as the rubbing strake held, I could save myself from being crushed and swim clear if I had to.

Flight Lieutenant Frederick Rutland, Royal Naval Air Service,
HMS Engadine

Signaller Ganderton witnessed this rescue:

Then I saw what was surely as brave a deed as any in that great battle. Lieutenant Rutland quickly seized hold of a rope, tied a bowline round his body and, telling the men to hang on to the other end, made his way forward a little towards the bows, swung himself over the bulwarks and quickly lowered himself down between the two ships. The men begged that they might go, but he forbade them to risk their lives. A confused scene of tossing water is my only impression of that moment, as he edged his way aft. I scarcely dared look down from my lofty vantage point at the end of the bridge. Now a man dangling in space, now lost to sight in a roaring cascade; a sickening thud that made the heart stand still as the ship struck. Still that persevering and gallant figure fighting on. A gasp of dismay as the rope slackened, but only for a moment. Now he had hold of the wounded man. Feverishly the men began to haul away at the rope and willing hands were stretched out to receive the poor crushed burden from the grasp of his brave rescuer. No, he did not live, poor fellow. He expired as he lay on the deck, his back broken it was said – but he was just able to whisper "Thank you!" before he died to the man who had risked his own life so fearlessly to save him. That was perhaps his greater reward as the Albert Medal which he afterwards received.[69]

Signaller H.Y. Ganderton, HMS Engadine

Captain Molteno was the last to leave the ship:

Finally, the Commander reported all hands were on board the Engadine, and he and I then jumped on board and the Engadine went astern to clear the sinking ship. As we left the old Warrior we gave her three hearty cheers. Every big sea washed over her decks and water poured down through the huge rents in the upper deck on to the main deck.

Captain Vincent Molteno, HMS Warrior

...so after everybody was aboard the Engadine she pushed off, leaving the old 'Warrior' to her fate flying the distress signal from her yard arm. As we sailed away from her the Captain said let us give three cheers for the old ship which we served so well. All eyes turned to the fast sinking ship, three mighty cheers rang out from the men who were all fatigued from the past 48 hours experience, and then as I looked at our skipper I could detect a tear wet his eye, something unusual for a strong hearted man like him, but he had a corner in his heart for everybody and a heart as good as gold.

Stoker Philip Brady

Warrior's surviving crew, 743 of them, had been rescued just in time:

Grappling irons and ropes were cast off at 08.25 and gathering speed we left the doomed ship – a truly forlorn spectacle. Derelict, batted and battle scarred, forsaken at the last, heaving in a queer dying convulsive sort of manner and yet with the White Ensign proudly flying at the mast head, her Battle Ensign. Warrior's crew gave their old ship a cheer and there were tears in her Captain's eyes. That was the last glimpse of the old Warrior we had before she was lost sight of in the mist, and vanished forever beneath the waves of the cold grey North Sea.

Signaller H.Y. Ganderton, HMS Engadine

HMS *Warrior* was abandoned about 160 miles east of Aberdeen in a rising sea at 8.25 a.m. on Thursday 1 June when her upper decks were only four feet above the water, and she sank soon afterwards.

The crew of *Engadine* gave their cabins to the survivors from *Warrior*, and the vessel's wardroom was turned into a hospital for the injured.

Stoker Philip Brady told Robert Church in 1972 that once on *Engadine* they could not account for one man from Dublin called Bolger, who had been overcome with fatigue and had stayed on *Warrior* until her final plunge into the depths. He had apparently crawled on to a piece of her wreckage and had been picked up by a fast Royal Navy destroyer – and was waiting for the rest of his shipmates on the dock at Rosyth when *Engadine* arrived there.

Brady also stated that while sailing back to port:

> Everyone agreed that Sir R. Arbuthnot had made a mistake going in between the lines of the enemy.

HMS *Engadine* took the *Warrior*'s surviving crew of 743 men back to port at Rosyth[70] and the thirty-six badly wounded men were taken to the Queensferry Hospital for surgery and treatment. Soon after the ship arrived, Captain Molteno issued the following order:

> I am proud to be in command of such a fine body of men. You behaved magnificently and I have just applied to the Admiralty to keep you all together and to again put me in command of you 'Warriors'. I am proud of you and have asked for leave for you all to go home and see your friends and you can 'cock a chest' for you will get 10 days, but if any of you have got to fill casualties I hope you will keep up the traditions of the Warrior and go with a cheer. Your courage was magnificent, not one had any thought for himself, but everyone tried his best to save his ship and render aid to the wounded and dying. I would not have believed it possible for a ship to get into 'hell' and come out again with so many survivors. We had 60 brave men killed,[71] 28 seriously injured and 15 slightly wounded – and I will see that the Warrior's wounded will be well looked after. Now men, I hope you will all enjoy yourselves at home and I know that your people will be jolly well proud of you, and well they may be.
>
> *Captain Vincent Molteno, HMS* Warrior, *First Cruiser Squadron*

The gallant Captain was cheered by the ship's company when they were all safely landed.

SA Newspaper, *10 June 1916, p.456.*

It may have been only on arrival at Rosyth that *Warrior*'s surviving crew heard that another of their sister ships in Arbuthnot's First CS, the armoured cruiser *Black Prince*, had been sunk during the night action with the loss of 857 men. Of the four ships of the First CS that had started the Great War chasing the *Goeben* and had stayed together to fight at Jutland, only HMS *Duke of Edinburgh* survived that battle.

That Friday morning the uninjured survivors rushed to the local post office to send telegrams to their families to reassure them they were safe. But the men were not able to stay at Rosyth for long – Admiralty signals read:

> Crew of Warrior will have sufficient clothing to travel in by Saturday evening. There is no reserve of bedding or sufficient clothing for kitting up men in this port. Submitted Officers and men of Warrior may be sent to their depots on Saturday and granted leave after kitting up.

> *Reply:* Approved.

The surviving crew members were sent back by train to their home ports, in most cases either Portsmouth or Devonport.

> …the *Engadine* arrived at Rosyth in the Firth of Forth. With us there the Chaplain held a memorial service for all that had been buried at sea, then we left the ship that saved all our lives to have a square meal, the first since we were in action. Then we travelled the train to Portsmouth to get some new clothes for us as the reader will understand all our belongings went down with the ship.
> Then we were sent home on 14 days leave.
>
> *Philip Brady*

Signalman Poole concluded:

> And so, by grace of God and the skill, devotion to duty, sound judgement and the seamanship of Captain Molteno of HMS *Warrior* and the Captain of *Engadine*, I and many others of the *Warrior's* crew escaped a watery grave in those wild stormy seas after the Jutland Battle.
> I understand the *Warrior* went down soon after we abandoned her. HMS *Engadine* with all the survivors sailed under the Firth of Forth Rail Bridge on the morning of 2 June 1916. To me Scotland was a beautiful sight after the horrors of battle.

The survivors were sent to Plymouth for kitting up and to prepare for a new ship. On the way to Plymouth the train stopped at Exeter, and it was here that my souvenirs rolled up and labelled in my great coat were deposited in the left luggage office. In the train my shipmates begged me to share the Union Jack with them and so it was cut up into pieces about a foot square and shared out.[72]

Signalman Reuben Poole

The Official Dispatches for the Battle of Jutland show that the Admiralty was very concerned about the possible loss of secret codes and cyphers from the ship which might be picked up by the enemy, just as the Allies had obtained German signal books from destroyed or captured ships at the start of the war. A series of signals was sent to the Captain of the *Engadine* during its voyage back to Rosyth:

What is position of *Warrior?*

Reply: *Warrior* abandoned 57° 21' N., 3° 20' E., at 7 a.m. 1st June.

Was *Warrior* sunk?

Reply: *Warrior* was afloat when I left her. The after part and midship part of upper deck was awash. Captain stated she was making water fast and did not expect her to float for more than one hour.

A sufficient force should be sent out as soon as possible to find *Warrior*.

Detail four Destroyers to accompany 3rd L.C.S.[73] and bring In *Warrior*.
    Please direct Captain of *Warrior* to report whether all secret and confidential matter was removed from *Warrior* or destroyed.

Reply: Captain of *Warrior* reports Cyphers thrown overboard, also Signal Books in use. When abandoned stem of ship was 2 or 3 feet above water, stern about normal draught, every sea washing over upper deck, at least 2 feet of water on main deck, decks and bulkheads terribly shattered by shell fire and no longer water-tight. Ship settling down, stability gone, consider no chance of remaining afloat in increasing heavy weather prevailing, probably sank in 2 or 3 hours at most.

At 8 p.m., 2nd June, Third Light-Cruiser Squadron and three destroyers sailed from Rosyth to join in the search for *Warrior*.

At 9.30 a.m., 4th June, Rear Admiral Commanding, Third Light-Cruiser Squadron, reported his position and proposed abandoning search at 8 p.m.. and return to harbour. This was approved and squadron arrived at Rosyth 6 a.m., 5th June.

Captain of *Warrior* reported by telegraph that cypher and signal books in use were thrown overboard when ship was abandoned.[74]

The Admiralty eventually accepted that Captain Molteno had no alternative but to abandon his ship and that it had sunk with its cyphers and codes.

Molteno was awarded the order of St Anna with Swords for his exceptional performance at the battle.

Engineer Lieutenant Geoffrey Morgan was recommended for promotion to Engineer Lieutenant Commander by Captain Molteno, who gave Morgan the following citation:

> Utmost gallantry and conspicuous devotion to duty in remaining in the engine rooms after the explosion and endeavouring to take action for the safety of the ship, by which delay he was imprisoned under the grating for over two hours, and very narrowly escaped losing his life by drowning, scalding and suffocation. Was almost overcome when rescued. He afterwards took part with energy and coolness in the work of salving the ship.

In his 1972 questionnaire the researcher Robert Church asked each of the surviving crew members who had contacted him whether the man had received any specific award for his action at Jutland. Invariably the response from the *Warrior* sailors was 'No' or 'Recommended, but did not receive anything'.

Nearly all members of the armed forces who served in the Great War, including George, were given the British War Medal and the Victory Medal after the war ended in November 1918. George also received the Star Medal 1914–1915, awarded to all service personnel who served in theatres of war before 31 December 1915.

In April 1918, two years after Jutland and when serving with the destroyer flotilla of the Harwich Force, George was also awarded the Distinguished Service Medal (DSM). This was a decoration established in October 1914 and given to personnel of the Royal Navy and members of the other services, up to and including the rate of Chief Petty Officer, for bravery while on active service at sea.[75] On the reverse of the medal is the inscription 'For Distinguished Service'.

The citation in the *London Gazette* dated 7 June 1918 states that this medal was given to George and the other listed officers and men for 'Miscellaneous Services' during the war; services which would have included his bravery and resourcefulness in that wrecked and flooded engine room on HMS *Warrior*. George, as an Engine Room Artificer, was of Petty Officer rate. Might he have been the un-named Petty Officer, one of the three survivors of *Warrior's* port engine room, 'who absolutely refused to recognise the horror of the situation and kept talking and cheering us up to the very end', and to whom Engineer Lieutenant Geoffrey Morgan said he owed his life? Perhaps, perhaps not, but George did tell his daughter Beryl that he helped to keep *Warrior* afloat by keeping her engines going, and so he certainly went through the same hell as those other engine room men during that night of 31 May 1916.

As for the Admiral who had taken all 903 of the ship's company on his flagship HMS *Defence* to their death, and had ordered the *Warrior* to engage the enemy in such a reckless manner with the loss of seventy-one of her crew:

> *Admiralty, 11th August, 1916*
>
> The KING is pleased to approve of the posthumous honour of Knight Commanderships of the Most Honourable Order of the Bath being conferred on the late Rear Admiral Sir Robert Keith Arbuthnot, Bart., C.B., M.V.O., killed in action on the 31st May, 1916, in recognition of services mentioned in the Commander-in-Chief's despatch of 24th June, 1916.

Those who go on the scenic six-mile 'Hall Walk' around the Fowey estuary in Cornwall from Bodinnick to Polruan can visit the beautifully named and lovely church of St Willow at Llantiglos, where the author Daphne du Maurier was married.

In the churchyard is the grave of a casualty of the *Warrior* at Jutland:

a young rating named William Wyatt, who was a carpenter on the ship. The headstone tells a tragic family story:

In loving memory of William the beloved husband of Avilla Wyatt
(late master mariner) died April 1st 1916 aged 53 years.

Also of William Richard
Their beloved and only son who was killed in the naval battle
on HMS *Warrior* May 31st 1916 in his 24th year.
In health and strength he left his home, not thinking death so near,
It pleased the Lord to bid him come, and in his sight appear.
Greater love hath no man than he who lays down his life for his friends.

Also of Elsie Gladys their beloved daughter
died April 27th 1893 aged 2 years 6 months.

And of Avilla
The beloved wife and mother
who died February 14th 1944, age 73 years.

Reunited.

U-Boats

When British warships returned to Rosyth the day after Jutland their crews were hissed and booed by some of the townsfolk. It should have been the great sea battle for which the warring powers had been preparing for over a decade in the Anglo-German naval arms race, and Britain had expected another victory to rank with Trafalgar over a century earlier. The indecisive outcome of Jutland was seen at the time as a failure by the Royal Navy, whose heavy losses compared to those of the enemy were a terrible shock and bitter disappointment to the British public.

Jutland demonstrated the limitations of the fleets of huge, heavily-armoured dreadnoughts and battlecruisers, their inflexibility in the fast-moving conditions of naval warfare, and potential vulnerability to mines and torpedoes. Jellicoe's much-criticised decision to turn away the Grand Fleet at the battle was based on his justifiable concern that superior German gunnery and the enemy's U-boats and destroyers would attack and sink too many of his battleships. Although not a factor at Jutland, the advent of aerial bombardment was another looming threat to large naval fleets.

After Jutland naval strategy on both the British and German sides changed for the remainder of the war. The irony of the pre-war Anglo-German arms race was that after May 1916 the capital ships of the Grand Fleet, in which so much hope and money had been invested and which had built up so many expectations, remained largely inactive at Scapa or Rosyth. They did however retain their power as a deterrent, for Germany's High Seas Fleet also stayed in its ports at Wilhelmshaven and Kiel for the rest of the war, apart from a few ineffectual sorties.

In response to the German U-boat campaign, smaller, faster and more flexible Royal Navy vessels – light cruisers and particularly destroyers – were deployed to protect Allied merchant shipping, and so became vital to Britain's very survival. The problem for the Admiralty was that they did not have enough destroyers to fulfil this role.

After his return from Jutland and two weeks' leave, George was transferred on 14 June 1916 to HMS *Vivid*, the shore base at Devonport. George's work at *Vivid* involved the maintenance and repair of the engines of the many naval ships based in Devonport during the war. He remained working there for the next year until he joined his next ship, a destroyer.

While at *Vivid* George was able to go back most nights to his nearby home in Beresford Street and his wife and baby daughter. That stable domestic life, despite the continuing horror of the Great War, would have aided his recovery from his own 'shell shock' experience of a battle during which many of his colleagues in *Warrior*'s engine rooms were killed or drowned. In those days there was little or no formal support for battle-scarred servicemen.

By the time George returned home from sea in June 1916 the conditions of war had produced major transformations in the lives of civilians in England. In Devonport itself, the merger of the Three Towns in 1913 had made Plymouth a much larger conurbation, which was now surrounded by army training camps. The coast of south Devon and Cornwall was lined with barbed wire and trench defences in the event of enemy invasion.

The Defence of the Realm Act 1914 (DORA), passed in the first week of the war, had introduced martial law throughout the country for civilians, along with censorship of the press and letters, and the internment of alien nationals. Under the National Registration Act 1915 all citizens were required to carry formal evidence of their identity. Church bells, bonfires or fireworks were prohibited; photography, sketching and even the keeping of pigeons were banned in certain areas around military or naval installations and bases, such was the concern about German espionage and sabotage. The Government assumed powers to requisition any land, factories or workshops. Further regulations under DORA were issued throughout the war, such as restrictions in the opening hours of public houses and the introduction of British Summer Time to extend daylight hours for extra work.

Soon after the outbreak of war, over 32,000 Canadian soldiers arrived in Devonport, brought across the Atlantic on thirty-three liners. Some of these Canadian soldiers paraded on Plymouth Hoe after a church service on 18 October 1914, and shortly afterwards ninety-two trains were used to take them from Plymouth to Salisbury Plain, with their military vehicles driving in convoy through Devon to their new camp in Wiltshire. The Canadian troops were the first influx of many overseas servicemen who came to Plymouth from across the British Empire during the war, including turbaned Sikh warriors of the Indian Army who disembarked at Devonport in 1915[76]. Tragically some men who had travelled across the globe to fight did not even make it to the trenches of the Western Front. In 1917 a train carrying troops from New Zealand was involved in an accident at Bere Ferrers station, just outside Plymouth, and ten of the soldiers died.

Hospital trains started to arrive in Plymouth loaded with wounded soldiers from the fighting in France as early as August 1914, and many men from the town itself were included in the army's casualty lists.

On the naval side, there were significant losses of sailors from Devonport, a manning port for the Royal Navy. Only two days after the outbreak of war in August 1914, HMS *Amphion* hit a mine in the North Sea and sank. HMS *Monmouth*, one of the two armoured cruisers sunk at Coronel on 1 November 1914, was also a Devonport ship which went down with all of its 735 hands. At the battle of Jutland in May 1916, five of the British ships that were sunk were manned by Devonport crews, as were at least four of the badly damaged ships in that battle. The majority of the 804 sailors killed when the Devonport ship HMS *Vanguard* blew up at Scapa Flow in July 1917 because of faulty cordite storage were from Plymouth.

A week after Jutland there was more bad news for the British public. Lord Kitchener, the Secretary of State for War, was drowned on 5 June 1916 after HMS *Hampshire*, which was carrying him on a diplomatic mission to Russia, hit a German mine off the Orkneys. Kitchener's military decisions, particularly concerning the Gallipoli campaign, had been controversial and had been criticised by other ministers. But he was known throughout the country as the face on the famous army recruitment posters, stating 'Your Country Needs You'. He was still a very popular figure, as most British people regarded him as the embodiment of a strong war leader, and his death was a severe blow to them.

That news was soon overtaken by further terrible military losses on the Western Front. One month after Jutland, the Battle of the Somme began on 1 July 1916, and some 20,000 British soldiers were killed on the first day alone, the largest ever loss in a single day suffered by

Britain's army. The Somme offensive dragged on until mid-November, becoming a stalemate bogged down in torrential rains and mud. There were hundreds of thousands of casualties on all sides, and this campaign brought little real advantage to the Allied cause.

Since the start of the war, British society on the 'Home Front' had undergone huge changes to their way of life, experiencing the extensive defence restrictions, national identity registration, the employment of women and the appalling statistics of military and naval deaths. But the years 1916 and 1917 really brought the concept of 'total war' to the civilian population of Great Britain, beginning in January 1916 with the introduction of conscription.

Until the passage of the Military Services Act that month, the men fighting in the war were all volunteers or regular troops. This legislation required single men and childless widowers between the age of nineteen and forty-one to enlist, and the age limit was later raised to fifty-one years. It was possible to apply to local tribunals for exemption from service, for example if a man was an essential war worker, physically unfit, a conscientious objector or ran a business which would fail if its owner went to war.

The second development which affected the whole British population was the real threat of national starvation in 1917. At one stage in that year Great Britain's food reserves were reduced to only six weeks' supply.

At the start of the war in 1914 the British had decided to intercept any ship, including neutral ones, taking supplies to Germany, even if it were food for its population, an act which was technically in breach of international law under the Hague Convention 1907. In turn, German U-boats started to sink Allied merchant shipping, initially adhering to the practice of 'prize rules', whereby the submarine surfaced and allowed the merchant ship's crew and passengers to escape in boats before the ship was sunk. The British tactics of disguising decoy Q-ships as merchant ships left U-boats vulnerable in this situation and the Germans abandoned prize rules. From 4 February 1915 the Germans declared a war zone around the British Isles and their U-boats began to attack all merchant vessels within that zone without warning.

This unrestricted policy antagonised neutral nations whose ships sailed in British waters or imported commerce to Britain. In May 1915 a German U-boat torpedoed the liner *Lusitania* off the south coast of Ireland with the loss of 1,195 passengers and crew, including 128 American citizens. This brought the threat of America entering the war on the side of the Allies. In August 1915 German U-boats sank another British liner, the SS *Arabic,* without warning off the Irish coast, and some forty passengers and crew drowned, including two Americans. Renewed anger in the United States caused Germany to change its policy and halt its indiscriminate attacks from 1 September 1915.

The positive outcome of the Battle of Jutland in 1916 for Great Britain was that the German High Seas Fleet mostly remained in port for the rest of the war. On 1 February 1917 Germany instead reverted to a policy of unrestricted U-boat attacks, which became its main naval strategy.

The Imperial German Navy – the *Kaiserliche Marine* – set itself a target of destroying at least 600,000 tons of supplies being shipped to Great Britain each month. Allied commerce was attacked in the Atlantic, the Irish Sea and English Channel, the North Sea and the Mediterranean. In March 1917 the Germans sank 500,000 tons of shipping, and the following month, April 1917, over 1,000 Allied merchant ships were sunk, mainly by German U-boats, with the loss of 869,000 tons of cargo. Some 4,000 merchant crewmen were drowned on these ships over a period of three months in the spring of 1917.

The German submarine attacks posed a terrible threat to the survival of Great Britain in 1917, and the British Government was desperate to find a way to combat this U-boat offensive. The answer came with the adoption of the convoy system: the use of Royal Navy ships, mainly destroyers, to escort fleets of merchant ships in a convoy that zigzagged across the seas.

Convoys had been successfully used since the start of the war on cross-Channel routes for troopships and coal ships, and it was a technique that had been used by the Royal Navy with sailing ships in earlier centuries. But the proposal to use convoys to protect transatlantic commerce was vigorously opposed by Admiralty officials and by many senior officers, including Jellicoe, now the First Sea Lord. They thought that it would be far too difficult for the Royal Navy to shepherd merchant ships zigzagging across the ocean and that a large convoy would pose a much easier target for U-boat attacks. It was also the case that the Navy could not spare the number of destroyers that would be required to escort the convoys as they were needed to screen the Grand Fleet's battleships.

Despite his serious reservations, Jellicoe agreed to experimental convoys early in 1917 for the ships bringing coal from Scandinavia, and in May 1917 on the supply route between Gibraltar and Britain. These trials proved successful, and in May 1917 the first convoy across the Atlantic set out from Virginia in the United States, with further convoys following throughout the summer. These reached Britain too, with only the straggler ships being sunk by the German U-boats. The Admiralty established a complex administrative section, based in Plymouth, to manage the routine convoys of between twenty and fifty-four merchant ships, plus escorts, that brought food, fuel and other essential supplies to Great Britain for the remainder of the war.

Some 2,000 Allied warships and 4,000 British merchant ships were painted in special camouflage colours, a scheme known as 'dazzle painting' devised by a marine artist and Royal Navy reservist called Norman Wilkinson. Dazzle distorted the outline and size of the ships at sea and confused German U-boat crews trying to identify a target through their viewfinders. Convoys were also protected as they approached or left British ports by the airships and aeroplanes of the Royal Naval Air Service, which had considerable success in preventing U-boat attacks. During the whole war only one vessel was sunk by a German submarine on a convoy escorted by an aircraft.

Germany's resumption of unrestricted submarine warfare proved to be a mistaken strategy, as it was one of the main reasons why the United States of America entered the war on the side of the Allies on 6 April 1917. America was unprepared for war, and the first squadron of US ships only arrived in Scapa Flow in December 1917. It would take nearly a year before American soldiers started to arrive in Europe in significant numbers. But the establishment of the convoy system in 1917 put in place the means of later bringing their troopships plus large quantities of US vehicles and supplies across the Atlantic.

During the Great War, German U-boats sank some 40 per cent of the British merchant fleet, and 14,000 merchant seamen died, but most of these losses were before the adoption of the convoy system. By January 1918 the Germans' monthly figure for sinking British merchant shipping was down to 300,000 tons. Over 16,000 merchant ships crossed the Atlantic between May 1917 and November 1918, and the Germans sank only 138 of these.

There were significant food shortages in Britain by the end of 1917, and to reduce malnutrition in poorer communities the British Government introduced rationing in February 1918. But Germany's blockade of Great Britain and the attempt to starve its population into defeat failed, largely because of the Royal Navy's convoy system.

Destroyers were the preferred escort ship for commercial convoys. When stationary, a destroyer could use hydrophones lowered into the water to detect submarines, but these were rarely responsible for the sinking of U-boats and not nearly as effective as ASDIC, or sonar, was to prove in the Second World War. Of far greater assistance was the Admiralty's intelligence unit in Room 40, which often intercepted and decoded the wireless messages of German submarines, and so was able to pass information as to their location to escorting destroyers on a convoy. This was the fast destroyers' opportunity to assume an offensive role and to counter-attack an enemy submarine with their quick-firing guns, torpedoes and depth charges, or even to ram the U-boat with their strengthened hulls.

Throughout the war, but especially after Jutland, destroyers were engaged more actively in the naval campaign, on raids, patrols and, from 1917, convoys, than the Grand Fleet's capital ships. But the great shortage of destroyers during the final two years of the Great War meant that many convoys had to be escorted by old, often obsolescent, cruisers and by small ships such as sloops and gunboats, or even private vessels such as trawlers.

On 1 June 1917 George was promoted to the rate of Chief Engine Room Artificer, second class. The following month, on 11 July 1917, George left HMS *Vivid* and Plymouth for Scapa Flow to join HMS *Sturgeon*, one of sixty-two Admiralty R-class destroyers, the last class of destroyers to have three funnels. Launched on 11 January 1917, *Sturgeon* was capable of a speed of 36 knots from her two steam turbine engines. She carried a complement of eighty-two men and was armed with three 4-inch guns, an anti-aircraft gun and four torpedo tubes. *Sturgeon* was part of the Eleventh Destroyer Flotilla, a formation with two flotilla leader ships (larger destroyers which provided space, equipment and staff for the flotilla commodore), and between seventeen and twenty-one destroyers. George also worked on the flotilla's depot ship, HMS *Blake*, which, given the confined space on destroyers, supplied the flotilla ships and provided a base for the destroyer crews when off duty.

The Eleventh Destroyer Flotilla was attached to the Grand Fleet, which was still based at Scapa Flow and was now under Admiral Beatty's command, although it later moved to the enlarged base at Rosyth in April 1918. The Eleventh Destroyer Flotilla's established role was to provide an escort screen against enemy attack for troop ships and the battleships of the Grand Fleet, as it did at Jutland when it was also involved in the night action. From the spring of 1917 the flotilla's new roles were to engage in anti-submarine operations and to escort convoys.

George joined the Eleventh Destroyer Flotilla in July 1917 when it was assigned to Scapa Flow, just after regular convoys for merchant shipping had been introduced. The destroyers from Scapa, including his ship *Sturgeon*, escorted the coal and iron ore convoys on the dangerous Scandinavian route from neutral Sweden and Norway. The convoys sailed through the North Sea, across the waters of the northern British Isles and into the North Atlantic and Irish Sea to ports in the northwest such as Belfast, Liverpool and on the Clyde. These convoys were at the mercy of appalling weather conditions as well as raids by German U-boats and surface ships, and two such convoys were attacked in October and December 1917 with serious losses.

An officer who also joined George's ship HMS *Sturgeon* at Scapa in July 1917 was a twenty-year-old sub-lieutenant called Patrick Blackett, who later became an eminent scientist, won the Nobel Prize for Physics in 1948 and was ennobled as Baron Blackett. George Lancaster, Blackett and the eighty other members of the ship's company shared the cramped, uncomfortable and poorly ventilated accommodation on the destroyer, where it could be difficult to find a regular space for a hammock. The sailors on destroyers, far smaller than the armoured cruisers on which George had served previously, were subjected to the violent pitching and rolling of the seas, and seasickness was more likely to affect the crew. In bad weather huge waves washed over the decks, every item on board was usually soaking wet and it was difficult to produce decent food.

However, many naval men preferred life on a destroyer to being on a big ship, as with a much smaller ship's company the rules and regulations were not necessarily so strict, and more flexibility was allowed. The men knew each other better and could develop a more personal rapport.

George stayed at Scapa Flow with the Eleventh Destroyer Flotilla as a Chief Engine Room Artificer (second Class) until 1 March 1918 when he transferred south with HMS *Sturgeon* to the port of Harwich in Essex. *Sturgeon* was now part of the Tenth Destroyer Flotilla in the Harwich Force commanded by Commodore Reginald Tyrwhitt, which also included submarines under the command of Commodore Roger Keyes.

The Tenth Destroyer Flotilla comprised four flotilla leader ships, twenty-four R-class destroyers, four paddle sweepers and the depot ship HMS *Dido*. This destroyer flotilla and nine light cruisers formed the surface ship element of the Harwich Force. Its commander, the able and highly regarded Commodore Tyrwhitt, was determined to attack the enemy at every opportunity, possessing what Arthur Marder refers to as the Nelsonian attribute of 'offensive spirit'. Throughout the war his Harwich Force ships were engaged on scouting and reconnaissance operations and several raids, including attempts to stop the Germans laying mines in the Channel. Marder states that no other naval unit during the Great War spent so many days at sea and suffered so many losses as the Harwich Force.[77]

The role of destroyers such as HMS *Sturgeon* on the Harwich Force was to defend the route into the Thames Estuary and the eastern approaches to the English Channel from the North Sea, liaising with the ships of the Dover Patrol. The Harwich destroyers were also engaged in escorting commercial convoys between the neutral Netherlands and England, bringing much needed supplies of food from Europe on a convoy route which was nicknamed 'The Beef Trip'.

On 11 March 1918, when George was part of its crew, HMS *Sturgeon* and two other Harwich Force destroyers, *Thruster* and *Retriever*, attacked an enemy German U-boat SM UB-54, which was part of the Flanders Flotilla of the German Imperial Navy based in Zeebrugge. This U-boat had sunk fourteen Allied merchant vessels since June 1917, and so her sinking with all hands by the depth charges of these three British destroyers was a good result for their crews.

This action is probably one reason why on 20 April 1918 George was awarded the Distinguished Service Medal for 'Miscellaneous Services', which was listed in the *London Gazette* on 7 June 1918.[78] This award was not handed out to servicemen on a routine basis – it was given to comparatively few lower deck men, given the size of the Navy, for genuinely distinguished service in wartime actions. The authorities in the Admiralty responsible for such awards would have reviewed George's career throughout the war, and noted his service on HMS *Warrior* at the Battle of Jutland – in which only 10 per cent of the then serving Royal Navy took part – and his role on active service with the Harwich Force. This medal was the culmination of George's fighting career during the Great War and meant a great deal to him.

George stayed with HMS *Sturgeon* until 1 October 1918 when his service contribution during the war was also recognised by his promotion from the lower deck to the warrant officer rank of Acting Artificer Engineer. Although the rather unprepossessing title of 'Artificer Engineer' sounds similar to his previous rate of Chief Engine Room Artificer, an Artificer Engineer was in fact a more senior position than a CERA or Chief Petty Officer. This new rank of Engineer Warrant Officers, known as Artificer Engineers, had been introduced by an Order in Council dated 18 May 1897, and was open to ERAs or CERAs of at least ten years' service who had passed a prescribed examination. As an Acting Artificer Engineer, George wore a narrow purple stripe and curl on the sleeve cuff of his uniform, and was entitled to carry a naval sword.

In October 1918 the German Admirals Scheer and Hipper planned to draw out the British Grand Fleet again for another major battle in the North Sea. But the crews of the German High Seas Fleet at Wilhelmshaven mutinied and refused to put to sea – the Fleet never left port. The Allies' armies on the Continent finally won the gruelling, bloody land battle in the trenches, and the Great War ended on 11 November 1918 with the signing of the Armistice in a railway carriage in the Forest of Compiègne, near Paris.

Under the terms of the Armistice the Imperial German Navy had to surrender its fleet to the British. On 20 November George was still with the Harwich Force and would have witnessed the first batch of German U-boats surrender to Commodore Tyrwhitt in the harbour at Harwich, which soon had over 100 German submarines moored there.

On 21 November, the British Grand Fleet of forty battleships and battlecruisers and some 150 cruisers and destroyers, under the command of Admiral Sir David Beatty, sailed out of the Firth of Forth into the

North Sea to meet seventy warships of the German High Seas Fleet for its formal surrender, which was code-named 'Operation ZZ'. The Royal Navy crews and guns were ready for action in case the Germans reneged on the terms of surrender, and the British fleet formed into two columns to surround the German fleet. Beatty sent out the order: 'The German flag will be hauled down at sunset today and will not be hoisted again without permission'.

This extraordinary meeting of the two fleets in the North Sea was reputed to be the largest assembly of warships ever in one place, and marked the bitter but peaceful conclusion of the Anglo-German naval arms race which had dominated the pre-war strategic planning of both countries.

Beatty's ships escorted the German High Seas Fleet to Scapa Flow in the Orkneys for internment. Seven months later, on 21 June 1919, the German commander at Scapa heard an incorrect report that the Versailles peace talks were about to fail. Fearing war might be resumed, he ordered his crews to scuttle their ships rather than allow them to be passed to the Allied Powers. Seventy-two German warships, over 400,000 tons, were deliberately sunk in Scapa Flow by their crews, the largest ever loss of shipping in a single day.

The number of British and Empire servicemen killed in the Great War, either in action or who died of wounds or disease, plus those missing presumed dead, totalled some 890,000. In comparison to the huge tally of soldiers who died, the Royal Navy's losses of some 39,000 were relatively light. This and the indecisive outcome of the Battle of Jutland have created a view in some quarters that the Navy contributed little to Great Britain's victory over Germany. This disregards several vital contributions that the Royal Navy made in the conduct of the war.

The ships of the Royal Navy had successfully transported over five million men and their equipment, vehicles and supplies across the English Channel to France to fight in the trenches. The Royal Navy's shelling of German ports enabled those Allied forces to land in Europe relatively unharmed.

The Battle of Jutland was a strategic victory for the British that meant the threat of the *Kaiserliche Marine*'s surface fleet to the British Isles was removed, and Great Britain remained, for a few more years, the supreme maritime power across the globe. Instead the Germans switched from surface ships to submarine warfare, and the Royal Navy's convoy system in 1917 and 1918 was a vital factor in undermining the offensive of German U-boats and saving the country from starvation.

The blockade mounted from the outset of the war by the Royal Navy of German ports and its interception of shipping to Germany had by 1915 cut that country's imports by 55 per cent from pre-war levels. Supplies to the enemy of food, fuel and other essential raw materials were stopped, and the lack of fertilisers vital for agriculture also caused food shortages. Rationing was introduced in Germany as early as January 1915, and the country manufactured ersatz food products such as powdered milk to supplement subsistence diets. Nevertheless the people of Germany and Austria-Hungary suffered badly throughout the war with widespread malnutrition, and food riots and looting were common. Official statistics state that what became known as the 'hunger blockade' by the Royal Navy caused the death of some 763,000 German civilians from malnutrition and disease.[79] It certainly created the conditions whereby the Kaiser's sailors at Wilhelmshaven were prepared to mutiny in October 1918 and the German population was ready to concede defeat a month later.

These successes of the Royal Navy and its role in the Great War are often overlooked. The naval engagements in that war, and the failures, also taught the Navy valuable lessons. Jutland demonstrated the inflexibility of large battle fleets, the vulnerability of fast but lightly armoured battlecruisers to accurate gunnery over long distances, and the importance of the proper storage of explosives and anti-flash precautions. After that battle the Navy also adopted measures to improve its communications at sea and its ability to engage in night fighting.

The effective use of convoys, the more extensive deployment of submarines and the advent of aerial warfare were vital developments in the Great War, from which the Royal Navy also learnt important lessons. Those lessons, and the consequent changes in naval strategy and operations, were to prove vital to the survival of Great Britain in the next world war, just over two decades later.

George's father, George Lancaster, 1893

Young George, 1905

St. John's Ramblers' Club Calstock, 1908

The Lancaster family, 1909

HMS *Warrior,* 1914

Able Seaman Alfred Swain (on left) and crewmate from HMS *Warrior* in Egypt, October 1914

HRH The Prince of Wales and George, August 1919

George's card from Estonia, December 1919

George's wife Ida with daughter Beryl and dog, Malta 1924

George and Beryl, Torquay 1925

HMS *Berwick* officers, Hong Kong 1928 (George under gun on right)

Celebrating Emperor Hirohito's coronation, Yokohama, Japan 1928

George's daughters Ida and Beryl, 1928

George's wife Ida and Beryl with the 'Baby Austin', 1937

Young Ida, 1937

George, 1937

Atlantic Crossings

HMS Dauntless, Bermuda – 3rd April 1919
*Just a line before the mail leaves tonight to let you know we are expecting
to go to Barbados from here and I have heard that we might get back by
the 27th of the month. I hope our little one is all right as this also leaves
me. I went to Hamilton today but it is very small. Hoping we shall soon
be together again.*
Your ever loving husband George xxx

1919 was an extraordinary year for George. He crossed the Atlantic four
times, sailed to the far north of Europe twice, saw active service when
his ship shelled both Russian and German troops (in different actions),
cruised the Caribbean, met the Prince of Wales and visited the major cities
of Eastern Canada.

The Great War had cost the lives of over 8.5 million people from
the victorious Allies and the defeated nations combined, with millions
more wounded, taken prisoner or missing. Some 890,000 of the dead
were from Britain and its Empire territories.

This horrific carnage was, however, quickly and hugely surpassed in
1918–1919 by the global influenza pandemic that broke out towards the
end of the war and spread throughout every continent. The estimates vary
wildly, but the more recent researched statistics indicate that this virulent
disease killed a total from all countries of between 30 to 50 million people
worldwide. In Great Britain as many as 250,000 died, including thousands
of servicemen, their resistance to infection weakened by conditions of war.
In his book *The Sailor's War 1914–1918* the historian Peter Liddle wrote:

> ...the influenza pandemic...was seriously affecting the fighting
> efficiency of the Navy in the weeks before the Armistice. Plymouth
> and Devonport, for example, were hit desperately hard; the rows of
> tombstones of boys from the training establishment there stand today
> as sad witness that the young and fit were not spared in their vigour.[80]

One week after the Armistice, on 19 November 1918 George joined HMS *Dauntless*, a *Danae*-class light cruiser built in 1916 with a total crew of 415 men, based at Harwich in Essex on the North Sea coast. After witnessing the U-boat surrender that month and taking some leave over Christmas, he spent the first six weeks of 1919 in Harwich with his ship, the crew following an established naval routine as recorded in the log book:[81]

> Typically at around 9 a.m. they have Divisions, prayers and physical drill. At around 4 p.m. they have Quarters. The hands spend a lot of time cleaning the ship and also painting. There are often training classes at instruction. On Sunday morning they have Divine Service and are Mustered by Divisions and if in port they land Church Parties. When at sea they exercise the sea boats' crew several times a day.
>
> While in Harwich, each afternoon, some of the crew have leave, until 10 p.m. for the men and 5.30 p.m. for the boys.

As Europe moved into 1919 its populations faced a world of collapse. In November 1918 the German Empire was replaced by the Weimar Republic, and Kaiser Wilhelm was sent into exile in the Netherlands. Emperor Franz Joseph had died in 1916 after ruling the Austro-Hungarian Empire for nearly sixty-eight years to be succeeded by the Emperor Charles. After the Armistice in November 1918, and in the face of nationalist movements, the Dual Monarchy of the Habsburgs was dissolved and Charles renounced his right to rule in both Austria and Hungary. The Ottoman Empire, which had been failing for decades, finally crumbled, and after the Russian Revolution in 1917 brought the Bolsheviks to power, they assassinated the Tsar and all his family in July 1918.

In contrast, the overseas territories of the British Empire were at their fullest extent in 1919. The Royal Navy, with over 400,000 officers and men at the end of the war,[82] maintained a chain of naval bases and stations across the globe. The log book of George's ship, HMS *Dauntless*, recorded her day-to-day activities from January to December 1919 and provides a detailed and fascinating insight into the voyages of a Royal Navy warship as it served the global interests of the British Empire.

On 11 February 1919 HMS *Dauntless* set sail down the English Channel for Plymouth, where the ship berthed for two days, giving

George time to take shore leave to see his family. On 14 February it left harbour again, sailing past the Eddystone and Lizard Lighthouses and the Peninnis Lighthouse on St Mary's in the Scilly Isles, and out into the Atlantic. HMS *Dauntless* had been assigned to service on the Royal Navy's North America and West Indies Station, and was heading for the Caribbean.

It was a rough passage for them through stormy seas, with waves up to thirty-five feet in height which damaged some small cutter boats stored on the ship's deck and carried off a mast. On 20 February the ship changed course to ascertain if a passing steamer called the *Roman* required assistance. Two days later *Dauntless* arrived at the dockyard in the British colony of Bermuda where the Navy's North America and West Indies Station had its permanent establishment, with an additional summer base in Halifax, Nova Scotia.

After four days in Bermuda, they were off again to Cuba, arriving at Havana on 1 March where the ship's crew fired a twenty-one-gun salute to the Cuban flag. The Republic of Cuba had been a Spanish colony until 1902 when it gained its independence, and this was clearly a goodwill 'flying the British flag' tour by HMS *Dauntless*. Over the next few days the ship received visits from the British *Chargé d'Affaires* and later the Cuban Minister of Marine and the Cuban Secretary of War, each of whom were greeted with a salute of seventeen guns.

Dauntless stayed in Havana for over a fortnight. Some American naval ships arrived while they were there: a gunboat, six submarine chasers and the warship USS *Cincinnati*, but otherwise little happened to disturb the routine of drills and inspections, painting, polishing and cleaning the ship and washing clothes. During these stays in the Caribbean islands, the log book states that:

While in port…each afternoon, some of the crew are given leave, until 11 p.m. or 7 a.m. for the men and until around 6.30 p.m. for the boys. A Patrol is landed at around 8 p.m..

On 17 March the ship left Havana to sail to another Cuban port, Santiago, where the British Consul visited her, and there were further gun salutes to the Governor of Santiago and a visit to a Cuban gunboat with reciprocal salutes.

The next stop was Kingston, Jamaica, where they arrived on 20 March, in very heavy rain, thunder and lightning, for a stay of four days before returning to Bermuda, which they reached, after a further four days' sailing, on 28 March.

George purchased several picture postcards on his visits ashore to these Caribbean islands. There are postcards showing street scenes in Jamaica in his collection, and several views of Havana in Cuba. One of the Cuban cards is of a fruit stand, and on the back George has written:

My Darling Wife,
I have enclosed some photos which you will be interested in, doesn't this
P.C. make your mouth water but Havana is not a patch on Jamaica
for fruit.

The cards from Havana are views of the Cathedral and the grand Spanish colonial buildings, wide avenues and promenades of the city. One shows smart, prosperous looking couples, the men wearing panama hats and blazers, the women in full-length dresses and elegant feathered hats, strolling along the Avenida del Golfo – this is some forty years before the revolutionary Cuba of the Castro era.

From late March *Dauntless* and her crew spent a fortnight in Bermuda, again occupied with routine duties and watching various ships of the United States Navy arriving in the harbour, also on courtesy visits, firing twenty-one-gun salutes which were duly returned. The Governor of Bermuda visited the ship and His Excellency received a seventeen-gun salute.

On 9 April *Dauntless* left Bermuda again, this time sailing for Barbados where she arrived on 12 April. Three days in Barbados, and she was off to Grenada for a two-day stay where the crew had training classes and instruction for non-swimmers, and a visit from the Governor of Grenada – yet another seventeen-gun salute for him. This was followed by a short overnight trip to Port of Spain and Point Pierre in Trinidad for refuelling of the ship, and then it was back to Bermuda via Grenada, with a sighting of Antigua on the starboard bow, arriving in harbour at Bermuda on 24 April.

Dauntless stayed in Bermuda for five days, during which two court-martials were assembled on board the ship – but the log book gives no further details. On 29 April *Dauntless* slipped anchor and set sail on a calmer return voyage back across the Atlantic, where they arrived a week later on 6 May, sighting St Michael's Chapel on Rame Head before proceeding into Plymouth Sound and mooring in the Hamoaze.

After a fortnight's leave in Plymouth, George departed again on HMS *Dauntless*, this time for a month-long trip to the Baltic,[83] returning to Devonport on 16 July 1919.

On 2 August George and his ship proceeded out of Plymouth Sound, and in thick fog sailed down the Cornish coast, past Polperro Coastguard Station and the lighthouses at the Lizard and Bishop Rock and out into the Western Approaches, the expanse of waters between the English Channel, the Irish coast and the Bay of Biscay. HMS *Dauntless* was again crossing the Atlantic, bound for Canada as one of the naval ships escorting Edward, Prince of Wales (later Edward VIII and the Duke of Windsor), on his official visit to Canada.

The Prince of Wales was twenty-five in 1919, and this was the first of several quite arduous global tours on which his father, King George V, sent him across the British Empire to thank the colonies for supporting Britain in the Great War. The monarch and his Government also hoped that the Prince's tours would boost the standing of George V as the King and Emperor among his subjects overseas at a time when so many other crowned heads, including the emperors of Germany, Austria-Hungary and Russia, had fallen from power.

The young Prince of Wales had already established his reputation as a playboy, and by 1919 was in a secret relationship with Freda Dudley Ward, the first of his affairs with married women. His despatch abroad was intended to make him focus on his royal duties and to remove him from scandal at home. The Prince and his entourage sailed on the battlecruiser HMS *Renown*, and on the first outward stage of the Canadian trip the escorting light cruisers were George's ship *Dauntless* and HMS *Dragon*.

HMS *Dauntless* first sailed to St John's, Newfoundland, passing close to several icebergs on 6 August – the ship was on a similar course to that of the *Titanic* which had sunk off Newfoundland only seven years earlier. After two days in St John's, where the ship refuelled, it put to sea again, altering course to avoid an iceberg and sighting HMS *Renown* and HMS *Dragon* bearing east. *Dauntless* joined company with those other ships the following day, 11 August, at Conception Bay, Newfoundland, which was just around the headland from St John's, and all three anchored in the bay.

Prince Edward's imperial tour of Canada was under way. While in Conception Bay, the *Dauntless* log book records that 'One detective and one writer of HRH Prince of Wales's staff joined ship.'

The three ships sailed into harbour at St John's, and at noon the crew of *Dauntless* 'Manned ship and saluted HRH Prince of Wales going ashore with 21 guns'.

The next day, 13 August, the Prince himself came on board: '11.30 a.m. HRH the Prince of Wales walked around ship and inspected ship's company. 1.50 a.m. HRH left ship'.

A photograph of this occasion shows George standing on the end of a row; the officer next to him is being spoken to by the Prince of Wales, and George, looking straight ahead of him and no doubt feeling rather anxious, with his ceremonial sword by his left side, is about to be inspected by the Prince himself. For George, after ten years' service in the Royal Navy, this must have been one of the proudest moments in his career.

The Empire trip started on 14 August. Over the next few days *Dauntless*, as an escorting ship, sailed with HMS *Renown* and HMS *Dragon* to St John's in New Brunswick, where George bought four postcards, and then on to Halifax in Nova Scotia and to Charlottetown on Prince Edward Island. From there, on 20 August they proceeded across the Gulf of St Lawrence and down the St Lawrence River to Québec, which they reached on 21 August.

As they arrived in the French Canadian city they saw the spires of Notre Dame de la Garde and St Joseph de la Délivrance, and after dressing the ship overall with ceremonial flags (a regular occurrence on this Empire trip) they 'fired Royal Salute 21 guns on HRH landing'.

On 24 August: 'Five officers and 100 Ratings left ship for Niagara Falls & short tour as guests of Canadian Government'.

George went on this excursion and his postcard collection includes ten cards with views of the Niagara Falls, including two of the frozen falls in winter, one splendidly surrounded with several embossed coats of arms in gold and the Union Jack.

HMS *Dauntless* remained in Québec for a fortnight, and during this time George also visited the Canadian capital, Ottawa, as well as the cities of Montreal and Toronto, which are all situated to the southwest of Québec and could be reached from there by train. George's postcard views of Toronto include pictures of the Canadian National Exhibition of 1919 which was held there in that 'Year of Victory'. This was a huge event, showcasing the industry, agriculture, art and commerce of Canada, with many special attractions. The Prince of Wales was the chief VIP guest, and photographs and newsreel film of his visit show him in army uniform on horseback being greeted at the exhibition by thousands of Canadians.

While HMS *Dauntless* remained berthed in Québec, the Prince of Wales departed for his three-month Empire trip of Canada, travelling by train across the country to Calgary in Alberta and British Columbia on the west coast. He also visited New York and Washington in the United States, and did not return home until November 1919, when his ship, HMS *Renown*, was accompanied by two other cruisers, HMS *Danae* and HMS *Constant*.

Edward proved himself a very popular figure in Canada and the United States, and his North American tour was highly successful. After this royal visit, King George V, normally slow to praise his sons, wrote to Prince Edward, saying:

I offer you my warmest congratulations on the splendid success of your tour, which is due in great measure to your own personality and the wonderful way in which you have played up. It makes me very proud of you and makes me feel very happy that my son should be received with such marvellous enthusiasm of loyalty and affection.

After his visit to Washington, the Prince was also praised by the diplomat Lord Reading, who wrote:

The Prince has proved a better Ambassador than all of us rolled into one. He has caught the American spirit, so difficult to understand quickly, and has done more in America to make their people comprehend the strength of the democratic support to our Monarchy than all books and articles and propaganda.

At the end of the Prince's first Empire trip, the officers of HMS *Renown*, HMS *Dragon*, HMS *Dauntless*, HMS *Danae* and HMS *Constant*, including George, each received a signed photo of the Prince of Wales to mark his 1919 tour to Canada, accompanied by a short letter headed 'York House, St James Palace, SW' which states:

> Equerry in Waiting is desired by the Prince of Wales to forward to you the accompanying souvenir as a memento for the services which you rendered to His Royal Highness during his tour, August and November 1919.

HMS *Dauntless* left Québec on 3 September for the voyage home, sailing via St John's, Newfoundland, before crossing the Atlantic in the company of HMS *Dragon*. They arrived back in Devonport on 12 September, sailing into Plymouth Sound past the Eddystone and Breakwater lighthouses. After securing alongside HMS *Liverpool* at No. 5 buoy in the Hamoaze, the crew of *Dauntless* were paid a war gratuity and given a week's general leave.

George had been an Acting Artificer Engineer since the end of the war, and in May 1919 Captain Symonds, his commanding officer on HMS *Dauntless,* wrote on his naval record that George was 'zealous, hardworking, thoroughly reliable'.

On 24 September 1919 George sailed on *Dauntless* for a second trip to the Baltic, this time for three months. While he was in the Baltic his new rate was confirmed as 'Artificer Engineer with seniority' on 1 October 1919.

George achieved this promotion to confirmed warrant officer rate not just because of his length of service at sea and his continuous good conduct. Then thirty-three, he had to pass a qualifying examination which could only be taken before the age of thirty-five. This tested his professional and educational ability, his technical and executive expertise and high standard of seamanship.

Three months later, in January 1920, George's rate was raised again to 'Warrant Engineer'. His rapid advancement over eighteen months from being a CERA to an Artificer Engineer and then to Warrant Engineer was in fact a significant promotion for him. After over ten years in the Royal Navy George was still determined to improve his position in life. In an era of rigid naval hierarchy, a man like George who started on the lower deck as an Engine Room Artificer had to show exceptional ability in order to progress up through the ranks.

Bolsheviks!

In December 1919 George sent a couple of postcards home to his wife Ida and his five-year-old daughter. Both cards have a photograph of him in his naval uniform on the front with a sketch of the ship, HMS *Dauntless*, and a black and white drawing of a polar bear on a rock. But he writes on the back:

> *I am afraid we have rather overdone the atmosphere of cold on the picture by including the Polar bear which of course do not exist in the Baltic Sea.*
> HMS *Dauntless*, Reval, 8th December 1919

Reval is now called Tallinn, the capital of Estonia, one of the Baltic states. George may have joked about the absence of polar bears, but the reality was that he and his shipmates had already spent several months in 1919 sailing in the dangerous waters of the Baltic in the middle of a war zone. He had been living in very harsh conditions on board ship off a remote island in the eastern Gulf of Finland, only thirty miles away from the enemy's naval base at Kronstadt and very near to Petrograd, one of Russia's major cities.[84]

George was on his second trip to the Baltic that year. His ship, *Dauntless*, had completed a month-long tour there in June and July 1919, and had returned for a second trip of three months from September to December 1919. So what was he doing in the Baltic?

Russia had fought alongside the Allied Powers against Germany and Austria-Hungary from the start of the Great War, but by 1917 its armies had experienced several defeats and the Russian people were suffering terrible privations and poverty.

The first Russian revolution of February 1917 had led to the abdication of Tsar Nicholas and the establishment of a provisional Government, which was dominated by mainly liberal politicians. In the second revolution of October 1917 the more radical Bolsheviks under Vladimir Lenin seized power and established the Soviet Union.

Lenin decided to negotiate peace with Germany. Despite the excessive demands of the Germans and the opposition of many Russians, including members of the Bolshevik Party such as Trotsky, Soviet Russia agreed to the Treaty of Brest-Litovsk with Germany in March 1918, by which large parts of Russian territory, including tracts of Georgia and the Ukraine, were ceded to Germany. Estonia, Latvia, Lithuania and Finland were ostensibly to become independent republics, although in reality they were to be fiefdoms of Germany, which intended to exploit the valuable resources of these Baltic states.

The opposition within Russia to the peace treaty with Germany, and the rule of the Bolsheviks, who were now instituting a one-party state through terror and oppression, led to the Russian Civil War of 1918–1920. The Bolsheviks were called the 'Reds' and their opponents, despite being made up of a diverse range of conservative, liberal and socialist groups with very different objectives, were together called the 'Whites'.

In July 1918 the Bolsheviks murdered Tsar Nicholas and all his family and servants at Yekaterinburg in the Urals. The British Government had been prepared to offer asylum to the Tsar, but King George V, despite being Nicholas's cousin, had blocked this as he feared that the Tsar's presence in Great Britain might provoke an anti-monarchist movement against his own throne.

After Lenin's seizure of power and the Tsar's assassination, many of the Allied Powers feared that the Bolshevik Revolution would spread across Europe and beyond. Britain, the United States, Canada, France, Italy and Greece all sent forces to aid the opponents of Bolshevism and to support the new republican movements in the Baltic states of Estonia and Latvia. Lithuania was also fighting for its independence, but did not receive significant support from these western Allies, as its troops were helped by German forces.

At the Peace Conference in Paris which had opened in January 1919, President Woodrow Wilson of the United States pronounced the principle that 'all nations have a right to self-determination'. On the face of it this gave the Allied Powers a reason to support the spread of the nationalist movements that were developing across Europe and the Middle East following the post-war collapse of the Austro-Hungarian, Russian and Ottoman Empires.

After centuries of Swedish rule, since 1721 Estonia had been subject to the control of the Russian Empire, and a nationalist movement seeking independence had been growing since the mid-nineteenth century. In February 1918, as the Russian troops retreated, the Estonians made a formal Declaration of Independence – but then Germany occupied Estonia. After the Armistice in November 1918, Germany formally handed over political power to the Estonian Provisional Government, but Estonia and its neighbour Latvia still had to continue fighting against renegade German troops as well as Soviet Russia's forces, which were moving west into the Baltic states.

Winston Churchill, back in the Cabinet as the British War Secretary, was particularly committed to resisting the 'Reds' despite the reservations of the Prime Minister, Lloyd George, and the opposition of the small Labour Party. The Cabinet supported Churchill, and in December 1918, only a month after the end of the Great War, a Royal Navy squadron of cruisers, destroyers and minesweepers commanded by Rear Admiral Sir Edwin Alexander Sinclair was sent to the Baltic under the code-name 'Operation Red Trek'. His orders were rather vague – 'Show the British flag and support British policy as circumstances dictate'.

The expedition started badly with the sinking of HMS *Cassandra* on 6 December, when it struck a mine in the Gulf of Riga and ten of its crew were drowned. However, the squadron reached ports in Latvia and Estonia, and in addition to delivering supplies it was able to support the fledging Estonian army by shelling Bolshevik troops. Sinclair's ships also helped keep the sea lanes open to enable 3,000 Finnish volunteers to reach Estonia to join its army of independence.

The Royal Navy captured two Soviet destroyers, the *Spartak* and the *Avtroil* which had been shelling the dockyard at Reval, and handed them over to the Estonian Provisional Government to use for its own Navy. Despite British protests, the Estonians later executed many of the Bolshevik crew of these ships.

Sinclair returned home, and in January 1919 a second squadron of light cruisers and destroyers under the pugnacious Rear Admiral Sir Walter Cowan arrived in the Eastern Baltic, where he was later joined by some French warships. In the course of a thirteen-month campaign from December 1918 to December 1919 Britain committed 238 Royal Navy vessels and approximately 25,000 British servicemen to fighting in the Baltic, and it took on a leading role in the intervention of the Allied

Powers in the Russian Civil War and the new Baltic republics' fight for independence.

After returning to Devonport from the Caribbean in early May 1919, the crew of HMS *Dauntless* spent a month in Plymouth, where George was able to take shore leave to be with his family. On 5 June 1919 Captain Cecil Pilcher joined the ship to replace the outgoing captain, and two days later, on 7 June, HMS *Dauntless* set sail again. She stopped for a week in Rosyth before setting off on 16 June for Copenhagen in Denmark, where the ship berthed for only a few hours.

That night *Dauntless* proceeded into the Baltic in the company of other naval ships and arrived the following day, 20 June, at the city port of Libau (also called Liepāja[85]) on the coast of Latvia. Here they picked up a senior officer named Commodore A.A.M. Duff, who was in charge of the British naval operations in the western Baltic, whom they immediately took back to Copenhagen with his staff.

Once in the Baltic, and throughout the ship's time there, the log book regularly refers to 'Out Paravanes' and 'In Paravanes'. These were torpedo-shaped devices towed alongside the ship to cut the mooring cables of underwater mines so that they rose to the surface where they could be destroyed. HMS *Dauntless* was operating in a war zone.

From Copenhagen they sailed to Danzig, and back to Libau on 25 June where they stayed for a fortnight. While they were there, the Treaty of Versailles was signed on 28 June 1919 and the crew 'Dressed the ship with masthead flags in celebration of the signing of Peace'. Otherwise the time was spent in gunnery and target practice, course and speed trials with other ships and Lewis gun practice for HMS *Dauntless*'s complement of forty-two marines. On 5 July divers were sent down into the Inner Naval Harbour of Libau to recover arms and ammunition sunk by Russians. The crew were also able to take some shore leave in the Latvian port.

Several other British warships came in and out of Libau harbour during this period, and also a French warship, the *Téméraire*, and the American ship the USS *Evans*. On 6 July 1919 *Dauntless* left Libau with seven White Russian officers on board, whom they landed next day at Reval before sailing on to Björkö Sound, arriving there on 8 July.

Björkö Sound is in the remote Beryozovye Islands in the far eastern end of the Gulf of Finland.[86] In July 1905 it had been the location of a strange and secret meeting between those two difficult cousins, Tsar Nicholas II and Kaiser Wilhelm II, when they each sailed into the Sound on their respective yachts and agreed a mutual defence pact, the Treaty of Björkö. The treaty came to nothing as Russia was already committed to support France.

In June 1919 Rear Admiral Cowan, the leader of the Royal Navy squadron, had decided to move his own base from Reval in Estonia to Björkö Sound as his ships would be better placed there to mount an offensive on the Soviet Navy based at Kronstadt, and to support the White Russians' objective of taking Petrograd from the Bolsheviks. By July there were many Royal Navy ships anchored there, including George's ship, and they were only thirty miles from their enemy's ships at the Russian naval base of Kronstadt, which guarded the passage to nearby Petrograd.

While at Björkö Sound, working parties from the ship were employed at the island's air station, but after only three days there *Dauntless* sailed back across the Baltic to Copenhagen via Libau and Reval, and then home to Plymouth, arriving in Devonport on 16 July.

The month that HMS *Dauntless* had spent in the Baltic may have seemed uneventful, judging by its log book entries. But the full extent of this cruiser's activities would not have been recorded in the log book, and the ship played its part in Cowan's overall mission.

Between December 1918 and December 1919 the British naval ships delivered some £100 million worth of arms and equipment to the Whites' counter-revolutionary movement and to the Latvian and Estonian armies, as well as food to avert famine. The Royal Navy also helped the White Russians to blockade Petrograd to stop the Soviet Baltic fleet from sailing out from its naval base at Kronstadt. The British mine-sweeping operations in the Baltic and support for shore landings in areas under Bolshevik control in Northern Estonia assisted the Estonians in pushing back the Red Army.

At this time the British secret intelligence service was sending agents into Russia to spy on the Bolsheviks. A flotilla of small coastal motorboats under the command of a Royal Navy officer called Lieutenant Augustus Agar was based in Finland, just over the Soviet frontier, to ferry British agents in and out of Petrograd. They included a British spy called Paul Dukes, who had infiltrated the Bolshevik Government and taken photographs of top-secret documents.

There were significant British losses in the course of the fighting. On 9 June two Bolshevik destroyers raided Björkö Sound, sinking the Royal Navy submarine L 55 with the loss of its entire crew of forty-two officers and men, and on 15 July two British minesweepers were sunk, with the loss of twelve naval ratings. On 31 August the destroyer HMS *Victoria* was sunk by a Soviet submarine and eight men drowned, and HMS *Verulam* hit a mine on 3 September resulting in the death of fifteen crew members.

In return the British campaign had its successes. In June and August 1919 the British carried out two raids on the Soviet fleet in Kronstadt Harbour. The first was led by Lieutenant Agar using coastal motorboats ('CMBs'), and they sank the Soviet cruiser *Oleg* and a depot ship, for which action Agar won the Victoria Cross. On 18 August the Royal Navy aircraft carrier *Vindictive*[87] in the eastern Gulf of Finland sent eight aircraft to attack the Russian ships at Kronstadt in a combined operation with a force of eight CMBs, which torpedoed and sank a submarine supply ship and a Soviet dreadnought and badly damaged another battleship. Fifteen of the British crew died in the raid, and the survivors were decorated for bravery, with two officers being awarded the Victoria Cross.

The Royal Navy had earlier in 1919 evacuated many White Russians from ports in the Crimea in Southern Russia on the Black Sea, including the Tsar's mother, the Dowager Empress Marie, and seven members of her family, who escaped just before the Bolsheviks arrived and were taken by the British to Malta. In late 1919 the Allies were also supporting a humanitarian rescue mission to pick up thousands of White Russian refugees fleeing the Bolsheviks through ports in the Baltic and to take them into exile in western Europe. HMS *Dauntless* may well have picked up some White Russian refugees in 1919.

After returning from their first trip to the Baltic and a fortnight's shore leave in Devonport, HMS *Dauntless*, and George, sailed off for their second tour across the Atlantic that year. This time it was to act as one of the escort ships on the Prince of Wales's Empire Trip to Canada, from which they returned in mid-September. The year 1919 continued to be eventful for the ship and her crew, as on 24 September they were off again, sailing straight back to Copenhagen and on to Latvia, reaching Libau on 28 September.

Two days after they arrived, a tragedy occurred. Stoker Petty Officer Sidney Riggs fell overboard from a liberty boat and was drowned at the age of twenty-six. He was a Plymouth man, and his death must have shocked the whole ship's company, including George who probably knew this seaman well. A court of enquiry was held on board the ship the next day.

On 2 October, HMS *Dauntless* left again for Björkö Sound via Reval, destroying mines on the way. This time she stayed at Björkö for over a month, from 3 October until 5 November 1919, sending working parties ashore, carrying out control drills and firing practice and going to sea for exercises. The transcriber of the online log book records that:

> …while at Biorko Sound: each afternoon, when not at sea, some of the crew are given leave until 5.30 p.m.; each evening the ship is darkened, a searchlight is burnt on the Western boat entrance and usually one 6" gun crew are closed up.

The crew of *Dauntless* also saw active service while based at Björkö, as in the autumn of 1919 the White Russians mounted an offensive on Petrograd, with gunfire support from Royal Navy ships.

On 14 October *Dauntless* was at sea, and the log reads:

> In company with Estonian Navy. 10.30 a.m.: Doubovski Point – S18W 3.7 miles. Opened fire on Bolshevik Battery. 11.09: Ceased firing. Course and speed various to Westward in Koporskaya Bight to communicate with Estonians.

On 21 October three Russian destroyers were sunk in a British minefield while attempting to defect to Estonia, with the loss of 485 men on board.

On 26 October Rear Admiral Cowan inspected the ship's company on *Dauntless*, which then spent its last ten days at the Sound going out to sea and returning to Björkö, probably engaging in the Royal Navy's blockade of Petrograd. There was an air raid alarm one afternoon and the crew manned the ship's high-angle guns in case Soviet aircraft approached.

On 27 and 31 October the bombardment of two Soviet sea forts by HMS *Erebus* provided support to the White Russian army's offensive against Petrograd, but this action marked the end of active British military support for the White Russians. At home Lloyd George's Government was faced with anti-war sentiments and increasing opposition to the British intervention in the Baltic, and the supply of arms to the Baltic for the White Russians had already stopped in late September 1919.

The White Russians' campaign failed to capture Petrograd, and by the end of 1919 they were in retreat.

The Estonians were in secret peace negotiations with the Russians by November 1919, and in February 1920 Russia recognised the independence of Estonia by the Treaty of Tartu and renounced all its rights to Estonian territory.

The thirteen months of the Baltic campaign had cost the lives of 111 British servicemen. But the Royal Navy's activities in the Baltic, including the Kronstadt raids, had succeeded in that they considerably reduced the threat of the Soviet Navy to the Baltic states in 1919 as they fought for freedom from domination by Russia.

The Russian Civil War was fought during 1920 across the lands of the former Tsarist Empire between the Bolshevik Red Army and the White Russian forces. The figures are estimates, but in addition to approximately 350,000 soldiers killed in the fighting, and another 450,000 servicemen who died from disease, the Bolshevik secret police, the Cheka, executed some 300,000 'enemies of the people' in their 'Red Terror'. Nearly half a million Cossacks were also killed or deported, and 100,000 Jews were killed in pogroms in Ukraine, mainly by White Russians.

The Civil War was a catastrophe for the Russian people. The three years of civil war, coming immediately after over three years' fighting in the Great War, caused extreme economic devastation and hardship. Millions of the civilian population died of typhus and typhoid, drought and famine between 1920 and 1922. Some estimates put the death toll at nearly ten million, and many historians regard the Russian Civil War of 1918 to 1920 as the worst civil conflict on record.

Although the British intervention in the Russian Civil War was ending in late 1919, George's ship saw further active service in the Baltic in the last weeks of 1919, this time against Germans.

Since June 1919 the Latvians and Estonians had been fighting German troops to the south. These were the right-wing Freikorps and the Baltische Landeswehr militia from Prussia, who had attacked Latvia in contravention of the orders of Germany's new Weimar Government. These militia were not prepared to accept Germany's defeat and were determined to prevent the spread of Bolshevism to their Prussian landed estates by colonising territory in the buffer states of Lithuania, Latvia and Estonia. A German 'Iron Division' under General von der Goltz, supported by brutal Freikorps militia, marched from Lithuania into Latvia, and a pro-German puppet state was established there. The Iron Division was advancing towards Estonia with the same intention.

In October 1919 British and French ships had shelled the Freikorps troops who were fighting the Latvians near Riga. In November the German Iron Division was trying to capture the port of Libau in Latvia. HMS *Dauntless* arrived back in Libau on 5 November, and early the following morning, its log book records:

> 4.40 a.m.: Exercised action. Opened indirect fire on German Positions to Eastward. No.5 gun burst. No casualties. Gun out of action.

> 6.10 a.m.: Ceased fire.

> 5.40 p.m.: Carried our short burst of fire as in morning watch.

HMS *Dauntless* engaged in further shelling of German positions to the east of Libau on 8 and 9 November, and again on 11 and 12 November. On 13 November the French warship *L'Ancre* arrived at Libau to join the several Royal Navy and French ships already there. The following day, 14 November, *Dauntless's* log book records several hours' action:

> 6.00 a.m.: Opened indirect fire on German positions between NE and ESE.

> 7.30 a.m.: All ships in harbour firing.

> 8.35 a.m.: Action stations firing full salvos. Letts [i.e. Latvians] driven back from front line.

> 11.00 a.m.: Firing continued (two or three gun salvos).

12.30 p.m.: Letts recovered front line.

1.45 p.m.: Ceased firing.

That evening HMS *Galatea* arrived in port, diverted from her voyage home to Britain in order to replenish the ammunition of the Royal Navy force at Libau, including that of HMS *Dauntless*, which fired four more rounds at German positions the following day. HMS *Whitley* also arrived, carrying Latvian troops, followed by HMS *Verdun* and HMS *Valkyrie*, with yet more British and French ships arriving and some departing over the next fortnight.

The Allied Powers clearly committed significant resources to supporting Latvia, and by the end of November the Latvians had succeeded in expelling the German troops from their country.

On 23 November HMS *Dauntless* left Libau to return to Björkö Sound, where she stayed for a fortnight until 5 December. The conditions for the crews of the British ships in Björkö in those weeks as the Finnish/ Russian winter set in must have been very harsh. The naval reason for her return to Björkö is not stated in the log book, although reference is made to submarines – H28, H30, H42 and H51 – sailing, and others – H21 and H48 – being secured alongside the ship, so *Dauntless* was probably picking up the crews of these boats.

Soon after *Dauntless* arrived at Björkö a court martial of a Lieutenant G.D. Salmon was held on board the ship for 'improperly forsaking station', and he was discharged to HMS *Vindictive* to be punished for his offence.

At that time of year it must have been very difficult for a light cruiser such as *Dauntless* to operate in the freezing waters of the Baltic, and on 5 December the ship left Björkö Sound and the next day arrived back at Reval. The eastern Gulf of Finland would be frozen by mid-January and naval activities would have to cease regardless of the political situation.

It was from Reval that George wrote his two postcards home on 8 December 1919:

My Darling Wife,
I have ordered some of the ship's Xmas cards but I don't think they will reach the ship from the printers in time for me to send. These will have

to take their place. The only wish I can send is that we may have the
happiness of being together this Xmas.
Your Ever Loving Husband, George

The second identical postcard with the same date is addressed:

To My Darling Little Ida – with best wishes for Xmas and hoping I can
be home when Father Xmas comes down the chimney to fill her stocking.
From Daddy xxx

HMS *Dauntless* sailed from Reval to Libau on 10 December, but her log book records that the ship then remained in the Latvian port for the next two weeks. On 19 December *Dauntless* 'Landed a party of Officers and men as guests of Lettish [Latvian] Commandant for expedition to scenes of fighting during November'.

George was perhaps included in the party. His ship was still berthed in Libau on 22 December (the last date recorded in the log book) and so he was unable to celebrate Christmas 1919 in Devonport as he had hoped. But he may have known by then that his wife Ida was expecting their second child.

Many accounts of the Allies' intervention in the Russian Civil War dismiss their campaign as a failure. Their ships had nevertheless performed an important role in the fight of the new republics of Latvia and Estonia to win independence by helping to keep the sea lanes across the Baltic open, and undermining the threat of the Soviet fleet by assisting in the blockade of Petrograd and raiding Kronstadt. The Royal Navy also helped the Latvian and Estonian resistance to the German Iron Division's attempt to colonise the newly independent republics of the Baltic.

The Estonians themselves were very grateful for the Allies' contribution to their fight for independence in 1918–1919 and regarded the British, along with the Finns, as having been vital allies in their 'Freedom War'. The leader of the Estonian army in 1919, General Johan Laidoner, later said:

I am sure that without the arrival of the British fleet in Tallinn in December 1918, the fate of our country and our people would have been very different – Estonia and, I believe, other Baltic states would have found themselves in the hands of the Bolsheviks.

The Estonian Freedom Cross was awarded to 128 British citizens by Estonia for their role in the War of Independence 1918–20.

In England a memorial in a Portsmouth church commemorates the 111 dead British servicemen of the 1918–19 Baltic campaign. And over eighty years later, on 20 July 2003 in the Church of the Holy Spirit in Tallinn, British and Estonian dignitaries attended a service to unveil a plaque in memory of the British servicemen killed in the Estonian fight for independence. The inscription reads:

> The Unveiling and Dedication of the memorial to the 14 Royal Navy Officers, 92 Ratings, 4 Royal Air Force Officers and one Airman killed in action in the Baltic waters 1918–1919.

The subsequent history of Estonia over the next half-century brought invasion, repression and tragedy. In their 'non-aggression' pact made in August 1939 the two dictators, Hitler and Stalin, divided eastern Europe into 'spheres of influence', and the Baltic states, including Estonia, were allocated to the Soviet Union. In 1940 Estonia was annexed by Russia and Stalin's secret police deported thousands of Estonians to Siberia in June 1941. Once Russia changed sides and joined the Allies in 1941, Germany occupied Estonia from 1941 to 1944 with a fascist regime imposing more terror.

In 1944 Russia again took over Estonia and subjected its people to persecution and totalitarian rule. Many more Estonians whom the Soviets regarded as potential threats to their rule were sent to prison camps in Siberia. On a single day, 25 March 1949, a mass deportation of over 20,000 Estonians, including women, children and the elderly, took place. Many of them died in the camps and the majority never returned to their homeland. Latvia and Lithuania were also subject to Soviet occupation from the end of the war, and their populations suffered mass deportations and deaths between 1944 and the late 1950s.

These Baltic states remained Soviet satellites throughout the Cold War until the collapse of the Soviet Union. Estonia became an independent state again in 1991 and, along with Latvia and Lithuania, joined the United Nations and NATO.

But nearly a century on from 'Operation Red Trek' the threat to the Baltic states from Russia remains. On 2 May 2014 the BBC issued the following press release:

Britain has joined with other NATO countries to provide extra security for Latvia, Estonia and Lithuania – all in response to the crisis in Ukraine.

The Baltic states, all close to Russia, have no fighter-aircraft and have for years been dependent on the alliance for protection. Four RAF Typhoon fighters are part of a NATO force of 20 jets now guarding the Baltics.

A total of 100 British troops arrived in Estonia for a training exercise with that country's defence forces.

A Baltic Footnote – Danzig

In January 1920 George was promoted from Artificer Engineer to the rate of Warrant Engineer, and he remained in Devonport at HMS *Vivid* engaged in the routine work of maintaining and repairing the warships patrolling the Western Approaches and the English Channel, and going on sea trials to test the ships' engines. His second daughter, Beryl, was born at home in Beresford Street on 3 June 1920 and he was overjoyed to be in Plymouth to see his new baby's first few months, especially as he had missed these when Ida had been born in 1914.

Later in 1920 George was back in the Baltic on another mission, to the Free City port of Danzig. His ship HMS *Dauntless* was part of a British naval force that was present in Danzig throughout 1920.

The city of Danzig (now called Gdansk) is a port on the Baltic Sea at the mouth of the River Vistula on the borders of German East Prussia and Poland. For centuries Danzig had been a busy and prosperous trading centre as its medieval merchant guilds had joined the powerful Hanseatic League, the confederation of market towns and cities in northern Europe which controlled maritime trade in the Baltic and North Sea from the late Middle Ages until the eighteenth century. It gained special privileges and held the status of a semi-independent city under Polish suzerainty until 1793, when it became part of Prussia. By the Great War the majority of its citizens were German, some two million of them.

At the Paris Peace Conference in 1919 one of President Woodrow Wilson's 'Fourteen Points' had been to guarantee an independent Poland with access from its capital Warsaw via the Vistula and through Danzig to the Baltic Sea. France and Poland therefore proposed that Danzig be incorporated into Poland.

This proposal was resisted, primarily by the British Prime Minister, Lloyd George, who feared the consequences of placing so large a German population under Polish rule. Lloyd George proposed that instead of being in either Germany or Poland, Danzig should become a Free City under the protection of the League of Nations. Poland would be given access to the Baltic through a corridor of Polish territory leading to the sea. The Treaty of Versailles was signed on 28 June 1919, and under its terms the Free City of Danzig was to be formally created and placed under the administration of the League of Nations. But the predominantly German communities in two East Prussian districts within the proposed Polish Corridor had protested at being put under Polish rule, and so – largely due to negotiations by Lloyd George – the Treaty directed that plebiscites should be held for these populations to vote whether they wished to be in Germany or Poland.

The German troops left Danzig and the Corridor Territory early in February 1920, and shortly afterwards an Allied force, commanded by the British General Richard Haking, landed at Danzig. He brought troops of the First Battalion of the Royal Fusiliers and a French battalion which occupied Danzig itself, plus the First Battalion of the Royal Irish Rifles and an equivalent force of Italian soldiers who occupied the plebiscite districts. The role of this military mission was to ensure that the autonomy of the Free City was secured and that the plebiscites were properly conducted without interference from either Poles or Germans unhappy with the Treaty's provisions.

The plebiscites were held in the East Prussian districts on 20 July 1920, and over 96 per cent of the population voted to remain in Germany. The width of the proposed Corridor was therefore reduced, with the majority of the people living within it being Polish.

British and other Allied troops remained in Danzig throughout that year until the formal proclamation of its status as a Free City on 15 November 1920, after which they left for home. That month HMS *Dauntless* was in Danzig, probably to transport British forces back to Great Britain.

George was clearly impressed by the Baltic architecture in the historic centre of Danzig, with its many towers and spires, its bells and fountains, and old multicoloured, pantiled stone buildings. He bought several picture postcards with views of the high-gabled merchant houses on the waterfront of the Old Town, the fifteenth-century quayside Crane (once the biggest working crane in the world), the Bourse (stock exchange) and the medieval basilica of St. Marienkirche, still said to be the largest brick church in the world.

It was during this trip to Danzig that Captain Cecil Pilcher, the commanding officer of HMS *Dauntless*, found himself convening a naval court to try thirteen crew members of a Royal Fleet Auxiliary tanker, RFA *Prestol*, for mutiny.

Royal Fleet Auxiliary ships were deployed to carry fuel, ammunition and other supplies to Royal Navy ships, and to transport troops and equipment. Their crews were mainly civilian merchant seamen, and not members of the armed forces. The RFA *Prestol* had been in the Baltic since December 1918 and was not a happy ship – one of its officers had already been court-martialled and six crew members had been charged with desertion. On 15 November 1920, when *Prestol* was in the harbour at Danzig, thirteen of its crew made complaints about lack of leave and the conduct of the Chief Officer and refused to return to work. Two of the stokers then threatened the ship's Chief Officer and the Chief Engineer with revolvers, 'using the most insulting language'.[88]

The Master of the *Prestol* reported the situation to Captain Pilcher on HMS *Dauntless*, as he was the senior naval officer in Danzig at that time. He sent a Royal Navy boarding party to *Prestol* to arrest the mutinous crew members and station a military guard on board. On 19 November Captain Pilcher held a naval court on HMS *Dauntless* under the Merchant Shipping Act to try the mutineers, with himself, the British Consul in Danzig and the Master of another RFA ship sitting as judges. One seaman was found guilty only of quitting the ship without leave and had to forfeit fourteen days' pay. The other twelve crew members were all found guilty of quitting the ship without leave and disobeying lawful orders of the ship's Master, and they were both fined and sentenced to various terms of imprisonment in British prisons.

Danzig retained its status as a Free City state until 1939. In the 1930s the local Nazi Party took control of the city's council and initiated a campaign of anti-Semitic persecution of the Jewish population there. In October 1938 the German Foreign Minister Ribbentrop demanded the return of Danzig to Germany, and Polish opposition to this over the next year was used by Hitler as an excuse to attack Poland itself. When Hitler's armies invaded Poland in September 1939 at the outbreak of the Second World War the Germans abolished the Free City, and Danzig was incorporated by Hitler into the German Third Reich.

After the end of the war in 1945 Danzig was placed back into Poland

and came under the rule of the Soviet Union during the Iron Curtain era. The city was renamed Gdansk, and drew worldwide attention again in 1981 when Lech Wałęsa, the founder of the Polish Solidarity movement, organised a strike of shipyard workers there which led to a wave of strikes across Poland, and the subsequent imposition of martial law in the country in December 1981 under General Jaruzelski.

As for HMS *Dauntless*, she arrived back in England in March 1921. George remained with the ship until the following year, and Captain Pilcher reported on his official naval record that Warrant Engineer Lancaster was a 'Good Engineer Officer. Zealous, efficient, of studious habits. Careful and capable, of genial disposition'.

Smyrna

After another year working at the shore base *Vivid* in Devonport, on 24 May 1922 Warrant Engineer George Lancaster was ordered to join HMS *Diligence*, a destroyer depot ship of the Royal Navy's Mediterranean Fleet based in Malta. His naval record states that he took passage on a merchant steamship, the SS *Nyanga*, from England to Malta on 16 June 1922, and a photograph of him, wearing his naval white uniform, shows him chatting to civilian passengers on deck as they sail across the Mediterranean.

Ida and her two daughters followed him to Malta on another civilian passenger steamship two months later, in August 1922. But when they arrived in Malta they found that George had sailed off on HMS *Diligence*, with several other Royal Navy ships, to Smyrna, a city in Turkey on the coast of the Aegean.

Smyrna is now called Izmir, 'a contemporary, developed, and busy commercial centre' according to its current tourism website, and a popular holiday destination in Turkey to where many Britons fly on package tours for the sun, beach and sea.

In the early twentieth century Smyrna was the second largest city in Turkey and a wealthy, enlightened, cosmopolitan port where a number of Europeans lived and worked. Some long-established European traders had founded merchant dynasties known as 'Levantines', such as the Girauds, the Patersons and the Whittalls who were originally from England. These rich magnates controlled the city's shipping, banking, insurance and mining industries, and they employed thousands of workers in their factories, packing and exporting cotton textiles, carpets and dried fruit across the world. Their families lived in splendour in luxurious mansions on vast estates with many servants and retainers, and owned yachts and summer houses on the Aegean islands.

The European and Greek quarters of the city were in its northern districts. There were 320,000 Greeks living in Smyrna, the largest community in its very diverse population. The Greeks were Orthodox

Christians, and their businessmen ran the trade in figs, sultanas and apricots, and owned a number of other major businesses, based mainly along the waterfront. Aristotle Onassis, the future Greek shipping tycoon, was an eighteen-year-old resident in Smyrna in 1922.

The Muslim Turkish community lived mainly in the south of the city near the Ottoman Governor's Mansion and the Turkish army barracks. The Turks numbered some 140,000 people, mainly traditional artisans and craftsmen living in the poorer, overcrowded streets in the area below Mount Pagus. They took little part in the international commerce of the city, but controlled its politics.

There was also a wealthy Armenian quarter with some 10,000 residents who were Orthodox Christians, part of an Armenian population originally from Eastern Turkey. Their people had suffered appalling massacres and deportations in the 1890s and during the Great War under the rule of the Islamic Ottomans. Between April and June 1915 the Ottoman Government of Turkey killed between 800,000 and 1.5 million Armenians by massacring the men of military age and deporting the women, children and old people, sending them on death marches to internment camps in the deserts of what is now northern Syria, then within the Ottoman Empire, where they died of typhus, starvation or dehydration.[89]

There was a Jewish quarter in Smyrna, and, most recently arrived, a community of Americans who ran various commercial enterprises such as a liquorice factory. They found the city so congenial that they named the district where they lived 'Paradise' and established the American International College and a YMCA.

International banks, shipping and insurance companies maintained offices in Smyrna. Theatres, the opera house, grand hotels, sporting and country clubs, department stores, cafés and bars flourished, and the standard of living and cultural life was exceptionally high, certainly compared to the rest of Turkey. Every day passenger ships from across the Mediterranean and from Great Britain called at the port, bringing wealthy travellers to enjoy the sights and delights of this exciting city.

What also distinguished Smyrna was confirmed by the 1913 census. Its Christian residents, the Greeks, Armenians, Europeans and Americans, were more than double the number of the Muslims, and the city had the largest Christian population in the Islamic country of Turkey. The resulting sectarian tensions were to determine the city's fate after the Great War.

Smyrna was in the region of Western Anatolia in Asia Minor, part of the Ottoman Empire, which had been established in 1453 when Mehmet II conquered Constantinople. Since then the Ottoman Sultans had been powerful for centuries, ruling land across the juncture between Europe and Asia. But by the early twentieth century it had been ailing for many years, and the final stage of its dissolution was accelerated by the revolution of the 'Young Turks' against the Sultan's rule in 1908.

Turkey controlled the trading routes from the Black Sea ports such as Odessa and Sevastopol in the Crimea through the Bosphorus and the Sea of Marmara to the Mediterranean. This was a vital sea route for the passage of Russia's naval and merchant ships.

The strategic importance of these sea routes meant that many of the European nation states were now jostling for power and influence across the territories of the Ottoman Empire as it collapsed. But it was Germany in particular that seized the opportunity of aligning itself with the new leaders in Turkey. After the arrival of the German battleships *Goeben* and *Breslau* in Constantinople in August 1914 and their nominal handover to Turkey, it had sided with Germany in the Great War, entering the conflict on 28 October 1914.

The European residents of Smyrna survived the Great War, even though many of their home nations were at war with Turkey, thanks largely to the actions of its cultivated and pro-western Turkish Governor Rahmi Bey, who skilfully managed to protect the city's various expatriate communities from deportation or internment.

Smyrna emerged largely unscathed from the war, but the Allies' victory over Germany and Turkey led to the final disintegration of the Ottoman Empire. On 12 November 1918, the day after the Armistice, an Allied fleet of British, French and Italian ships arrived at Constantinople, and the following day 3,000 British troops marched into Constantinople and occupied the Turkish capital city for the next three years.

Early in 1919 the victorious Allied Powers met at Versailles to deal with the future of various European countries according to the US President Woodrow Wilson's principle of self-determination. They then began the prolonged negotiation of what became in August 1920 the Treaty of Sèvres to conclude the peace between the Allies and the Ottoman Empire and draw the new borders of its former territories.

Greece did not accept those agreed borders and would not ratify the Treaty of Sèvres. The British Prime Minister, David Lloyd George, had promised Greece that it could have territory in Asia Minor ceded from Turkey. Lloyd George had an exaggerated and sentimental notion of Greece as the cradle of classical civilisation, and encouraged the Greek Prime Minister in his ambition to establish a 'Greater Greece' in the former territories of the Ottoman Empire.

This was challenged by Turkish republicans led by Mustapha Kemal, later known as Ataturk ('Father of the Turks'), who became the first President of Turkey. In 1918 Kemal's Turkish National Movement was determined to preserve Turkey as an independent state in the face of Greece's plans to occupy former Ottoman lands.

The conflict between Greece and the Turkish National Movement over which country would secure the lands of the collapsing Ottoman Empire resulted in the Greco-Turkish War of 1919–1922.

On 15 May 1919 the Greek army, supported by British Royal Navy ships led by their flagship HMS *Iron Duke*, landed at Smyrna. The Greek occupation was initially peaceful, but following gunfire, allegedly from Turkish opposition, local Greeks and Greek soldiers rioted against the Turkish population over the next two days. Shops and houses were looted, with many cases of beatings, rape and murder. While some twenty-two to thirty-two Greeks were killed, the figure for Turkish deaths was 300–600.

The Greeks occupied Smyrna for the next three years, and the Greek Governor restored a largely stable regime within the city. But in the course of the ensuing Greco-Turkish War, fought out in the remainder of Anatolia, many other sectarian massacres and atrocities occurred, committed by both sides against Greek and Turkish civilian populations. The last and worst of these occurred, again at Smyrna, in September 1922 when Turkish troops led by Mustapha Kemal arrived to retake the city from the Greek occupiers.

After some successful military campaigns into central Anatolia, the 200,000-strong Greek army had suffered a major defeat fighting Kemal's nationalist army in August 1922 and had been forced into a retreat to the coast. Some 50,000 Greek troops arrived in Smyrna. By early September they were joined by over 150,000 Greek civilian refugees who were fleeing their homes in Anatolia away from the victorious Turkish soldiers.

On 3 September 1922 George's ship, HMS *Diligence*, arrived in the port of Smyrna, one of eleven Royal Navy ships including HMS *George V*, HMS *Iron Duke* and some destroyers. They were joined by three large American destroyers and a number of French and Italian warships. Their mission was to evacuate the Europeans, Levantines and American nationals from the city, and the ships of each of these countries had been instructed to maintain strict neutrality and not to take on Greeks or Armenians. The mission of the British ships was to pick up 1,200 British refugees, but no non-British nationals. On Friday 8 September the British landed a force of 200 heavily armed marines to guard the British consulate, fire station and telegraph company, but not private properties.[90]

The Great Fire of Smyrna which destroyed most of the city was probably started on 12 September by Turkish soldiers, although many Turkish historians still challenge this, claiming it was started by Greeks or Armenians. The fire spread to the waterfront, trapping an estimated 500,000 refugees along the two-mile stretch of quayside between the burning warehouse buildings and the sea. They were desperate to escape by ship from marauding Turkish troops who were looting, raping and killing throughout the city, and here on the quay they faced death by drowning, fire or massacre by the Turks.

As the situation became more horrific, some of the international group of naval commanders at the scene felt compelled to depart from their governments' official policy of neutrality and to rescue Greeks and Armenians from the quayside, with scores of them swimming around the ships begging to be saved. The British ships were at last authorised to take on board refugees of all nationalities who were in danger. In late September 1922 the Royal Navy ships at Smyrna, together with Greek ships under American control, evacuated some 177,000 refugees as the crisis and chaos escalated, and they took them to safety on nearby Greek islands, mainland Greece, Malta or the port of Alexandria in Egypt.

Remarkably, one of the most graphic surviving accounts of what happened in Smyrna over the next few days was written by a shipmate of George. Charles James Howes was a Chief Petty Officer on HMS *Diligence*, and soon after leaving Smyrna he wrote, in his own hand, a seven-page description of what he had seen. The original account is now held at the Imperial War Museum in London, available for public inspection.

It is a difficult read in parts, and while the following extract is most of the letter, it omits some of the more horrific detail. As a Chief Petty Officer, Charles Howes would have worked closely with Warrant Engineer George Lancaster on their ship, and may have shared a mess on board. Surely some, perhaps even much, of what Howes saw from his ship moored in the harbour at Smyrna would also have been witnessed by George.

Smyrna, September 1922

I wonder how many Britishers were at the evacuation of Smyrna? If there were any they will hear me out in any statements set below, and having emerged safely from that hell make them realise whether this was a horrible nightmare or reality. When we arrived on Sunday 3rd September 1922 everything was normal and nobody in Smyrna seemed to realise to what inhumanity the Kemalists would stoop.

From the 3rd up to the 6th the Greek Army, or rather the remains of it, arrived in Smyrna and immediately embarked on the Greek Steamers which were waiting there.

I have observed different types and nationalities of armies during my career and I do not hesitate in saying that they were the most dilapidated, filthy, untidy, slouching lot of humans I have ever witnessed wearing uniform. Of course it was not the poor devils' own fault, as supplies of food had not reached them for 12 days, the only substance they had was fruit which they had stolen on their disorderly retreat. Haggard, hungry looking, some bare footed and unshaven, 50,000 of these soldiers passed through Smyrna. No officers, no regulations, no marching, just sloughing along in twos and threes as fast as their stumbling legs permitted.

Our naval force was landed for the purpose of assisting the Greeks to surrender the town to the Turks. I do not wish to be political, or pass political comments on why we did not resist, nor yet through the evacuation fire a shot at the Turks, but this I will say, whereas 50,000 Greeks left the town without the least resistance, the small naval Patrol landed could have prevented the Turkish Army from entering Smyrna. I said Turkish Army, but when they eventually did arrive there were barely 400 Turkish cavalry. Although the Turks have always been charged with barbarism and bloodshed it was discovered that all these acts were committed by a crowd of roughs called Cheetaks.[91] After a Turkish Regiment had passed through a village these brigands, scoundrels, call them what you like, followed in the rear of the regulars and committed most of the acts for which the army was accused, including looting, murder, rape and everything else which is beyond the understanding of Christian Faith.

However, when the Turks did arrive… I think one of the most daring things occurred just as they entered. Bear in mind all our imaginations had been conjuring up Turks cutting everyone down, without word or sign, so that is why I call the following act brave. The Cavalry were approaching at the canter, the horsemen brandishing their swords and yelling at the tops of their voices, when Captain Thesiger of HMS *King George V* stepped into the middle of the road and held up his hand. The leader gave a blast on his whistle, commanded silence and dismounting held out his hand, rather a curious act for a cut-throat to do you would agree. The Turk began in French and as our Captain was pretty well versed in this language they conversed as follows:

"Who are you and why do you stop my army?" began the Turk.

Captain replied, "I am a Captain in His Majesty's Navy and have been commissioned to assist in the surrender of this town to you. Everything is peaceful and you will meet with no resistance, but if you enter yelling and brandishing your scimitars you will undoubtedly be asking for trouble."

This rather amused the Turk as they walked towards the town together. When they arrived at the Sea Front the Captain of the Turkish Cavalry mounted and proceeded to lead his men through the town.

There were approximately 20,000 people on the front and when the cavalry appeared a terrified shriek went into the air "The Turk, the Turk". As if by magic the whole front was cleared and in less than ten minutes only a few casual stragglers remained. The cavalry advanced at a walk without any interruption until they were almost at the other end of the Front when the mischief started. A Greek and his family were hiding behind some sacks, and on a sudden impulse he picked up his rifle and fired at the leader of the Turks, giving him a nasty gash on the cheek. Then another miraculous thing happened, quick and quite cool he got off his horse, walked over to the Greek, took his rifle, broke it across his knee and sent him on his way without even touching him.

The only trouble in the city now was caused by the Greek and Turkish civilians who started to murder and loot, only individual cases at first but it had a demoralising effect on the Turks who had evidently intended on Mustafa Kemal's promise to Great Britain to avoid as much bloodshed as possible. Various Greek civilians started sniping at the Cavalry and then human nature came to the fore. It rankled in the brains of the Turks as the thought of the horrible massacres which occurred when the conditions were reversed and the Greeks entered Smyrna in 1919. Their first act was to start on the Armenians which they did with vengeance, and blood flowed freely and horrible ghastly were the ways of death meted out. No doubt the atrocities I set below will disgust some people, others will feel a pang of pity, but I will here give a list of some of the atrocities committed.

The harbours were littered with dead bodies, orders were given for all nationalities to evacuate but even then the majority did not realise how grave the situation was and a number endeavoured to keep their businesses open. The Turkish Infantry arrived; 200 Armenians, to escape death by stabbing, sought refuge in their church, and many and conflicting are the rumours concerning the start of the fire, but an American eyewitness declared that the regular Turks set fire to the church and then surrounded it. This occurred about midday on Tuesday 12th and with a strong breeze soon spread its way. Nobody on earth could have stopped the conflagration and the scenes of panic were pitiful to behold. All the people made for the jetty where British ships were attempting to take them out to refugee ships. The British ships HMS *Diligence*, *Iron Duke*, *King George V* and a few destroyers took part in the rescue work which, in my opinion, was worthy of the highest praise. With the approach of night the panic increased and so did the fire and by midnight 200,000 souls were between the blazing Hades and the deep Sea. The Turkish Cavalry were stationed to each end of the Front so that escape was an impossibility. The people were cut down right and left by the soulless devils who had broken their promise and the scene can only be described as worse than hell.

Our Blue Jackets,[92] eager to get the people on board nevertheless had to keep the crowd from rushing and so swamping the boats, had a terrible task. Right along the Sea Front was a wall of unbroken fire with flames 100 feet high, casting a vivid glow in the sky. The light was rendered at intervals by loud explosions and all the while the people in the rear were being massacred. In the words of our Commander-in-Chief (Sir John de Brook) the spectacle was 'magnificently terrible'. Bandits were in from the mountains behind, and taking advantage of the panic, started looting the shops, which had not already been burnt, and carried on highway robbery on a large scale. Their ardent belief was that death tells no tales, and after holding up anybody and obtaining their money they proceeded to stab them to death. Meanwhile the fire was roaring and raging fierce and its toll of victims increased. The heavens were lit by the flames and myriads of sparks flew skywards, the crackling of the wood and the collapsing of the houses sounded like a salvo of guns, the whole of Smyrna accepted that the Turkish quarter was now in the grip of the greedy fire, and out at sea could be heard the dull booming of the Greek battleship 'Kilkes' as she covered up the retreat of the last stragglers of the vanquished Greek Army.

As hard as our boats and sailors worked during the night in rescues, we didn't seem to make much impression in diminishing the crowd. Old women of 80 and upwards had all the household goods they had managed to rescue on their humped backs, cripples were staggering along the burning beach and were dropping on the way, skeletons and remains of crutches testifying to their fate.

Then came the blinded, led by instinct, mostly gasping and choking with fumes and ever the Turkish murderers carried on their nefarious blood spilling... Fire, murder and rape before we could get them aboard the Ships allotted. If hell is only a fierce damnation it is heaven like to this inferno.

We have just left Smyrna as I write this and we had many refugees aboard. Our doctor had the sick quarters full of different cases. One case is a doctor who was shot through both legs, his 'crime' being that he attended wounded on the beach, the remainder are women suffering from various injuries. One of the saddest cases I met was that of a little girl of 9 who, with her father and mother and baby in arms, was making her way to the boats when the parents were shot dead. This little girl picked the baby up off the ground, went dashing through the flames and reached the boat. She was attended to for burnt legs – and still these continue their raving arson and murders unchecked. Mustapha Kemal, the Turkish Nationalist Leader, pleaded to the allied authorities that his troops had got out of control, and he continued, "It is only human nature after all when these Turks had friends and relatives massacred in the same manner in 1919."

I do not think the majority of English reading people will believe this narrative and will say I exaggerate. Well here is the Truth, think of the old time torture, add to them the modern appliances for the destruction of mankind, exaggerate it as much as you like and you will not realise half the horrors of the evacuation of Smyrna.

Although the British Navy landed with arms but did not fire, and so plunge England into the War, the greatest credit is due to them for the splendid way they controlled themselves whilst these atrocities were committed all around them.

Charles James Howes

Most of the international fleet of naval ships had left Smyrna with their refugees over the weekend of 16/17 September, but there were still some 300,000 terrified Greeks and Armenians on the quayside, living in appalling conditions and threatened with massacre by the Turkish army.

Many of these refugees were rescued by a fleet of Greek ships, commandeered by Asa Jennings, the American manager of the YMCA in Smyrna, with the initially reluctant support of the Greek Government. The extraordinary story of Jennings's rescue operation, which saved over 200,000 of the refugees on the quayside, is recounted fully in Giles Milton's book.[93]

The death toll from the Turkish occupation of Smyrna ranks it among one of the most terrible episodes of ethnic cleansing of the twentieth century. The figures are not certain, but reliable sources have estimated that some 100,000 Greeks and Armenians, mainly Christian by faith, were killed and at least another 100,000 – some calculate 160,000 – were deported into the interior of Anatolia where most of them died.

After leaving Smyrna, the Royal Navy warships landed the Greek refugees on a Greek island, and took the Levantine families on to the naval base in Malta where they were housed, in poor conditions, in disused military barracks until they were able to establish new lives elsewhere in Europe or in the United States.

Those Greeks who had escaped from Smyrna to Greece to start a new life instead found it difficult to find jobs and many became homeless and destitute, treated badly by the indigenous Greek population – one notable exception being Aristotle Onassis.

George returned with his ship, HMS *Diligence*, to Malta to be reunited with Ida and his daughters, who had been left to find their feet in Malta alone while he was away at Smyrna.

After the Turkish troops defeated the Greek forces and recaptured Smyrna on 9 September, they advanced towards Constantinople (now Istanbul) and threatened to attack British and French troops stationed near the Turkish town of Chanak (in Turkish spelt Canakkale), which the British and French were guarding to protect the neutral zone in the Dardanelles.

The British Cabinet, a coalition of Conservative and Liberal ministers, met on 15 September 1922 and decided that British forces should maintain their positions. On the following day Prime Minister Lloyd George, supported by some Cabinet ministers, issued a communiqué threatening Turkey with a declaration of war by Britain and the Dominions of the Empire, which included Canada, Australia, New Zealand and South Africa, on the grounds that Turkey had violated the Treaty of Sèvres. Lloyd George did this in the absence of his Foreign Secretary, Lord Curzon, without fully consulting the Prime Ministers of the Dominions, and despite the fact that the French Prime Minister, Raymond Poincaré, had already ordered the withdrawal of the French troops at Chanak and persuaded the Turks to respect the neutral zone.

The threat of war was removed when the Turkish leaders ordered their troops to avoid any incident at Chanak and agreed to the terms of an armistice two hours before British forces were due to attack.

The British public was alarmed by the Chanak crisis and the possibility of going to war again. Lloyd George's rashness resulted in the calling of a meeting of Conservative MPs at the Carlton Club on 19 October 1922 which passed a motion that the Conservative Party should fight the next general election as an independent party. This decision had dire ramifications for Lloyd George as the Conservative Party made up the vast majority of the 1918–1922 post-war coalition between the Conservatives and the Liberals. Lloyd George had also lost the support of the influential Foreign Secretary, Curzon, who considered that the Prime Minister had been manoeuvring behind his back.

Following the Carlton Club decision, the MPs in the House of Commons voted 185 to 85 for ending the coalition, and Lloyd George resigned as Prime Minister, never to return as a significant figure in political life. The crisis in Turkey, and the Carlton Club decision and its consequences, also led to the demise of the Liberal Party as a major force in British politics.

In 1923 the defeat of the Greek forces by the Turkish National Movement forced the Allied Powers to abandon the Treaty of Sèvres. The Treaty of Lausanne between Turkey and the main Allied Powers, signed by Mustapha Kemal, recognised the Republic of Turkey. The Allies also sanctioned an exchange of populations, by which 400,000 Muslims living in Greece were sent back to Turkey and the remaining 1.2 million Greek Orthodox Christians living in Turkey were expelled from their homes to Greece.

Since then tensions between Greeks and Turks have endured, evidenced by the Turkish invasion of the Greek island of Cyprus in 1974 which led to the separate self-declared state of Northern Cyprus, and by continuing sovereignty disputes between Greece and Turkey over territorial waters in the Aegean.

Tragically, too, the ethnic cleansing of peoples with a different religious faith and the brutal displacement of populations that George witnessed at Smyrna was to be repeated time and again throughout the twentieth century, and into the next.

Malta

On 18 August 1922 the P&O steamship SS *Khyber* sailed from the Port of London. Its passenger list included the names of Mrs Ida Lancaster (aged thirty-five) and her daughters Ida (eight) and Beryl (two). This Peninsular and Oriental steamer was bound for Sydney in Australia, but many of its sixty-five passengers were to leave the ship at ports en route, in Malta, Port Said in Egypt or Colombo in Ceylon, or at Fremantle, Adelaide or Melbourne in Australia.

Ida and the girls joined the ship, along with other local women and children, when it called in at Plymouth. They were heading for Malta to join George, who had left them two months earlier in June 1922 for his posting to the Mediterranean Fleet. Malta was one of the few overseas naval bases at that time that allowed naval officers to have their wives and children living with them.

This was the first time that Ida had ever travelled abroad, or possibly even left her home town of Devonport for any significant period of time. It must have been a very difficult journey, travelling with two little girls on the ship down the English Channel, into the Atlantic and across the Bay of Biscay, down the Portuguese coast and through the Straits of Gibraltar into the Mediterranean. The single-funnelled *Khyber* was a comparatively small steamship, and conditions on board were probably fairly cramped and uncomfortable. Ida was the daughter of a master mariner and had been brought up by the sea, but that would not have prepared her for life on the ocean waves in rough weather with two young children suffering from seasickness.

By strange coincidence, Ida's brother David Horne, eleven years her junior, also left England that week. He was twenty-four, a labourer, and had been living at 71 George Street, Devonport, not far from his childhood home in Mutton Cove. He had decided to emigrate because of the lack of work and prospects in the hard economic climate of post-war England. On 17 August 1922 he sailed on the SS *Minnedosa* from Southampton, bound for Québec in Canada. It must have been an exceptionally emotional time for David and Polly Horne, waving goodbye in the same week to their daughter and two granddaughters as well as their only son as they all departed on long overseas journeys.

Ida Lancaster's companions on the SS *Khyber* were other naval wives travelling out from England to Malta, two of them with the only other children on the ship – Mrs Lilian Knight with eleven-year-old Ronald from Chatham, Mrs Vera Slocum, also from Devonport, and Mrs Ethel Toms, from Mutley in Plymouth, with her two-year-old son Stanley. Other women passengers going to Malta included Mrs Alice Law, Misses Mary Robertson and Florence Watts (both described as 'spinsters') and Miss Eleanor Mary Plumer, a thirty-seven-year-old lecturer from London. This lady was going to visit her parents in Malta as she was the daughter of Field Marshal, later Viscount, Plumer, Governor of Malta from 1919 to 1924. The Honourable Eleanor Plumer was herself an eminent academic who became the Principal of St Anne's College, Oxford, from 1940 to 1953.

The travellers on the *Khyber* were reminiscent of the cast of an Agatha Christie story between the wars. The male passengers were a varied group – two cable operators going to Malta, a Scottish bank assistant accompanied by his wife bound for Egypt, a couple of barristers for Ceylon, and an optician, a clergyman, a Roman Catholic priest, a merchant, a shipping manager and an umbrella maker all going to Australia: quite an assortment of British expatriates heading for a life in the colonies.

After a voyage of some ten days from England, Ida and the girls must have been very excited by their first glimpse of Malta as the SS *Khyber* sailed into the impressive Grand Harbour, lined by its huge pale limestone bastions, the Fort Elmo of Valletta on one side and the massive Fort St Angelo of Vittoriosa on the other.

Malta, with its adjacent islands of Gozo and Comino, had been a British colony since 1814. The Knights of the Order of St John had ruled Malta for over 250 years since 1530, securing Christianity there after defeating the Ottoman Turks in the Great Siege of 1565. But in 1798 the French forces of Napoleon had occupied Malta, and the 'Little Emperor' himself and his troops had plundered the island, taking treasures from its churches and palaces. In 1800 the outraged Maltese, supported by British warships, ousted the French after their two years of occupation. When in 1802 it was proposed to hand Malta back to the Knights, the Maltese themselves opposed this as by then the Knights were generally regarded as corrupt and discredited rulers. Instead Malta wanted to be 'under the protection and sovereignty of... His Majesty the King of the United Kingdom of Great Britain and Ireland'. In 1814 Malta became a British Crown Colony and remained so for another 150 years until it became an independent state in 1964.

Throughout the nineteenth century and into the late twentieth century until 1979 Malta was also an important Royal Navy base and army garrison for the British Empire – 'Fortress Malta'. After the opening of the Suez Canal in 1869 the Grand Harbour at the capital, Valletta, became a vital staging post halfway across the Mediterranean for British naval and merchant ships sailing to and from India, the Far East and Australasia.

Malta was not directly involved in the hostilities during the First World War, but its dockyard was an important supply and repair base for the ships of the British Mediterranean Fleet. Malta's hospitals and many private homes also received and cared for some 25,000 injured servicemen during that conflict, particularly from the fighting in the Dardanelles in 1915, and Malta became known as 'the Nurse of the Mediterranean'.

The end of that war brought unemployment and depression to Malta as Britain cut back on its defence expenditure, and many thousands of local men were laid off from their jobs in the naval dockyard and army garrisons on the island. Strikes and demonstrations about low wages and the cost of bread led to demands from Maltese politicians to the British for a new constitution. In June 1919 a public meeting in Valletta about constitutional reform turned into a riot and four Maltese men were shot dead by troops brought in to restore order.

A potentially explosive political situation was calmed by the then new Governor, Field Marshal Plumer, and following wide consultation the Maltese were granted a new constitution and self-government in April 1921. The Maltese were given responsibility for all their internal matters, while Britain retained control of defence and foreign affairs. The new Maltese parliament was opened by the Prince of Wales, later Edward VIII, on November 1921.[94]

When Ida and her two daughters arrived in Malta in late August 1922, it was not Maltese politics that caused them problems, but the international strife in Asia Minor. George was not in Malta to greet them as he had sailed off on HMS *Diligence*, with several other Royal Navy ships, to Smyrna in Turkey to rescue British nationals trapped in the city as Mustapha Kemal's troops arrived.[95] So Ida was left to settle into a new life with her young daughters in a country very different from home.

The main British naval base in Malta was situated across the Grand Harbour from Valletta in Cospicua, one of the 'Three Cities' bordering the Dockyard Creek and French Creek, the others being Vittoriosa and Senglea.[96]

The commanding officers, and some of the junior bachelor officers, were able to live in townhouses and apartments in Valletta, but since the early 1900s the married quarters for many of the service families had been in the St Nicholas Bastion in Cospicua. This was near the huge walls of the Verdala Barracks, built in 1853, which housed the British army garrison. It is likely that the Lancaster family lived either in these married quarters or possibly in local rented accommodation. Captions on family photos seem to confirm that they did reside in this area as one refers to Ida and Beryl at '1 Strada Irlandese in February 1924', and another to 'Julia, Beryl, Melita and Patricia on Margharita Square in March 1924'. The Strada Irlandese is a short residential road, now called the Triq Irlandizi,[97] only two streets away from the Verdala Barracks, and Margarita Square is situated nearby in Vittoriosa.

Much of the rather forbidding architecture of the bastions, forts, barracks and docks must have reminded Devonport sailors of the dockyard and Citadel at home in Plymouth. The Navy's Number 1 Dock was at the far end of the Dockyard Creek in Cospicua, surrounded by high impregnable walls. Nearby, on the Vittoriosa side of the Dockyard Creek, was the large and impressive Naval Bakery on the quayside with a clock tower modelled on Sir John Rennie's Clock Tower at the Royal Victualling Yard in Plymouth. This Naval Bakery building is now, in 2015, the Malta Maritime Museum.

As Ida and the girls settled into their new home in August, their first challenge was to cope with the searing late summer heat of a south Mediterranean island which was only 180 miles off the coast of north Africa. The hot sun and the intense blue skies would have been an extraordinary change for them from the wet and damp climate of south Devon.

The British naval community in Malta, like most expatriate communities across the globe, was a very insular and self-contained one, and there was probably little social interaction with Maltese people. But British families like the Lancasters would have experienced something of the island's Latin culture – the afternoon siestas, the Italian road names, the vibrant street life, the *dghajsa* (little boats similar to Venetian gondolas) in the harbours, the horse-drawn *karozzini* used for transport, and women wearing the *faldeta*, their traditional hooded headdress.

A young naval officer from Plymouth, Eric Brockman, a former pupil at Devonport High School for Boys, also arrived in Malta for the first time in the 1920s, and recorded his early memories of the island:

> Sunlight on golden stone, a childlike gaiety, courtesy, the smell of roasting coffee and black cheroots.

Brockman returned to Malta, and after marrying a Maltese girl he spent many years there, and wrote a book, *Last Bastion*, about the island, which gives a vivid account of its society and culture in the inter-war years. He wrote:

> Superficially, Malta in the twenties presented a picture of a feudal, Latin upper class, entrenched within a medieval, theocratic society, maintaining a gracious and cultured way of life at the expense of an under-privileged, illiterate and superstitious lower class, living on the fringe of absolute poverty. Insofar as this was a true picture, the British accepted and acquiesced in it, content only to interfere if the security of the fortress seemed threatened.[98]

The Lancasters were able to obtain the sort of English food they were used to at home from the shops run by the NAAFI,[99] which opened in Valletta in 1921 with its main establishment in St James Cavalier, a building forming part of the fortified city walls. The NAAFI provided food and other commodities and ran canteens and a social club for service personnel and their families. So sadly the British developed little or no taste for the Italian-based cuisine of Malta, which was also influenced by Arabic and French cooking, and in the 1920s by dishes popularised by White Russian and Greek refugees who had escaped to Malta from the Bolshevik Revolution and the atrocities at Smyrna. The

British wives may have bought fresh fruit and vegetables from the local food markets and perhaps even tasted some of the more exotic produce of the Mediterranean countries.

The British will have also seen some of the poverty of Malta in the 1920s, then an island of meagre resources and unproductive agriculture, high levels of illiteracy and disease, and with many beggars in the streets, where charitable care and support were provided by the Catholic Church.

For Protestants like George and Ida, from a 'low' Church of England tradition, living in an intensely Catholic country was a novel experience, with numerous priests, nuns and monks in the streets, and Malta's ornate High Baroque cathedrals and churches, roadside shrines and domestic religious icons on house walls and doors.

The English naval community worshipped in the dockyard church, or visited St John's, the Anglican cathedral in Valletta, but the strong religious faith and Catholic culture of the Maltese would have made an impression on the British families. The Maltese year was determined by the Church calendar, and its many religious feast days were marked by frequent carnivals, with street processions and floats, men on stilts and fireworks, always very popular in Malta.

The ancient and complex language of the island, Malti, derived mainly from Italian and Arabic, may also have been a subject of some curiosity, but the British residents did not need to learn any of its phrases as they were generally able to converse in English with the locals. In the 1920s English vied with Italian as the official language of Malta, and the choice between them became a matter of heated political debate – the Catholic Church supporting the use of Italian, and politicians such as the Anglo-Maltese Sir Gerald Strickland promoting English. The influence of the English lobby increased once Mussolini became Prime Minister of Italy in 1922 and over the following decade the threat to Malta of Italian Fascism produced a reaction against Italian culture and language on the islands.[100]

The British families' contact with the Maltese community may have been limited, but, like most of the other Navy wives, Ida paid a local woman to help her with domestic chores and to look after the children. In one photo of Ida with a young Beryl sitting on her lap there is a Maltese lady standing at their side, who may have been a maid called Melita.

There are several family photographs of Ida and the girls in Malta, always wearing wide-brimmed hats to protect them against the Mediterranean sun. They include ones of nine-year-old Ida with little sister Beryl standing in the middle of a tree-lined street near the barracks in Cospicua; mother Ida with Beryl in the Upper Barrakka Gardens in Valletta; Beryl sitting on steps stroking a large snoozing dog at her side – she was always a dog-lover. One photo shows mother Ida with Beryl, her sister Ida and another young girl standing in front of the well-known fountain in the San Anton Botanical Gardens in Attard. This town is in the middle of Malta, on the road to the old Maltese capital of M'dina, and the photograph confirms that the Lancasters went on excursions by motorbus or horse-drawn *karrozini* around the island while living there.

Another photograph shows a jolly social gathering of British men and women with a number of young children, all of whom are wearing large sunhats, sitting in front of their parents. A couple of the men are in their naval uniform; two others are holding babies. George and Ida are standing there, George in civilian clothes with a panama hat, Ida in a white dress with a sun hat, and the two girls sitting in front of them, Beryl on young Ida's lap. Malta had long been a welcome posting for Royal Navy officers and their families because of the British community's active social life there, which was, as a popular service ditty of the time suggested, a round of 'Balls, Picnics and Parties – Picnics, Parties and Balls'.

Young Ida, who was eight when she arrived in Malta, attended a school there for the children of British personnel, probably the Royal Naval School, which in the 1920s was located in Prison Street in Senglea and had about 250 English and Maltese pupils aged five to fourteen. Beryl was an infant throughout their stay in Malta, aged between two and four, and she remembered little of her life there. But the girls made friends with the other naval children, and also with some local children. Beryl even kept in touch with one Maltese girl called Vittoria for over two decades after the Lancasters left Malta. In 1946 Vittoria, by then working for the United States embassy in Palermo in Sicily, wrote to Beryl to congratulate her on her marriage.

While stationed in Malta, George furthered his studies to advance his career, perhaps wanting to make up for not having had a school education beyond the age of fourteen. On 17 August 1923, while in Malta, he obtained a Higher Education Certificate, First Class, awarded to him as 'Warrant Engineer RN', in English History – 90 per cent,

General Knowledge – 86 per cent, Geography – 83 per cent and Practical Mathematics – 75 per cent.

During this two-year posting with the Mediterranean Fleet, George went on tours of duty with HMS *Diligence* to the eastern Mediterranean. He again went to Port Said, where he had been based in late 1914 as part of the wartime operation to protect the Suez Canal, and this time while on shore leave George visited Cairo where he saw the Tombs of the Khalifa and of the Mamelouks, and bought cards with views of the city, and of *feluccas*, the traditional wooden sailing boats on the Nile. He also brought home a photo of a veiled lady entitled 'Femme de Harem'!

His postcard collection confirms that his other ports of call included Athens, where he bought views of the Acropolis and the Areopagus Hill, and Constantinople where he purchased a picture postcard of the Topkapi Palace and the Hagia Sophia, then still a mosque, seen from the Golden Horn, and two painted cards showing Turkish sailing ships and the Galata Bridge, with the Suleiman Mosque and the New Mosque in the background.

George also visited Palestine for the first time. Following the defeat and dismemberment of the Turkish Ottoman Empire in 1918, a League of Nations mandate had put Britain in control of Palestine in 1920, a mandate which was to last until 1948. HMS *Diligence* called in at the ancient port of Jaffa, now within Tel Aviv, where George visited the House of Simon the Tanner, reputed to be the place where, as related in the Acts of the Apostles, St Peter was staying when he had a dream that he was to found a new church. The Bible story also tells that St Peter resurrected a lady called Tabitha on the roof of this house. George bought a postcard of the House of Simon, and then went on to Jerusalem where he bought several more postcards – views of the city from the Mount of Olives, the Jaffa Gate in Jerusalem, the River Jordan and two other cards of holy sites in the city on which he has written notes. On one, a view across Jerusalem, he wrote:

This is the Mosque of Omar which covers the site of Solomon's Temple and inside it is the Rock of Abraham still.

George was referring to the beautiful Dome of the Rock, the most famous Islamic site in Jerusalem, and believed by some to be the biblical Temple of Solomon.

The other picture postcard is of the interior of Christianity's most sacred place of pilgrimage, and shows a religious service with a large congregation. George has written:

This is the Church of the Holy Sepulchre which covers the supposed site of Calvary, notice the guard of soldiers to keep the various sects from killing each other. Only the Greek, R.C.s and Armenians think this is the genuine place of Our Lord's Crucifixion and Burial.

His recent experience of sectarian killings at Smyrna no doubt influenced his comments. But as one brought up in the Church of England he was clearly a man of faith and his visits to these sites in the Holy Land must have meant a great deal to him.

George served with HMS *Diligence* in the Mediterranean Fleet for nearly three years, and the ship's Captain Hughes gave him this report:

V. energetic, capable and hardworking. G. appearance and manner. Tactful in dealing with both officers and men. Average physique.

In the summer of 1924 Ida Lancaster and her daughters left Malta and returned by steamship to Devonport, when young Ida was ten and Beryl a little girl of four. They were followed later by George on HMS *Diligence*, which returned to its home base in Devonport in late 1924 or early 1925. The family's two years' residence on the island must have been an extraordinary life experience for George's wife Ida, the only time she ever travelled overseas.

The Maltese people have a long tradition of uniting to resist or oust many of the foreign invaders who have attempted to exploit or subdue their island, including Arabs, Ottoman Turks and the French, but another test of their resilience was to come during the Second World War. Mussolini's air force attacked the island on 11 June 1940, the start of a ferocious three-year battle between the Allied Powers and the Axis forces of Italy and Germany for control of this strategically vital island on the supply route to North Africa and east of Suez.

During that war Ida and George's own memories of Valletta and the Three Cities must have been very vivid as, while they too endured the Luftwaffe in their own blitzed city, they read and watched the press and newsreel reports of the siege of Malta by German and Italian forces between 1940 and 1942. Much of the island, and particularly the areas of Vittoriosa, Senglea and Cospicua around the naval dockyard where the Lancasters had lived and George had worked, were very heavily bombed by the Luftwaffe. Between June 1940 and May 1942 there were over 2,000 air raids on Malta and 40,000 homes were destroyed.

The Maltese population suffered terrible hardships during those years. The Allies' ships were seriously impeded in the delivery of supplies of food, oil and ammunition to the island because of the enemy blockade, and the Maltese were nearly starved to death. But the islands held out against the Axis, refusing to surrender. Finally, in August 1942 a vital convoy of ships, code-named 'Operation Pedestal', reached the island after suffering the loss of many vessels and crew, bringing essential relief supplies to islands that might otherwise only have survived for another two weeks.

Before that, in April 1942 King George VI had awarded the George Cross 'to the Island Fortress of Malta to bear witness to a heroism and devotion that will long be famous in history'. By the summer of 1943 the Germans and Italians were capitulating in North Africa, and Malta was being used as the base for the Allies' invasion of Sicily.

Back in the 1920s, at the end of his tour of duty in Malta, George's commanding officer Captain Finlayson made the following report on him in December 1924:

> Zealous and energetic. Tactful. Good judgement. Exceptional initiative and reliability. Good command of men. A very hard and steady worker who has good control over his men. Even temperament and quiet disposition. Possesses a well-balanced mind and his decisions are good. Gets work done well and commands much respect from the men.

Once home in the UK in 1925, George found that the Royal Navy of the mid-1920s was a force much reduced from its strength at the end of the Great War in 1918, when it had over 400,000 men and women serving in a wide range of some 745 vessels.

The difficult post-war economic situation caused the Government in 1919 to adopt the 'Ten Year Rule' for all military planning, based on an assumption that there would not be another war for ten years. The proposed ten-year ban on warship construction was successfully resisted by David Beatty, by then Earl Beatty and the First Sea Lord, but later under the 1922 Washington Treaty between Britain, the United States, Japan, France and Italy those five victorious world powers agreed to restrict the construction of warships to agreed maximums. Britain and the United States were each allowed no more than 525,000 tons of capital ships. It was the Washington Treaty, not enemy fleets, which effectively ended the global maritime supremacy that the Royal Navy had maintained since its victory at Trafalgar in 1805.

When George returned home to Britain in the winter of 1924–25 the country was feeling the full impact of the cuts in Government expenditure known as the 'Geddes Axe'. In August 1921 the Prime Minister, Lloyd George, had appointed Sir Eric Geddes, who had been First Lord of the Admiralty from 1917 to 1919, to chair the Committee on National Expenditure. Following the Geddes Committee Reports, the Government made huge reductions in public spending by all Government departments.

The naval budget was drastically cut from £356 million in 1918–19 to £52 million in 1923, and it remained at that level for the next decade. Under the Geddes Axe, in addition to the reduction in warship construction, one in three captains was retired, and from 1925 the pay of newly recruited ratings was cut from 4 to 3 shillings a day.

Despite the cuts, George fortunately retained his naval employment and tried to improve his prospects as a naval engineer. After the war there was considerable naval opposition to the continuation, under the 1903 Selborne-Fisher Scheme, of the joint training of executive and engineering officers, the argument being that an officer could not be fully proficient in both areas. In the early 1920s the Admiralty dismantled the scheme, and separate training and the distinction between the two branches was reintroduced, with engineers being denied command of a ship, a policy which the Navy has maintained. The Royal Naval Engineering College at Keyham in Devonport, which had closed in 1910 following the introduction of the Selborne-Fisher Scheme, reopened in 1919 in anticipation of its abolition. On his return from Malta in 1924 George applied for a place on an advanced course at

Keyham, but was unsuccessful, his mathematics being too weak.

On 5 May 1925 he joined an S-class destroyer, HMS *Simoom* – named after a desert wind – on which he served for two years, still based in Devonport. George was living in Plymouth during the General Strike in Britain in May 1926, which underlined the depressed economic conditions and bitter social divisions of the time. The Trades Union Congress called a national strike of all workers in support of the miners after the mine owners in the private coal industry decided to reduce wages by between 10 per cent and 25 per cent. Over a million and a half workers from all industries across the country stopped working and the strike lasted ten days. In the southwest, over 80 per cent of employees on the Great Western Railway were on strike. In Plymouth tram workers tried to stop 'blackleg' staff from operating the city's trams on 8 May and there was a violent riot. Yet on the same day the local police played a football match with some strikers, who won 2–1.

In 1927 George was forty, a family man living in his own home in Plymouth with his wife and two young daughters. He had served in the Royal Navy for eighteen years, much of that time on ships overseas, including periods on active service in the Great War, and he now held the non-commissioned rate of Warrant Engineer. During these three years, 1925 to 1928, that George spent based in Devonport he was able to enjoy a peaceful family life there with Ida and the girls for the first time in his naval career, and this may have been one of the happiest periods of his life.

Family photos of the time show the Lancasters on excursions to Dartmoor or the beaches of South Devon, which they reached by trips on charabancs run by local transport firms such as Mumfords. They often went with George's sister Nell Ronson and her family of five children – her eldest girl, Miriam, was the same age as George's daughter Ida. Beryl's best friend from school, Doris Holder, sometimes also went along with her mother. The girls swam, six- or seven-year-old Beryl wearing a fetching swim-cap with her bathing costume. Their mothers Ida and Nell, and Mrs Holder, wore rather cumbersome dresses and skirts, while George usually dressed in a suit and wore a formal hat, even on the beach when building sandcastles with his daughters!

On 29 March 1927 George joined HMS *Berwick*, a new Kent-class heavy cruiser launched in 1926. After a year based in Devonport,

Berwick was commissioned in February 1928 on what the Navy called the 'China Station' in the Far East. George was to set sail on a two-year trip which would take him to coastal and inland China, and to Korea and Japan, countries and societies which politically and culturally were a world away from Devonport.

The Far East

Since 1865 the Royal Navy's ships of the China Station had patrolled the coast of China and its rivers, the western part of the Pacific Ocean and the waters around the Dutch East Indies, maintaining a presence in the British colonies in the Far East and supporting British commercial interests in the region.

The China Station fleet comprised mainly cruisers and destroyers, based either in Singapore, Hong Kong or, from 1898 to 1930, the island of Wei-Hai-Wei in the north-east of China, a territory which the British leased from the Chinese. The Royal Navy also patrolled the inland navigable rivers such as the Yangtze in shallow-draught gunboats and sloops. The ships on this station usually had a distinctive livery of a white hull and superstructure, and dark funnels. When George was posted to the China Station in 1928 its Commander-in-Chief was Vice Admiral Reginald Tyrwhitt, George's former commander on the Harwich Force in 1918.

In the nineteenth century the British Empire expanded across the globe through trade and commerce, missionary zeal and conquest. The extension of British power into China was a discreditable aspect of Victorian economic imperialism as it was accomplished by the enforced import of dangerous narcotics harmful to the Chinese population, despite the opposition of the Chinese Government. The East India Company and later British merchants, such as Jardine and Matheson, imported large quantities of opium grown in Bengal in British India into China.

This became a very profitable business for them, and for the British Government which benefited from the taxes paid on the trading income. When the Chinese rulers tried to stop these imports which were so harmful to its population, the British and French Governments sent armed forces to occupy several Chinese ports and cities. The outcome of these mid-nineteenth-century 'Opium Wars' was that the British and other European powers were able, through gunboat diplomacy, to impose on the Chinese unequal treaties which established several extra-territorial 'concessions' in China. These concessions were areas within a city or port controlled by foreign colonial powers, where the foreign nationals of those powers were able to trade freely without having to obtain visas, without paying local taxes and with immunity from Chinese laws. Christian missionaries were also given the right to preach their religion across China.

In the late 1920s the role of Royal Navy ships on the China Station and of the British army garrisons based in China was still to protect British commercial interests there. The need for such protection had become ever greater at a time of violent political change and turmoil in China. The attitudes of the Chinese to the British and other Europeans in their country at this time were still influenced by resentment of their treatment by the British in the Opium Wars of the previous century and hostility to the continuing privileges held in the foreign concession areas.

George kept a diary of his two-year trip, written in pencil in a small 4 x 6-inch Navigating Officer's Note Book. By this time he had taken up drawing and painting as a hobby, and he made some sketches and watercolours at the back of the diary, scenes of China and one of his ship *Berwick*. He also took several photographs on his tour and mounted them in an album, which survives along with the diary.

This China Station diary represents the only time in George's naval career of thirty-five years that he recorded his day-to-day routine of duties on board ship and his varied social activities over a period of two years. This chapter focuses on the diary entries in some detail as an account of the life of a naval officer serving overseas in the inter-war years.

In March 1928 George left Devonport on HMS *Berwick*, sailing out through Plymouth Sound:

> Saturday March 3rd, 1928
>
> *Left home with great regret, weather auguring well for a fine trip to Gibraltar. 2.15 past Breakwater, en route HMS Suffolk hoisted flag signalling their wishes pray 'bon voyage and au revoir'. Mount Edgcumbe and Cawsand Bay looked very beautiful in the sunlight on leaving.*

This was the start of his two-year trip to the Far East and a long period of separation from his wife and daughters. On the way out, the ship stopped for two days at Gibraltar, where George went ashore for a stroll and to play tennis, and took a photo of HMS Benbow leaving port. Then Berwick sailed along the north African coast to Malta, which of course George knew well and where he looked up several old friends.

Sunday March 11th

Arrived Malta 7 a.m., just the same as ever, noticed increase of motor buses. Visited Mr. and Mrs. Cowle, and Mrs. Borg, went to Dockyard Church, few familiar faces, saw Mrs. Lock afterwards.

Burnt 500 tonnes of oil on passage from home. Received second dose of inoculation, arm very painful indeed. Went to see Mr. Brincat, seemed pleased that I called.

Oiled ship in morning, received letters from Ida and the children.

George invited Mr Brincat and the Locks on board his ship for tea before his departure from Malta.

The ship sailed on through the Mediterranean to Port Said for refuelling, where nearby he saw 'the Orient liner *Orecoto* with interested passengers watching the ship, probably tourists'.

While at Port Said, George calculated it would cost £3,000 for his naval ship to pass through the Canal, with dues set at about 5 shillings per ton.

The tolls duly paid, HMS *Berwick* passed through the Suez Canal, where George took a photograph on deck of some crew at the ship's rail as the ship steamed along:

Remained on deck after divisions and watched different aspects of Canal, very monotonous, nearly all sand and mud.

On they sailed through the Red Sea, where they 'Started wearing Whites' (their white naval uniform for the tropics).

Saturday March 24th

Passed Farasan Islands known as Twelve Apostles, most desolate job for Lighthouse Keepers.

Sunday March 25th

Arrived Aden 6.30, weather very sultry.

215

The ship's crew had been ordered by the Commander-in-Chief of the Mediterranean Fleet not to refuel at Aden 'on account of plague' there, but during their short stop of less than an hour they did land ratings and stores in the port.

Monday March 26th

Before noon Somaliland on starboard side, 4 p.m. passed Socotra on port side.

Into the Indian Ocean and across to what was then known as Ceylon, now Sri Lanka, and they arrived at the capital, Colombo, where on 1 April George received mails dated 9 and 12 March brought out from home by the ship *Naldera*.

Sunday April 1st

Went ashore in the evening with Collins, had a walk around Colombo, afterwards met Pike and Greet, took a ride by motor car on to Cinnamon Gardens Museum Buddhist Temple. Caught in a thunderstorm and went aboard at 7 o'clock.

After a week of thunderstorms in Colombo, and some social visits to and from officers on other naval ships in the port, George spent Good Friday there. The next day *Berwick* left Ceylon and sailed on over Easter and the next few days into the Malay Straits, where there was an 'abundance of vegetation on many islands'.

On Friday 13 April they arrived at Singapore: 'Weighed myself at 11 stone 8lbs'.

Here George received more mail dated up to 21 March – his post from home was taking about three weeks to reach him. After three days in Singapore the ship then set sail for her China Station destination of Hong Kong, where she arrived after a six-week voyage on Friday 20 April 1928.

Arrived Hong Kong 16.30. Ship besieged by Washerwomen. O.O.W. Lieutenant Dallison dispersed them with hose. Posted first letter for transit 'via Siberia'. Weather wet. Temperature moderate.

On his first weekend in his new base of Hong Kong George visited another officer, Mr Brooks, on HMS *Durban* – he always referred to his colleagues in a very formal way. He visited the Warrant Officers' Club and 'had a walk around principal thoroughfares of Hong Kong' – surely quite an eye-opening introduction to China in 1928.

Over the next two years George would be based either at the Royal Navy's base in Hong Kong or in Shanghai, or at Wei-Hai-Wei island in northwest China on the shore of the Yellow Sea, sailing between these ports up and down the coast of China.

He would also receive a significant promotion and transfer to a river gunboat, HMS *Magnolia*, sailing with her up the Yangtze deep into inland China.

George had arrived in China at a turbulent time in its history. The Qing dynasty of the Manchu Empire, the last of a succession of imperial dynasties that had ruled for over 2,000 years, was overthrown by a revolution starting in October 1911. The last Qing emperor abdicated in February 1912, and was succeeded by the Republic of China.

The first President of the Republic was the revolutionary Dr Sun Yat-Sen, the leader and co-founder of the Chinese nationalist party, the Kuomintang, who died of cancer in 1925. George visited his tomb near Shanghai while based there. Sun Yat-Sen's rule failed to deal with the various brutal warlords who controlled, exploited and terrorised vast regions across China throughout the 1920s.

After Sun's death, the leadership of the Kuomintang passed to the military leader Chiang Kai-Shek, whose goal was to unify, industrialise and modernise the nation of China.

It was Chiang who in 1927–28 led his National Revolutionary Army on what became known as the 'Northern Expedition' from Canton in the south up to central and northern China to suppress the rule of the warlords, such as the Dogmeat General of Shandong and Zhang Zuolin in Manchuria. The Northern Expedition was alleged to be the largest military campaign anywhere on the globe between the two World Wars. After two years of brutal fighting, Chiang's nationalist forces, which at their peak totalled over a quarter of a million soldiers, overcame the warlords, and in 1928 this marked the unification of China under his Kuomintang Government.

It was not just the warlords whom Chiang Kai-Shek wished to control. In the late 1920s the Chinese Communist Party, whose leaders included Mao Zedong (Mao Tse-tung), was also challenging the Kuomintang nationalist party. There were communist and peasant uprisings across China in 1927 in many cities, including Shanghai, Canton, Wuhan and Nanchang, and in rural provinces such as Hunan, and these were brutally suppressed by the Kuomintang. The communists claimed that over 37,900 of their supporters had been killed in the repression that year.

The turbulence in Chinese politics was also affecting the international interests in the country. Anti-foreigner riots had occurred in several cities during the Northern Expedition in 1927, notably in Nanking when nationalist troops attacked the British, American and Japanese consulates, and a Royal Navy ship had evacuated British nationals to Shanghai. There were attacks on Christian missions in China, and in January 1927 the British concession in Hankow was occupied by demonstrators who fought with British marines. A boycott of British goods in Canton was organised by local trade unions which disrupted trade through Hong Kong.

The British armed forces were certainly not just standing on the margin of Chinese political events. Their role was to protect Great Britain's extensive commercial interests in the Far East and the lives of the many British nationals living and working in places such as the International Settlement in Shanghai and in the European concessions in cities such as Hankow.

George arrived in China in 1928 at a time of civil war and revolution. However, his diary refers only very occasionally to Chiang Kai-Shek, the background of nationalist/communist fighting at the time and the consequent movements of British troops.

Most of George's duties on the China Station involved routine naval exercises on HMS *Berwick*, usually with the other ships of the Fifth Cruiser Squadron – *Kent*, *Cumberland*, *Suffolk* and *Cornwall* – and with submarines. There were regular torpedo and gunnery firing trials, and at Hong Kong the ships would go out to Mirs Bay or Tolo Bay for weaponry practice.

As one of the main British colonies in the Far East, Hong Kong had the naval base HMS *Tamar* and dockyards for the supply, fuelling and repair of His Majesty's fleet. There was also a large military garrison of various army regiments, which in George's time there included the King's Own Scottish Borderers and the Berkshire and Hertfordshire Regiment.

In Hong Kong the catering for the non-commissioned officers like George – the chief petty officers and warrant officers – was done in their mess by an employed Chinese cook who would purchase all the necessary supplies and whose pay was funded from the officers' mess bills, each one paying a few shillings a month for their meals. The Chinese cook, or messman, would also recruit Chinese girls as laundry maids, who every day would collect, wash and starch the officers' uniforms and other kit, charging only a few cents for producing beautifully laundered clothes. This was clearly an important source of income for local people – as we saw, George had noticed on arrival in Hong Kong that the ship had been 'besieged by Washerwomen'!

The shore base HMS *Tamar* provided sports and social clubs for the Royal Navy in Hong Kong, such as the Warrant Officers' Club and the Kowloon Club, which offered the sailors overnight accommodation, restaurants, bars, cinema shows, tombola and other indoor recreational activities.

There was plenty of time for outdoor leisure in Hong Kong, such as taking motorbuses to explore the area, going for walks and picnics, and sea-bathing. George often took trips by motorbus out to the 'nice sandy beach' at Repulse Bay, on the south side of Hong Kong island, for a swim with his shipmates Collins and Down. They would also play tennis and cricket, and watch Navy football matches against HMS *Kent* and other ships. Inter-service matches with the army were a regular feature of the sporting activities. George took some photos of his shipmates on their excursions to the beach, posing in or by a rowing boat, some of the men in swimming costumes, or wearing shorts and panama hats. Two of the photographs show George himself on the boat with his friends, in shirtsleeves and sporting a fedora hat.

George's album contains many photos which he took in 1928 of local scenes and people in Hong Kong. He photographed junks and sampans in the harbour with Kowloon in the distance, a funeral procession with mourners carrying large Chinese lanterns, a bride being carried in a highly decorated sedan chair, a street tram, market scenes, a park with pagodas, a traditional gate, Buddhist prayer wheels and a bridge over a lake. Another photo shows a large open area – possibly the Happy Valley racecourse on Hong Kong Island – with a pavilion flying a huge Union Jack.

There are three photos of 'coolie women' – George using the then standard but now pejorative European term for Chinese unskilled labourers. He labels one such snap of women wearing traditional wide-brimmed hats and hauling a heavy load of wood on a cart as 'Coolie women as human horses'. Another shows a woman with a baby on her back while she carries a wooden pole across her shoulders with large loads of goods in baskets on each end. Other women are shown labouring in a stone quarry – 'Coolie women carving away Morrison Hill, Hong Kong'. A Chinese family with eight young children pose outside their home for a photograph with several British sailors, two rather skinny pigs in the foreground referred to as 'Chinese porkers' by George.

On 12 May 1928 a formal photograph was taken of the ship's company and the King's Own Scottish Borderers to be used for a combined Christmas card to send home to their families in due course. George took his own snaps labelled 'K.O.S.B.s' on board HMS *Berwick* and some of the troops sailing off in another vessel.

Two days later HMS *Berwick* left Hong Kong to sail north, up through the East China Sea to Wei-Hai-Wei, the British naval base on the Yellow Sea.

> Monday May 14th
> *Ship proceeded from Dockyard Wall at 8 a.m. to buoy. 11 a.m. Ship left for Wei-hai-Wei. Kings Own Scottish Borderers' pipe band played ship out of harbour. Compliment most appreciated.*

George of course was working as an engineering officer down in the bowels of the ship, and in the Far East this must have been extremely uncomfortable. He records 'engine room temperature 90 degrees'.

> Sunday May 20th, 1928
> *Arrived Wei-Hai-Wei 7 a.m. Read Thomas Hardy's Far from the Madding Crowd.*

So far from his native West Country, and working in such a different environment, he turned to an English novel for reminders of home.

The British leased Wei-Hai-Wei from China from 1898 until 1930 for a naval and fuelling base. It was an island off the Chinese coast in the province of Shandong in north-eastern China. The climate there was more comfortable in the summer than the oppressive heat of Hong Kong and Shanghai, and the base provided a sports ground, clubs and a naval canteen for the ships' crews and the garrison of British troops. The Navy also organised two-day sailing regattas.

Went ashore at Wei-Hai-Wei for a walk, watched tennis and cricket. Beryl's birthday.

His daughter Beryl reached the age of eight that day. George had left behind with his wife a gift of a Holy Bible, inscribed by him 'To Beryl from Daddy, June 3rd 1928'.

George kept active himself, playing cricket and tennis and often going on walks around the island with colleagues.

Friday June 8th
Played cricket match. W.O.'s v E.R.A's[101] – result first inning E.R.A.'s 132 W.O.'s 58. Second innings W.O.'s 43 finished about 6 p.m., played tennis with Walker and Collins at W.O.'s club.

Sunday June 10th
Commander-in-Chief inspected ship, remained for church.

George took more photographs of scenes in Wei-Hai-Wei: of Chinese male labourers, two sailors sitting on steps with three local children, traditional Chinese buildings and the docks.

While at Wei-Hai-Wei George's ship was engaged in several sea exercises, including night exercises with sister ships such as HMS *Cornwall* or ones with submarines, and on 'Full Calibre shoots' of the guns. In June 1928 he made one of his few references to the military situation:

Saturday June 23rd
P.M. 5.30 Left Wei-Hai-Wei for China Wang Tai with a Battalion of Berks & Hertfordshire Regiment

Sunday June 24th
Soldiers entrained in armoured train alongside ship. Object of landing troops is protection of K.M.A.1. Mines at Lwanchow from damage and occupation by Chinese Southern Army.

Monday June 25th

Received telegraphic signals of congratulations from Commander-in-Chief and G.O.C. [General Officer Commanding] on successful landing of T.R.E. Force and news of their safe arrival in mines at Kailan and Tongshan. 10 a.m. 'Hermes' arrived to relieve 'Berwick'.

10.30 left for Shanghai to relieve 'Cumberland' at S.N.O. Speed 140 Revs.

This is a rare insight in George's diary into the active service role of British forces in China at this time.

On 27 June the ship arrived at Shanghai on the Chinese mainland, the first of George's several trips to this city where he was to stay for lengthy periods over the next two years and parts of which he came to know well.

By the late 1920s Shanghai was the largest city in China, a port of over three million people situated near the mouth of the Yangtze river, a business and financial centre with numerous textile plants, factories and shipyards. The westerners who lived in its French Concession and the large Anglo-American International Settlement were responsible for managing the extensive foreign commercial interests in Shanghai, which represented a third of all overseas investment in China. Foreigners poured into Shanghai – some 8,000 White Russians arrived in the French Concession after the Bolshevik Revolution, along with Germans expelled from British colonies after the Great War. Of the half a million residents in the French area, some 19,000 were non-Chinese, and only 1,400 or so of them were French. One third of the city's cotton factories were owned by Japanese businessmen.

Thousands of refugees from the fighting between the Kuomintang and the warlords also fled into Shanghai as the Northern Expedition progressed during 1927–28.

Like most international seaports, Shanghai had a criminal underworld of gangs, protection rackets and secret societies, profiting from prostitution and the trades in opium and other narcotics. But Chiang Kai-Shek had few scruples about doing deals with the crime bosses as the people he really wanted to suppress were the communists.

Although foreign investment had brought gas, water and electric utilities, telephone lines, motorcars and trams to the city, Shanghai's millions of workers, and an army of beggars and hawkers, lived and worked in appalling, squalid conditions. In the fast-changing political climate in China, trade unions and labour organisations developed under the influence of the nascent Communist Party, and strikes were common.

In April 1927 Chiang Kai-Shek's nationalist forces, acting in conjunction with the criminal Green Gang, carried out a brutal purge of the Shanghai communists and of others in the city who were perceived as being too left-wing, killing hundreds indiscriminately and arresting thousands. The expatriate community in the compounds of the International Settlement and French Concession were protected from the terror by their countries' troops, including, in the case of the British, two planes of the Royal Air Force.

George first arrived in Shanghai in June 1928 just over a year after these events, and must have been aware of the dangerous political climate there. However, his movements around the city do not seem to have been too restricted, although Royal Navy personnel must have been warned not to go to certain risky areas.

A week after his arrival, George visited Shanghai for the afternoon with a couple of shipmates, Hicks and Collins. A few days later, on Sunday 8 July:

Went for a walk around Shanghai in the evening to Bubbling Well Road and back. Curious phenomena occurred at former billet of HMS Berwick where a water spout damaged a ship and mill adjacent.

Thursday July 12th
Anniversary of ship's commissioning. Concert on Quarter Deck. Dined with Captain.

Friday July 13th
French Bund[102] *illuminated, torchlight procession. Firework display. Anniversary of Fall of Bastille.*

The city seemed to have been celebrating Bastille Day a day early.

Saturday July 14th
Walked to Jessfield Park and back.

Jessfield Park was a large municipal park in the centre of Shanghai, which is still there, now called Zhongshan Park.

George's photographs show river scenes in Shanghai, including a shot of the famous Bund and the prominent colonial architecture of the large commercial buildings lining the waterfront. These included the massive domed structure of the Hong Kong and Shanghai Banking Company built in 1923 and the clock tower of the Shanghai Customs House, built the previous year in 1927.

Sunday July 22nd

Went to evening service Shanghai Cathedral, rather disappointed at absence of Choir.

After a five-week stay in the city, on 1 August 1928 HMS *Berwick* left Shanghai to sail back to Hong Kong, arriving in wet and sultry weather. The ship was there for a refit in the dockyard which lasted for six weeks, and George spent August and early September in the heat of Hong Kong. When not on duty, he was exploring the area, taking a tram ride to Shauriwan, walking to Repulse Bay, going to the cinema at HMS *Tamar* and watching the forces' football teams. He also visited and took tea with a couple called Mr and Mrs Hemer who became firm friends during his many stays in Hong Kong.

Berwick's refit was finished on Friday 14 September, and a few days later the ship was again played out of Hong Kong Harbour by the band of the King's Own Scottish Borderers as she sailed off to carry out full power trials of the ship in 'conditions unfavourable, heavy sea' before returning to Wei-Hai-Wei in time for a two-day sailing regatta.

On Monday 1 October 1928 George's diary records that he was summoned up to the Ward Room at the request of the Senior Engineer and congratulated on a promotion. His Certificate of Appointment dated 1 October 1928 confirms that he had indeed been promoted from Warrant Officer to Commissioned Engineer on HMS *Berwick*.

After nearly twenty years in the Royal Navy, at the age of forty-two he had finally attained the rank of a commissioned officer. At that time it was rare for men from the lower deck to be awarded a commission, and this was a real accolade for George in recognition of his long and creditable naval service.

Later that month, on 23 October, he saw a copy of *The Times* published on 3 October (it would have taken some two to three weeks for the paper to get out to the Far East), and this contained a list of the promotion of 'CD Engineers' (Commissioned Engineers) which included George's name.

The following week HMS *Berwick*'s new Captain joined the ship to replace the splendidly named Captain Wyker Sneyd. To mark the occasion a photograph of the two captains was taken with all the ship's officers and midshipmen, including George, on the deck in front of *Berwick*'s huge guns. The officers are all dressed in their whites and George is standing in the back row, immediately beneath one of the 8-inch heavy guns.

In early November 1928 *Berwick* left Wei-Hai-Wei to pay a goodwill visit to Tsingtau, a large city also in Shandong province to the south down the coast, which George says saw itself as the 'Riviera of the East' – it is now called Qingdao. Here George relates that a community of English children came on board for tea, about thirty-three of them, from some of the British expatriate families in China that the Royal Navy was there to protect.

The following day *Berwick* received new orders in official despatches from Shanghai. George's ship was to go to Korea, and then on to Japan to be present at the international Fleet Review to celebrate the coronation of Emperor Hirohito of Japan. Japan had been a naval ally of Britain during the Great War, assisting with operations against German ships in the Indian Ocean and the Pacific, and even sending a flotilla of Japanese destroyers to Malta to escort merchant convoys across the Mediterranean. HMS *Berwick* was one of a trio of Royal Navy ships, also including HMS *Kent* and HMS *Suffolk*, which represented Great Britain at the Fleet Review.

HMS *Berwick* left Tsingtau immediately on 9 November 1928 to sail east, first calling in at Fusan, a large port in Korea also called Busan (sometimes Pusan), which is now the second largest city in what later became South Korea. She arrived there on the day of the Japanese Emperor's Coronation.

Sunday November 11th
Went ashore to see Fusan. Fine docks and commercial facilities on landing.
Koreans in their national dress of white and Japs very conspicuous. Town

decorated lavishly for the Coronation celebrations. Watched women beating out clothes in stream when washing them, roads very rough, main street very clean but behind there is an amazing collection of shacks and smells. I saw a Korean wedding procession.

Watched fishing boats with brilliant flares at work in the evening to attract the fish.

George comments on the 'Japs being very conspicuous' in this Korean city. After years of Japanese migration into Korea, in 1910 Japan had annexed Korea, by which time there were over 170,000 Japanese settlers in the country. They were encouraged to move there and acquire land by the Japanese Government, who seemed to view Korea in the same way as Hitler was later to see the countries surrounding Germany as providing *lebensraum* (room to live) for his people. Korea remained a colony of Japan until the end of the Second World War and the defeat of the Japanese Empire.

From Korea, HMS *Berwick* sailed across the East China Sea on to Karatsue, its first port of call in Japan.

Arrived Karatsue 9 a.m. In the evening our ship illuminated (Dai Josai ceremony in connection with Coronation). Harbour very pretty and well wooded in surrounding country.

The next day on 15 November George disembarked in Japan.

Went ashore at Karatsue, interesting walk out into country. Typical country life of Japan represented. Saw wool made suitable for wearing. Weavers at work on looms. Straw rope being made. Women doing usual heavy work of pulling carts as in China. Most of country around consists largely of paddy fields for rice. Orange trees abound. Village very muddy but people seemed clean. Many houses glazed with rice paper windows. Curious steam trains running through streets.

George is clearly fascinated by the new sights and different culture that he is seeing for the first time in Japan.

On 16 November *Berwick* left Karatsue, and in very rough weather passed the towns of Shemina and Seka, and the local island ferries, into the Inland Sea, the stretch of water separating the three main islands of Japan. The ship anchored at Miyajima, then, as now, a popular tourist destination on an island an hour or so south of Hiroshima.

Saturday November 17th

Arrived Miyajima. Went ashore in afternoon to visit the island, considered one of the three beauty spots of Japan. For more than 18 centuries it has been a sacred island. The lives of the people centre around the temple which is one of the chief seats of Shinto worship. Behind is a park leading up to Mount Misen (1,789 ft), there are over 2,000 steps, climbed same and saw the shrine on the top with a wonderful view of the surrounding district. On coming down again visited the Buddhist Temple built in A.D. 802 with a five-storeyed pagoda adjoining. I saw the stable and sacred white horse. The Shinto Temple was first built in A.D. 592. Mornijitana Park is a veritable fairyland with Maple trees showing their Autumn tints. The main street consists mainly of shops selling toys and curios for tourists and many visitors must come in Summer to keep so many shops going.

George took several souvenir photographs in Miyajima which are in his album, showing the famous red Torii Gate sitting offshore in the sea, and the park at Mount Misen. He was clearly fascinated by this site as he also bought several picture postcards of the Torii, the temples and the park.

Two days later on 19 November *Berwick* left Miyajima and headed for Osaka, sailing in daylight through the tortuous channels of the Inland Sea.

On 21 November George sent a postcard from Osaka to his eight-year-old daughter which showed five Japanese mothers in traditional costume carrying their babies in slings on their backs:

HMS *Berwick*, Osaka, November 21st

My darling Beryl,

I am now sending you a Christmas card that I painted for you and also one that I bought for you. My ship is now in Japan and this picture postcard shows how the Japanese children are carried by their mothers, I have not seen very many prams yet out this way. I am very sorry I can't be at home with you this Christmas but I am hoping you will have a nice time and go

to a lot of parties. I shall be thinking of you all through the Xmas. Give my
love to Ida and Mummy.
Your ever loving Daddy xxx

On another postcard from Osaka on the same date to his elder daughter, Ida, he wrote:

I have not seen much of this place yet but it is a huge city and has
a population of nearly 2¼ millions. It is not very up to date as regards
roads and rather noisy.

From Osaka he was able to take an excursion on 23 November:

Went ashore at 8.30 for a trip to Kyoto. I caught 9.00 train and arrived at
about 11 a.m. Saw only a few objects of interest, 5 tow ropes of women's
hair and Marayama Park and Exhibition. Kyoto very beautiful city and
we were lucky to have a fine day for visit. Left Kyoto by electric tramway
at 5 p.m., arriving back at 6.30 p.m. (fare by electric 68 sen single, train
1.36 single). Received mails.

George also visited the Sumadera Garden in Kobe, a city west of Osaka where he purchased one coloured photograph showing lovely cherry blossom trees by the lake, and another of local ladies in kimonos and carrying parasols, seated in Japanese rickshaws pulled by men wearing their distinctive wide cone-shaped hats, called *kasas*.

While in Osaka an Officers' 'At Home' was held on the quarter deck of the ship with Japanese visitors invited on board, and George 'showed Japanese gentleman with knowledge of English around the ship'.

Leaving Osaka on 25 November, the ship arrived at Yokkaichi in Ise Bay on Wednesday 28 November.

Went ashore at Yokkaichi, walked out to grounds where there were cages
containing some monkeys and a bear, various birds etc. Took a country
walk. I saw women threshing rice with treadle machines, also making
straw rope. Dogs used for draught animals. Town very similar to Karatsue
but larger. I saw school children on way to visit ship. I.E.E. driven trains
running on narrow gauge rails.

On 1 December *Berwick* left for Yokohama to rendezvous the following day with her sister ships.

Weighed at 7 a.m., joined 'HMS Kent' and 'Suffolk'. Anchored for review of Japanese and International Fleet by His Imperial Japanese Majesty. Saw a few relics of the 1923 earthquake[103] on nearing Yokohama.

On Tuesday 4 December:

Emperor of Japan's Review of Japanese Fleet, weather very rough, warship conveying Emperor preceded and followed by battlecruisers, aeroplanes in formation flying overhead. Fujiyama snow-capped in distance, looked very beautiful.
   P.M. Officers invited to lunch on 'Konga', had a rough trip to and fro.

The following day the ship's company on HMS *Berwick* entertained some Japanese officers to another 'At Home', and in the evening George and his fellow officers visited a Japanese naval ship, HIJMS *Nagato*[104], where they were entertained by conjurers and wrestlers.

There is a photograph in George's album of one of these social events in Japan showing the officers of HMS *Berwick* standing in a group with several serious Japanese ladies and two young children, the women wearing their traditional dress.

On 6 December George took a day trip to the capital, Tokyo.

Landed at Yokohama and travelled up to Tokyo by electric train. Attended function at Japanese Officers' Naval Club. I saw Japanese dancers, tea on lawn of club.

He returned to Yokohama that evening, and next day he and five other officers attended a garden party given by the Mayor of Yokohama. This marked the end of George's tour around Japan, and next day his ship left for Hong Kong, arriving there six days later on 13 December.

Christmas Day 1928 was fairly uneventful: '*Cinema on quarter deck, weather nice*'.

Over the next week he met up often with his Hong Kong friends, Mr and Mrs Hemer, visiting their home and inviting them back for tea on his ship. On 1 January 1929 when George went ashore, Mr Hemer took him on a trip to the Chinese Bazaar in the Queen's Road and showed him 'various purchases in the curio line. Bedspreads, Swatow lace tablecloths, Kimonos, silk embroidered slippers, blackwood, cane chairs. Handbags of pig skin, bamboo work, pillow slips'.

George brought back many gifts from the Far East for his family, including a bronze table, white leather gloves and a set of black wooden boxes inlaid with mother of pearl, as well as the cane chairs and bedspread which he bought on this New Year's Day shopping trip. From Japan he bought as souvenirs a pair of ceramic figures, a pig-skin wallet and two painted and gilt views of Mount Fuji.

He returned the Hemers' hospitality by inviting them on board again on 9 January for the Ship's Concert for Officers and friends, and while making another visit to their house the next day, he 'saw the Governor riding around the Race Course, same day as his return from England' – a reminder of Hong Kong's colonial status under the British Empire which lasted until 1997.

Beryl wrote to her father while he was away at sea. On 12 February 1929 the eight-year-old girl wrote from 14 Beresford Street:

Dear Daddy,

I had a big surprise this afternoon because I was just at the door when the postman gave three parcels to Mammy. I had just come from school so I ran right indoors and we started to open them, Mammy was making pancakes for tea as it is pancake day today and she let some of them burn. Mammy says that you know how she can burn things!

I am delighted with my pencil box especially the fountain pen and I am writing this letter with it and it is much better to write with than an ordinary pen and Mammy says I must not take it to school.

Mammy is properly vexed that the photos have not come and she wants to know if they are still on your ship and Ida wants to know if they are in your desk or uniform pocket or any place in your cabin, she only meant it for a joke.

Granny was ever so pleased with her scarf. Mummy and me liked Ida's bag so much that we would like one ourselves that is if you can afford it.

Ida said she doesn't want us to have the same although I want the same.
Thank you ever so much for the presents.
Heaps of love from Beryl to Daddy xxx

After a month in Hong Kong, HMS *Berwick* sailed again for Shanghai, anchoring for a night on the way in Nimrod Sound (now Hsiang Shan Bay), which in foggy weather was 'a wild forbidding looking spot, apparently plenty of game to be shot here'. They proceeded to Woosung on the outskirts of Shanghai for a second night before sailing in the next day to dock at the city on 20 January.

George stayed in Shanghai for nearly two months from late January to mid-March 1929 on this trip, although his diary gives only a sketchy account of his duties and social activities during these weeks there.

Again his movements around the city seem to have been fairly unrestricted. He twice went out on walks to Bubbling Well Road where rich Chinese lived, and this time he saw the actual Well, and on another day he walked to Hongkew Park 'which consists mostly of football pitches'. The Ship's Company gave a concert at the Ferry Road Recreation Centre, with an audience mostly of soldiers, and a dance afterwards. Another dance at the Town Hall; a walk to Jessfield Park; a visit to the Union Jack Club with colleagues. George went for more walks through the Rue Du Consulate and down the Nanking Road. On 1 March he recorded his naval pay – 40 Hong Kong dollars at the rate of 10.66 dollars to the £1.

On 15 March 1929 *Berwick* left Shanghai for Woosung, and then received orders to sail up the Yangtze River to Nanking (Nanjing), the seat of the Chinese Government under Chiang Kai-Shek. This city had been the scene of the 'Nanking Incident' two years earlier in March 1927, when victorious nationalist troops had attacked and looted foreign houses and offices, including the British, American and Japanese consulates, and had shot dead two European Catholic priests and the American Vice-President of the University. The British consul was badly wounded, and American and Royal Navy warships had evacuated many of the foreign residents from Nanking to Shanghai, including several women and children.

By the time of George's visit in 1929 the political situation was clearly more stable.

Sunday March 17th

Arrived Nanking 3.30 p.m. Beautiful and sunny trip up Yangtze, country mostly flat and uninteresting. Plenty of wild duck on the river.

The following day George attended a lecture on the subjects of the Yangtze and Chinese topics given by the local river pilot, a Mr Pote-Hunt, which perhaps gave him the incentive for his next sightseeing trip on Monday 25 March:

Visited the Ming Tomb.[105] Took motorcar from Nanking out to Dr Sun Yat Sen's Tomb which stands on top of flight of 412 steps, interior embellished with black marble and overhead mosaic work. It took 3 years to do by Italian workmen. Roof supported by black marble pillars, and artificial wreaths from Chinese in different parts of World hung up. Afterwards motored back to Ming Tomb, saw the Temple of the Tortoise then through a long courtyard with carved stones, well worn down with age, and up through a tunnel to a temple above, in a state of ruin. Facing temple is a long avenue of stone figures and animals arranged in pairs. The Nanking City Wall is a massive one & about 28 miles around. Country looked very well cultivated and green with such heavy rain, as we experienced on trip. Arrived back at Nanking Pier at about 4.15 p.m. Had a wet passage off.

The Ming Tomb that George visited was the Ming Xiaoling Mausoleum where the Hongwu Emperor, the founder of the Ming Dynasty, is buried. There George took a photograph of the famous Elephant Road, which is lined by twelve pairs of six kinds of animals carved in stone, including lions, camels and elephants. George's other destination, the tomb of Sun Yat-Sen, the first President of the Chinese Republic, had only recently been completed following his death in 1925.

The following day, 26 March 1929:

Received commission and took Mechanics Exam.

George was still studying to work his way up the naval promotion scale.

On 28 March *Berwick* left Nanking and sailed back down the Yangtze for the open sea. Over the last two days of March George's ship was engaged in a series of sea trials of up to six hours' duration under 'unit conditions and cruising conditions', and on Easter Day they arrived back at Hong Kong, where he was to remain for another six weeks.

That April in Hong Kong his naval routine consisted of fleet exercises with sister ships such as HMS *Kent*, torpedo firing practice in the nearby bays and engine room inspections by the Admiral. When off duty he again went on social visits to the Hemers, took ferry and bus trips to Kowloon, Mong Kok and Castle Peak, walked and swam at Repulse Bay and watched the ship's team in football league matches. One Tuesday he and seven other members of his mess went for a picnic in Tolo Harbour, where the ship had anchored after firing practice. They played cricket and bathed there, and were surprised to see so many Chinese graves in the sides of the hills around this district.

One break in the routine was the arrival on 25 April of Prince Henry, the Duke of Gloucester, the third son of King George V, on the P&O steamer *Morea* en route for a royal 'Garter Mission' to the Emperor of Japan. At Hong Kong the Duke landed at the Queen's Pier with the Governor and transferred to HMS *Suffolk*, and when they left 'All ships manned and cheered as she went by with the Duke on the bridge at the salute'.

After this relatively peaceful springtime in Hong Kong, in mid-May George set off on HMS *Berwick* on a second trip to Japan, this time to Nagasaki, sailing in rough weather in the company of HMS *Seraph* and HMS *Serapis*. While at sea these two companion ships dropped depth charges and then sent out manned sea boats to pick up the number of fish thrown up from the sea by the explosions.

This trio of British ships arrived at Nagasaki on Friday 17 May, and George commented on the 'beautiful scenery around harbour'. But when he went on shore for a walk that Sunday, he thought:

> *...town rather disappointing, eventually got out of it. Saw children's sports up on hill above, band in centre of field which played only when actual racing took place. Crowds of Japs around watching and in their coloured kimonos made a gay picture. In the evening Mr Hutchinson invited me over to HMS Seraph to dinner.*

The next day he went on the Chief Petty Officers' trip to Hot Springs at Unzen which was 2,000 feet up in the hills. After two more days in Nagasaki, on 22 May they left for Wei-Hai-Wei and started a 'full power trial' with the ship. The reason for this six-day trip to Nagasaki is unexplained, but it gave George a further insight into the culture of Japan.

The weather was clearly becoming cooler as the crew 'changed into Blues'. However, it quickly improved as by Saturday 28 May they 'changed into Whites again'.

Life on the base at Wei-Hai-Wei that June included regular walks around the island, watching football matches between the teams of the Fifth Cruiser Squadron ships, with a satisfying 5–1 win by HMS *Berwick* against HMS *Cornwall*, and several more long-range gunnery and torpedo-firing exercises at sea.

On Monday 24 June, *Berwick* left Wei-Hai-Wei along with HMS *Kent* and a group of smaller ships – the destroyers HMS *Starling* and *Stormcloud* and the minesweeper HMS *Petersfield* – to sail across the Yellow Sea to a seaport called Chemulpo on the southwest coast of Korea, where they arrived the following day, 25 June.

Saturday June 29th, 1929

Went on shore at Chemulpo at 1.30, visited town and surprised to find the streets so smooth, wide and clean. Oxen used mainly for draught purposes and few horses. Koreans use hods on their backs for carrying loads on, when they want a rest they just convert it into a tripod arrangement which they stand on ground. Japanese are very conspicuous here but a large number of Koreans seen in their native dress of white with cone shaped hats as head dress in the case of the men. The rise and fall of the harbour as much as 37ft but a dock and lock has been constructed. An island called Getsubi is accessible by an embankment and we crossed over to it. The trees there are very beautiful but the sea views are marred by mud banks. There is a salt water bath for swimming and hot salt water indoor bath for bathing. A Berwick football team played the commercial school team and we watched part of the game. Afterwards we got into conversation with an English clergyman attached to the Theological College of Korean Native Church originally built by an ex-naval chaplain, Bishop Corfe.

On Sunday June 30th, the Bishop of Northern Korea, R.R. Dr Embling, preached at church. His address was very suitable to the occasion and everybody seemed interested in his account of the difficulties of missionary work in Korea generally. Met Reverend Leigh at his house and stopped until 11 p.m.

On 1 July the ship left Korea, and arrived the following day at Dairen (now known as Dalian). This was a seaport in northeast China on the tip of a peninsula in the south of Manchuria, the Chinese region that bordered both Russia and Japan, and where many settlers from both those countries lived, as George observed.

Tuesday 2nd July
10 am arrived Dairen, fine breakwater & dock accommodation. 4.30 landed to see town. Very nicely laid out and many large buildings to be seen. Yamatadori (the name of the street leading into the town) is very spacious. Population mostly Chinese and Japanese, sprinkling of Russians etc. Droskhys as in Russia plying for hire, also rickshaws numerous.

Japan, ambitious to establish itself as the dominant industrial nation in the Far East and Pacific, had already colonised Korea, and it also wished to control the resources of food, raw materials and minerals in the Chinese region of Manchuria. After its success against Russia in the Russo-Japanese War of 1904–5, Japan occupied the territory around the city which they renamed Dairen, increasingly replaced Russian influences in southern Manchuria, and extended Japanese interests there.

The Manchurian warlord Zhang Zuolin, who controlled most of the region, had fought Chiang's Kuomintang armies for several years. But by 1928 these two leaders were negotiating to form an anti-communist front together, and Zhang had agreed to hand Peking (now Beijing) over to Chiang's nationalists. On 3 June 1928 Zhang Zuolin was assassinated by Japanese officers, and Japan's imperial ambitions to dominate this region and beyond would eventually lead to its invasion of Manchuria in September 1931 and the Sino-Japanese War of 1937–1945.

Wednesday 3rd July
Party went to Port Arthur, from all accounts visit was only of historic interest. (George had not gone with them.)

George's ship stayed for four days in the Manchurian port of Dairen, where with other officers he attended the American Independence Day Ball on 4 July, as there were several US citizens in the city. His ship left

Dairen on 5 July in very foggy weather to carry out machinery flexibility trials and then return to Wei-Hai-Wei.

On Saturday 13 July the ship's officers organised another 'At Home' from 9 until 12 p.m. which was clearly quite a party:

> *Quarter deck decorated with lanterns worked by resistance that switched on different coloured lamps alternately. Fountains spraying water, revolving ball with mirrors to reflect spots of light, a streamer fountain etc.*

The next weekend, Sunday 21 July, George and his colleagues went on a boating picnic on Wei-Hai-Wei's mainland (Port Edward), and two days later, on Tuesday 23 July, they went ashore to see yet another football match, *Berwick* against *Kent*, which, after an exciting game, *Berwick* won 2–1.

On Sunday 4 August, George's naval service in China suddenly changed:

> *Surprised to receive orders to join HMS 'Magnolia' in place of Cd. Engineer E. Hoskin.*

China Station – The Yangtze

HMS *Magnolia* was a sloop on the China Station, a type of shallow-draught gunboat, in size something between a frigate and a corvette, suitable for patrolling inland along the rivers in China. As its name indicated, it was a sloop of the 'Flower Class' – popularly known as the 'cabbage class' – built during the Great War for roles such as escort duty, minesweeping and anti-submarine warfare. HMS *Magnolia* was of the *Acacia* class of these sloops and was launched on 26 June 1915.

On 5 August 1929, the day after receiving his orders, George transferred immediately to HMS *Magnolia*. Over the next two days he was at sea off Wei-Hai-Wei on his new ship, towing a gunnery target for HMS *Suffolk*, HMS *Cumberland* and his former ship *Berwick*. On 8 August *Magnolia* sailed for Shanghai, arriving two days later just as the port received a typhoon warning.

George spent the next seven weeks in Shanghai, but records his very various off-duty leisure activities only when on shore leave. On his first evening walk ashore on 13 August he 'noticed several improvements in Shanghai since last visit'. He accompanied his shipmate Hake for a visit to a bird shop, where Hake 'purchased four canaries at $1 each'.

On his days off that August George walked to Jessfield Park, watched polo teams at the racecourse, where the British beat the Americans by 7–6, and visited Luna Park for the dog races. In September, after dinner at Marcel's with the navigator and gunnery officer from his ship, they went to see a 'Talkie film' called *Alibi* which must have been one of the earlier talking pictures, as the first one, *The Jazz Singer*, had been released only in 1927. A week later he saw another film, *The Redeeming Sin*, at the Carleton Cinema, and then 'dined at the Masonic Club with Hake'.

Sunday 1 September is one of many entries throughout the diary where George records the exchange rate – 'Received 160 dollars, $1 = 1 and 8¾'.

His recreational outings also included a trip to the Canidrome in

Shanghai where he 'saw a performer with a motor car which turned a somersault', a visit to the Autumn Meeting at the Shanghai Races and an evening at the Luna Park dog racing track.

While George spent the summer of 1929 in Shanghai, his wife Ida was busy bringing up their two daughters back in Devonport. Like most naval and army wives, Ida was used to coping with the long separations from her husband.

She frequently spent time with her sister-in-law Ellen Ronson, whose husband Jack was another naval engineer who spent long periods away at sea. The Lancaster and Ronson families were friendly with the Elsons who farmed at Downhouse Farm at Stoke Climsland, a village across the River Tamar in Cornwall. Ida and Ellen would take young Ida and Beryl and the five Ronson children out to the Elsons' farm at Stoke Climsland for weekend stays and they all enjoyed their trips there. One photograph from a visit there in the late 1920s shows young Beryl with other children while her cousin Jack Ronson plays with a farm dog; another is a shot of Beryl standing on top of a wooden horse-drawn hay wagon along with Jack and the Elson children, her mother Ida standing in front of them with the dog.

For one summer holiday week in 1929 Ida and Ellen rented the old coastguard's cottage at Cellars Beach near Noss Mayo in South Devon on the Yealm Estuary. The two families travelled there from Devonport on a charabanc to Newton Ferrers, and then by rowboat across the river for a walk along Revelstoke Drive to the cottage on the cliffs by the edge of the sea. The joy of these days – playing on the sands, walking the coast, exploring the rock pools and swimming – compensated a little for the absence of the children's fathers.

On his last night in Shanghai on Sunday 6 October 1929, at the end of his seven-week stay there, George went to the evening service at the cathedral, where the Bishop of Northern China preached. The following day George left Shanghai on HMS *Magnolia*, sailing up the Yangtze for Hankow.

This voyage deep into inland China took five days, past the cities of Nanking and Wuhu, the ship anchoring each night on the river. They passed the Zhenfeng Pagoda at Anking (Anqing) on a bend in the north bank of the Yangtze. It was built in 1570 during the Ming Dynasty and was once used as a lighthouse. George thought it was the finest pagoda he had seen on the river.

The Royal Navy had about a dozen gunboats on the Yangtze, and these patrolled over a thousand miles of its waters to protect the British residents in the various ports on the river and ensure safe passage for the steamships that carried the goods and commodities of the British traders.

There were various hazards on the river, and not just the dangerous currents, whirlpools, shifting sandbanks and narrow navigable channels. Chinese merchants transported large cargoes of timber on huge rafts, the crews of which could only steer them with large oars. These rafts, which also carried small houses for the crewmen and their families and animals, drifted largely uncontrolled down the river, and there were frequent collisions with ships.

Chinese bandits boarding ships on the river and demanding money and free passage were another regular danger. In September 1926 there was a particularly serious incident when the troops of a local warlord seized two British merchant ships and held the six British officers hostage. The Royal Navy sent ships and armed forces on a rescue mission, and in the ensuing action many of the warlord's soldiers were killed, but the British naval commander and four of his men also died.

On 12 October 1929 HMS *Magnolia* arrived at Hankow where she stayed for a fortnight. Hankow (or Hankou) was one of the three cities located in central China which made up the metropolis of Wuhan on the banks where the Yangtze met its tributary, the Han River, the other cities there being Wuchang and Hanyang. After the Second Opium War of 1856–1860, Great Britain and other European countries had secured further trading concessions in Chinese ports, including from 1862 the one in Hankow.

Again George's diary records only his leisure time, including visits to the Zero Club for lunch and watching the Autumn Race Meeting at the Hankow Race Club, where the following day, Sunday 20 October, he dined with the ship's doctor: 'Lovely orchestra playing there and went to Victoria Cinema afterwards'.

Life for the Royal Navy officers in this concession territory, an outpost of British imperial power, seemed as comfortable and unchanging as it had been at the height of the late Victorian Empire.

But why was HMS *Magnolia* berthed in Hankow for a fortnight?

In the first weeks of 1927, during the Northern Expedition fighting between the nationalists and the warlords, the Kuomintang forces had occupied Hankow and were clearly intent on reclaiming the British concession territory for a unified China. The German and Russian concessions there had already ended in 1917 and 1920 respectively. An anti-British demonstration in January 1927 turned into a riot, and a mob attacked the British settlement in Hankow. A corps of volunteer male civilians resident in the concession were mobilised and joined by a landing party from the gunboat HMS *Bee*, and this combined force of only some thirty men with batons and bayonets protected the settlement while British women and children were evacuated by tugs to British steamships anchored in the river.

A month later, in February 1927, the British Government's negotiations with the Chinese nationalists and their foreign minister Eugene Chen resulted in the Chen-O'Malley Agreement which set up a joint British-Chinese administration of the Hankow concession. In 1929 the British concession finally ended, and the territory was handed over to the Chinese authorities. This seemingly minor event was significant in that it represented one of the earliest acts in the slow dismantling of the global British Empire, a process that would take some seventy years, culminating in the handover of Hong Kong itself in 1997.

The British had held their concession in Hankow since 1862 so there was a large British expatriate community resident in the territory. Anti-British and anti-Christian demonstrations were frequent and threatening. The role of Royal Navy ships like HMS *Magnolia* in Hankow in October 1929 was to protect and help evacuate the British community from the city, together with their personal belongings and papers, including potentially sensitive commercial and official records.

George of course could not relate this role in his diary, but it was undoubtedly a risky operation for his ship and her crew.

On Sunday 27 October HMS *Magnolia* left Hankow to sail back down the Yangtze to call in at Kuikiang (later known as Juijang) where another concession operated by the British had recently been ended by agreement with the Chinese. After anchoring here for an overnight stay, during which *Magnolia* may have picked up British nationals and/

or their papers and property, the ship sailed on past Wuhu, arriving back at Nanking on Tuesday 29 October.

The day after that they left for Shanghai, where they arrived in the afternoon and coaled the ship the following day. On Friday 1 November they sailed again for Hong Kong, arriving there on Monday 4 November. On Sunday 10 November, George had dinner and tea with his friend Mr Hemer, and then commenced a six-week period of shore leave in Hong Kong, recording two days later that he was 'accommodated at Kowloon'.

George's Chinese photograph album includes two photographs of him with other British men, all dressed in civilian suits, on the balcony of the large house in Kowloon where they stayed while on leave. Otherwise, his diary is sadly silent on his activities during these six weeks, and he records only that he went to the Hong Kong races on 16 November and 30 November.

On 23 December he 'went back to live in ship again'.

On 25 December, Christmas Day, he 'went ashore for a walk in evening'.

George remained with his ship in Hong Kong for the next month, and spent the first few weeks of 1930 engaged in sea trials and exercises, including firing exercises in Mirs Bay, and engine room inspections. The military situation had apparently become more urgent, as on 2 January *Magnolia* received a signal cancelling a proposed cruise to the Dutch East Indies, and on 15 January the ship 'landed 30 men of King's Own Scottish Borderers' somewhere which George does not identify. Then they went on a few days' voyage to Hoihow, which was 265 miles to the south, for reasons unknown, returning to Hong Kong and arriving there on 20 January after a 'very unpleasant passage against north east monsoon'. After his return, he saw his old ship HMS *Berwick* alongside the harbour wall.

On the social side, he visited his friend Mr Hemer's house twice – 'caught sampan back to ship from Praya East' – and went to dinner in Kowloon. On 25 January 1930 George visited the Chinese New Year Fair with Mr Cooper of HMS *Cornflower*. The centuries-old Chinese New Year celebration, also known as the Spring Festival to mark the lunar New Year, was a time for family gatherings and special dinners, traditional lion dances through the streets, fireworks, firecrackers and red paper decorations with messages of good fortune and happiness.

On 27 January HMS *Magnolia* left Hong Kong in rough weather along with HMS *Cornflower*, and four days later they arrived in Shanghai for a stay of over a fortnight, during which George had some new culinary experiences:

February 1st

Arrive Shanghai 10.30 a.m. alongside Pootung Wharf, went ashore in the evening landing at Wayside and walked to Nanking Road. Chinese New Year Festival and few shops open.

February 12th

Dined ashore with Doctor, saw film at Odeon called 'Volga Volga', caught 11.30 night ferry down.

February 14th

Visited Japanese restaurant with Navigator and First Lieutenant of 'Sepoy' and sampled suyikaki. Afterwards went to see Hai-alai[106] at Auditorium.

February 15th

Tipton entertained Doctor, Navigator and myself to Chinese 'Chow' party, courses consisted of shark skin soup, salted almonds, bird nest soup, chicken and ham, mandarin fish and ham, melon seeds etc. Found it difficult to use chop sticks.

February 18th

Left for Nanking.

On 20 February the ship arrived at Nanking, which was at that time the capital of China, where George spent the next three weeks. While there he 'received news of relief' – which meant that his time in China would be coming to an end as a relief naval officer would be taking his place on the station.

But it would be nearly another three months before the relief officer arrived from Great Britain, and in that time George returned from Nanking to Shanghai, where he was from mid-March to early April, back to Nanking for a fortnight and then to Wei-Hai-Wei on 18 April.

In Nanking he went to the cinema, and dined in the Ward Room Mess with the river pilot. In Shanghai he walked from Lai Road to the racecourse one day and met a Mr and Mrs Bruce, and the following week he attended the Shanghai Races one afternoon followed by an evening with the ship's navigator at the Lunar Park dog track. He went to the Odeon cinema with Mr Haynes, and on 25 March:

> *Farewell tiffin at Shanghai Club. Saw Lieutenant Jenkins off in the 'Rawalpindi' 16,000 tonne P&O Liner, great many passengers on board.*[107]

On 6 April, George arrived back in Nanking where he dined on board HMS *Cornwall* in the evening. He then makes some rare diary references to the military/political situation in China and the Chinese leader:

April 8th

> *Chiang-Kai-Shek crossed river to Pukow. Warships present manned Ship and fired salute, 21 guns.*

By this time the British Government had reached an accommodation with the Nationalist leader Chiang and was supporting him against the communists:

April 14th

> *Expected trouble from Communists at Oogee Factory. Landing party standing by for protection of Oogee. Raised steam to shift to vicinity of factory but Chinese authorities took action & at 11 a.m. orders cancelled.*

The following day George on HMS *Magnolia* set sail for Wei-Hai-Wei, and while en route in fine weather he received a signal concerning *Vindictive*. HMS *Vindictive* was the large troop carrier that transported naval crew and soldiers to and from England, and was shortly to complete an outward trip from Britain. George would be returning home on this ship. The next few days on Wei-Hai-Wei were eventful:

April 23rd

> *Landed for route march around Wei-Hai-Wei Island. HMS Vindictive arrives Hong Kong.*

April 24th

Tried to hold sports meeting for ship's company but heavy rain stopped our doing so.

April 25th

Afternoon held sports. Evening entertained by wardroom at US Club to dinner. After dinner played bowls, made score of 300.

April 29th

Dined with Captain, Mr & Mrs Gill, Mrs Dick and First Lieutenant, played card game called Newmarket.

April 30th

Noon, went to sea in response to SOS of unknown ship near SE promontory of Shantung. Picked up boat load of survivors and turned them over to D.H.K. tug, weather very foggy.

May 1st

Returned to Wei-Hai-Wei.

On 5 May, George's relief officer, a Mr Stonestreet, arrived, and after a few days' handover briefing, George departed.

May 9th

Left Wei-Hai-Wei in SS Shantien 9.45 p.m. Weather fine.

May 11th

Arrived Shanghai 6.30 p.m., HMS Suffolk's boat sent punctually.

He spent a week in Shanghai, staying on HMS *Suffolk*.

May 14th

Walked to Jessfield Park with Wynne and Prior, visited the zoo, had tea and arrived back on board at 7 p.m.

May 18th

Went to Jessfield with Wynne.

*Left HMS Suffolk 6.40 a.m. to pick up HMS Vindictive at Woosung.
Raining very heavily.*

Having joined HMS *Vindictive* at Woosung, which was just outside
Shanghai, he sailed back to Hong Kong for his final week in the Far East
after two years on the China Station.

May 23rd

*Arrived Hong Kong 7 a.m., visited Kowloon to see Hocking and Daniel
in evening.*

May 25th

*Went to Repulse Bay in afternoon, met Tink and Richards who gave me
a lift back by their car.*

May 26th

Went out to see Mr & Mrs Hemer to say goodbye.

May 27th

Left Hong Kong 6 a.m.

May 31st

Arrive Singapore, paid £9 and 10 shillings.

George spent two days in the Crown Colony of Singapore where the British
were building a huge naval base to defend, if necessary, their interests in
the Far East against the expanding Japanese Empire. On his voyage home
on *Vindictive* he was able to spend a few interesting days in Colombo,
the capital city of Ceylon, then another Crown Colony (now Sri Lanka):

June 2nd

HMS Iroquois commissioned. 11 a.m. left Singapore for Columbo.

June 6th

*Had middle watch, arrived on deck just too late to see HMS Berwick pass
at 12.30 a.m., clock put back one hour.*

Arrive Columbo 5.30 p.m., weather cooler than at Singapore.

June 8th

Went ashore at 4.30, walked to Cinnamon Gardens. Columbo natives seem to be en fete at fair in a field near town which interested me. Columbo a garden city around Cinnamon Gardens area. There are a fine collection of trees. Everything was nice and green after heavy rain in forenoon. Walked back via Galle Face jetty. Very heavy surf running on sea front.

June 9th

Mr Rice came aboard.

June 10th

Left Columbo 6 a.m. Weather fine.

It was a rough and hot passage across the Indian Ocean:

June 14th

Fed up with incessant rolling and stuffy atmosphere due to heavy south west monsoon. Heavy seas shipped on deck, port in cabin closed and cabin fan broke down to make things worse. Expect to arrive Aden 10 a.m. on 17th.

June 15th

Weather worse than ever, tremendous seas over ship, wind gale force. Expect to make Cape Guardafui [in Somalia] tonight.

June 16th

Entered Gulf of Aden during morning watch, weather easier, able to open cabin port.

June 17th

Arrived Aden 11 a.m., oiled and left 6.30 p.m. Weather extremely hot and engine room intolerably so. Howard and Mercer went sick which placed us in four watches.

Weather extremely hot, sea water 90°.

Weather rough through strong head wind. Ship much cooler but necessity of keeping cabin port closed rather trying.

The last fortnight of the voyage was more comfortable, but his shipmate Tink was clearly suffering:

2 o'clock entered Gulf of Suez.

3.45 a.m. stopped, entered canal about 5 a.m., arrived Port Said 3.30 p.m. HMS Medway *and four submarines present. Left Port Said 11 a.m. Passed German warship* Karlsruhe *on way out, temperature much cooler.*

Nice weather still, arrived Malta 2 p.m. Tied off at Bighi Bay under hospital.

Tink sent to hospital.

Left Malta 9 a.m.

Steaming 165 revs along the African coast, weather very good.

Arrive Gibraltar about 4 p.m., left at 7 p.m.

Pass Ushant about 9 p.m. It started to rain.

Home again. Tied up at number 1 jetty 9 o'clock.

With that final understated comment, George's two-year posting on the China Station was over, and after a six-week return voyage from Hong Kong he was back in Devonport with his family.

Over the next fifteen years George would read in his newspapers of events in China at many of the places where he had lived or visited.

A year after his return home, on 19 September 1931 the Japanese invaded and occupied the Chinese region of Manchuria, an act of war that went unchallenged by the League of Nations. Many commentators regard this as the beginning of a near-decade of international failure to resist both Japanese imperialism and European fascism, a catalogue of inactivity and appeasement which led to the Second World War.

From 1937 to 1945 China fought against further Japanese aggression in the Sino-Japanese War. In November 1937, after the three-month Battle of Shanghai, Japan captured that city. The Japanese army then advanced on the capital, Nanking, in December 1937, where over a six-week period its soldiers committed the atrocity known as the 'Rape of Nanking' – it is estimated that 250,000–300,000 Chinese were massacred, with rape and looting widespread.

The Japanese Empire's global ambitions resulted in its attack on the United States at Pearl Harbor on 7 December 1941, after which the United States entered the Second World War. The war in the Far East ended with the dropping of the first atomic bombs on the Japanese cities of Hiroshima and Nagasaki on 6 and 9 August 1945. George had visited Miyajima near Hiroshima and also Nagasaki on his trips there in 1928 and 1929. These bombs resulted in Emperor Hirohito accepting defeat and agreeing to the unconditional surrender of Japan on 15 August, despite the opposition of some of his fanatical military leaders who attempted an unsuccessful coup against him. Many felt that Hirohito should have been tried for war crimes and atrocities, both in the war against China and in the Second World War, but he was not, and he remained Emperor of Japan until his death in 1989.

After the defeat of Japan, the civil war in China between the Nationalists and the communists resumed and, after the death in the fighting of some five million Chinese, the communists under Mao Zedong were victorious. Chiang Kai-Shek fled to the island of Formosa off the Chinese mainland, where he established the separate state of Taiwan and ruled as a dictator – the *Generalissimo* – until his death in 1975, aged eighty-seven.

Mao's People's Liberation Army marched into Shanghai in May 1949. The Canidrome and the Shanghai racecourse, where George had enjoyed many sociable hours with his colleagues, became the sites of public trials and mass executions of thousands of opponents of the Communist Party. In 1951 alone some 300,000 people were killed in Shanghai by Mao's regime.

The Korea which George had visited in 1929 was split into two nations following the Korean War of 1950–1953, and North Korea became the 'rogue state' which over sixty years on is ruled by a dictator and is considered a major nuclear threat to world peace.

China has become a world superpower and in recent years has challenged Japan over their competing territorial claims to islands in the East China Sea. China has also accused Japan of renewing its aggressive militarism of the 1930s.

On 14 January 2015 a BBC press release stated:

Japan's parliament has approved its largest ever military budget, the third rise in defence spending in as many years.

Since WWII the country has been constitutionally bound not to deploy combat troops abroad.

However, Japan says China now poses a threat to its interests in the East China Sea and that it must boost its military capabilities in response.

The Thirties, and Gibraltar

I expect you were very interested to hear the proclamation of King Edward VIII and although I wish the new King a long reign, I hope the announcer was wrong when he said you would probably never hear anything like it again in your life time. It is very possible that you may live to hear another Queen Elizabeth proclaimed to the Throne.

(George's letter to Beryl, February 1936.)

When George arrived back in Great Britain in July 1930, the country was in the grip of austerity.

The Stock Exchange Crash in New York in October 1929 had precipitated a global Great Depression which extended to Great Britain, whose world trade halved between 1929 and 1933, as did British steel production. In the summer of 1931 there was a run on the pound in the City of London and the country was suffering a huge trade deficit. By the summer of 1932 unemployment had reached a record figure of 3.5 million, with many more people in only part-time employment.

In 1931 the Labour Prime Minister, Ramsay MacDonald, crossed the party divide to join a National Government with the Conservatives (an act for which the Labour Party never forgave him). The Government embarked on a drastic programme of cutting the pay of public sector workers, including the civil service, the police and the armed forces. For the Royal Navy, the Admiralty announced all men being paid on the 1919 pay scales would now be put on the lower 1925 scales, which meant that many older sailors lost 25 per cent of their wages, while naval officers lost only 11 per cent – this compared to cuts of 10 per cent in the Army and Royal Air Force.

The discontent that this wage cut provoked in the crews of Royal Navy ships led to the 'Invergordon Mutiny' in September 1931. The Atlantic Fleet, which was in the Cromarty Firth anchored at Invergordon, had been ordered to sea, but the crews of four battleships refused to raise anchor and signalled that they were 'on strike'. The crew on the cruiser HMS *Norfolk* issued a manifesto which was smuggled to the other ships and read:

> We, the loyal subjects of His Majesty the King, do hereby present to My Lord Commissioners of the Admiralty our representative, to implore them to amend the drastic cuts in pay which have been inflicted on the lowest paid men of the lower deck. It is evident to all concerned that this cut is the forerunner of tragedy, misery and immorality amongst the families of the lower deck, and unless a guaranteed written agreement is received from the Admiralty and confirmed by Parliament, stating that our pay will be revised, we are resolved to remain as one unit, refusing to sail under the new rate of pay. The men are quite agreeable to accept a cut which they consider reasonable.

The news of the British sailors' 'mutiny' – more of a strike, and certainly not a violent uprising – went quickly around the world, and caused such shock that the pound plummeted on foreign exchanges and the National Government was forced to abandon the Gold Standard. The Admiralty backed down and agreed that the Royal Navy's sailors would have the same 10 per cent pay cut as the other armed forces were receiving. The strike was called off, and the ships sailed for their home ports. Although the Admiralty had said there would be no victimisation of the crews concerned, thirty-six ringleaders were subsequently dismissed, and seven ships' captains were relieved of their commands.

The impact of the so-called Invergordon Mutiny on the other ports of the Royal Navy, including George's home base in Devonport, must have been immense. Nothing like this had been experienced in the armed forces in living memory. For many it was a symbol of the decline of the Royal Navy as the Senior Service of Britain's armed forces. The amount spent on the naval budget had been drastically cut throughout the 1920s, in particular by the Geddes Axe, from £356 million in 1918–19 to £53 million in 1932–33. The Navy's manpower of over 438,000 in 1918 was reduced to 90,000 by 1932.

From October 1930 George was serving on HMS *Carysfort*, a cruiser on which he served as a Commissioned Engineer. This ship was part of the reserve of the home fleet based in Devonport, and George also worked on HMS *Comus*, which was a tender to HMS *Carysfort*.

George was living in Plymouth with Ida when they received a visit from her brother, David Horne, in the summer of 1931. He had left England in 1922, aged twenty-four, to emigrate to Canada, looking for work and a better life. He now returned to Devonport at the age of thirty-three to visit his parents and three sisters, clearly more prosperous as his occupation on his ship's passenger list was shown as 'Motor Business'. But Ida and George were scandalised to learn that he was living 'in sin' with a woman in Canada and appeared to have no intention of getting married.

In the 1930s cohabitation out of wedlock was still regarded as highly immoral by the majority of British men and women, especially the 'respectable' middle classes, at a time when churchgoing was the norm and people were expected to abide by certain uniform standards of conduct. On 15 August 1931 David Horne sailed back to Montreal from Southampton on the passenger ship *Duchess of York*. He had little further contact with his eldest sister Ida, although by the late 1930s he had returned permanently to England to live in Hornchurch, Essex, still working in the motor trade.

On 7 December 1931, at the age of forty-four, George transferred to HMS *Dart*, a fishery protection gunboat captained by Lieutenant Commander Charles Adams. It was Adams who wrote this report on George in his naval record:

> V shy and simple, portly and rather ludicrous figure but an engaging personality. Taken charge of department and firmly maintained machinery in high state of efficiency and cleanliness. Loyal. V. tactful and reliable. Sound common sense. Well read and interested in current events – March 1933.

George's previous commanding officers had valued his quiet reserve. Perhaps the unkind 'shy and simple, portly and rather ludicrous' comment, inconsistent with the later remarks, was that of a younger officer, with limited sensibilities, who could not perceive the character and qualities of the older man.

Following the abolition of the Selborne-Fisher Scheme, the snobbish culture of executive deck officers looking down on their engineer colleagues may also have persisted. But another of Admiral Fisher's reforms to open up the rigid social structure of the Senior Service was to prove of benefit to George when in February 1933 he achieved a further promotion from Commissioned Engineer to the rank of Lieutenant Engineer. This came at a late stage in his career but marked a significant achievement for him.

An officer called Anthony Miers, who had also served on HMS *Dart*, wrote George a letter marked from the 'Army and Navy Club, Pall Mall, SW1' on 27 February 1933 on hearing of his promotion.

Dear 'Chief' [108]
A thousand congratulations. I am most frightfully bucked to see at last the reward of all your labours. It is a splendid show.

I would have sent you a wire only (a) I have no money (b) your letter says you are on patrol and I don't know where to send it.

I only wish I were there to join in the celebrations and I hope you do not leave the ship. Thank you for your awfully kind letter and I shall always treasure many happy memories of the 'Dart', particularly of my messmates. I hope some day we may serve together again. Best of luck always.
Yours with very great delight,
Anthony Miers

Our 'shy and simple' George was clearly liked and respected by his colleagues and senior officers. He kept in touch with Lieutenant Anthony Miers, who wrote another warm letter to George in Gibraltar, still addressing him as 'Chief', from the submarine HMS *Resolution* in Hong Kong in 1935. Miers wrote that he had a 'wizard captain and a wizard crew', but he said he loathed China. He asks after George's daughter and signs off 'Please give my best to your missus and I shall hope to have the pleasure of coming into see you when I get home…wishing you the best of luck.'

Despite Lt. Commander Adams' comments, George maintained a good relationship with that officer too, as in 1939 he did a painting of HMS *Dart* and sent it to Adams as a gift on the occasion of his wedding. Charles Adams' letter of thanks to George in February 1939, written from Antwerp, says:

My dear Chiefy,

After the wedding – which I surprised myself and girl by enjoying – we walked around the presents and there I saw your watercolour sketch of the 'Dart'. Someone had unpacked it without telling me, and dear man how delighted I was to see it. Thank you very, very much – it is simply grand of you. I must tell you that a very critical N.O. said to me "That man knows how to paint a ship."

Thank you again, old shipmate – and again for giving me so much pleasure, you and old Carson between you, for that hero has sent me a cigarette box of hen wood.

Yours aye,

Charles Adams

After serving on HMS *Dart* for eighteen months, on 1 April 1933 George moved from that ship to the Mechanical Training Establishment at HMS *Victory*, the Royal Navy shore barracks at Portsmouth, where his duties included being an Instructional Officer for Leading Stokers' classes. He remained at HMS *Victory* for nearly two years, but his time in this post, away from home but not at sea, may not have been a happy one.

George's natural reserve, always an element in his character, combined with a possible lack of confidence to produce a mixed and rather critical officer's report in December 1934 from Engineer Commander Baker:

> Loyal and capable. Rather lacking in personality and would do better if he asserted himself more. Sound common sense. Generally v. reliable but apt to give information without having thoroughly investigated the question.

On 22 February 1935 George joined HMS *Shamrock*, a destroyer of the Mediterranean fleet based in Gibraltar. In May that year King George V celebrated his Silver Jubilee, marking his twenty-five years on the throne, and in Plymouth a Silver Jubilee service was held on 6 May 1935 at St Andrew's Parish Church, the city's mother church. The service was for the city's schools, and George's daughter Beryl, nearly sixteen, attended with her class from Devonport Secondary School for Girls.

By this time George was out in Gibraltar, the promontory located adjacent to southern Spain on the narrow Straits between Europe and North Africa at the entrance to the Mediterranean. It is known to British servicemen as 'The Rock', from the great limestone ridge whose sheer cliffs rise above the territory with views across the Straits to the coastal mountain of Jebel Musa in Morocco. This and the Rock were reputed to be the Pillars of Hercules of Greek mythology, marking the edge of the ancient world.

Gibraltar was captured from Spain by an Anglo-Dutch force in 1704 in the War of the Spanish Succession, and was ceded to Great Britain by the Treaty of Utrecht in 1713. The British established a naval base and dockyard there, and for 300 years Gibraltar has been, and in 2015 remains, a British Overseas Territory, despite Spain's frequent attempts to reclaim it and to obstruct access in and out of the confined territory, which is only 2.6 square miles in area.

Along with Malta and Suez, Britain's possession of Gibraltar allowed its Royal Navy to control the Straits of Gibraltar, one of the vital staging posts and 'choke points' on the sea route to the Middle and Far East, India and Australasia. George had called in at Gibraltar several times during his naval career, but his service on HMS *Shamrock* from February 1935 until September 1936 was the first time he had been stationed there.

George was based in Gibraltar during the period when, across the border in Spain, the Spanish Civil War was being fought between the Republican Government of Spain and General Franco's right-wing Nationalists. Although the British Government was neutral as far as the Spanish Civil War was concerned, the historian Antony Beevor suggests, in his definitive study of this conflict,[109] that many Royal Navy officers in Gibraltar were sympathetic to Franco's Nationalists, particularly following the scare of the Invergordon Mutiny in 1931, which had raised the spectre of a socialist uprising in Britain. British warships may even have assisted the Nationalists by supplying ammunition to them via Gibraltar together with intelligence on support by the Russians to the Republicans.

Many refugees who were sympathetic to Franco fled the fighting by crossing into Gibraltar, and they gave British journalists accounts of alleged atrocities by the Republicans. Despite maintaining an official line of non-intervention in the Spanish Civil War, the British Government, and in particular the Foreign Secretary, Anthony Eden, pursued a policy which on balance appeared to favour the victory of the fascist forces of Franco, supported by Hitler and Mussolini, rather than see the victory of a Republican Government which was perceived as communist. In Gibraltar itself, the Royal Navy may have provided communications facilities for a German general to enable him to speak to his superiors in Germany, Italy and Portugal, and the battleship HMS *Queen Elizabeth* was actually deployed in order to prevent Republican warships shelling Algeciras.

Not surprisingly, George gave no indication of these events or of naval sympathies in his letters home, where in any event the British population was more concerned about the position of their monarchy. King George V died on 20 January 1936, to be succeeded by the Prince whom George had met on his Canadian trip in 1919 and who now became King Edward VIII. A month later, on 12 February 1936, George wrote from HMS *Shamrock* in Gibraltar to his daughter Beryl, who had written to him about the passing of the King and how she had felt about it:

My Darling Daughter,

I was delighted to get your letter of the 22nd and the nice present you sent me for my birthday and am sorry I am so long in acknowledging it. If the ship moved about to enable us to see fresh places I would write more frequently and describe my impressions of such new places, but we seem fated to remain at Gib until my time expires to leave, and very glad I shall be when that time comes because I am fairly looking forward to being with you again after such a long exile.

I was interested to read your account of listening to the announcements about the King dying. It must have been very solemn to hear Big Ben striking in intervals of the last moments of the late King's reign. I expect you were very interested to hear the proclamation of King Edward VIII and although I wish the new King a long reign, I hope the announcer was wrong when he said you would probably never hear anything like it again in your life time, it is very possible that you may live to hear another Queen Elizabeth proclaimed to the Throne.

I was pleased to know you liked my watercolours enough to stick them in your autograph album. I have not done any more lately, but will send you on some from time to time when I am able to settle down to some more painting and am sorry I have not included something in this letter.

Last week I climbed up the Rock for the first time since I came here. It is rather steep in places, but on a lovely day like last Wednesday when I made this effort it was worthwhile. In places it is awfully nice up there, lots of wild narcissi and flowers I don't know the names of are out now, and the trees and shrubs are beginning to look nice after the rains. There are lots of places I have not seen as yet on the Upper Rock. I have not explored the galleries or a large cave called St Michael's Cave which is one of the sights of the fortress. When I came down I was fortunate to see the 'Ceremony of the Keys' being carried out by the Gordon Highlanders, it is on Wednesdays that this is performed now. The Pipers marched to Government House where the Key Sergeant comes out with the Keys and takes up position between an escort for the Keys behind the band, which then plays along the Main Street to a place called Grand Case Mates. There the Pipers played for about half an hour slow marches and quick, they looked very fine in their elaborate kilted uniforms. At one time all the gates leading into Gib were locked regularly at Sunset every evening, but now the gates leading into Spain are the only ones shut, the present ceremony is just to keep up the tradition and is purely spectacular.

Give my love to Mummy and Ida, may God Bless and keep you safe in health and grant I may see you soon again,

Your ever loving Daddy xxx

George's comments about the new King are remarkably prescient. In 1936 Edward VIII remained unmarried at the age of forty-one, and his reputation for being interested in a succession of married women was no doubt well-known in the higher levels of society and to others with whom Edward regularly mixed, such as naval officers. When, as Edward, Prince of Wales, he had travelled on HMS *Renown* for his Empire Trip to Canada in 1919, he had just embarked on an affair with Freda Dudley Ward, the wife of a Liberal MP, a liaison which was to last for many years. In the early 1930s, another of the Prince's mistresses was Lady Thelma Furness, the wife of Viscount Furness, a shipping magnate.

In 1934 Thelma introduced Edward to Mrs Wallis Simpson, a divorced and remarried American who had come to London with her second husband, Ernest Simpson. The Prince, who 'had caught the American spirit' on his trip to the United States in 1919, became infatuated with Wallis. But Edward's father, George V, was horrified by the prospect of his son and heir forming a long-term relationship with a woman whose status as a divorcee would be unacceptable to the majority of his British subjects and in the Dominions of his Empire such as Canada and Australia.

In 1935 the old King said of Edward to his Prime Minister, Stanley Baldwin: "After I am dead, the boy will ruin himself in twelve months" – and he was also heard to say "I pray to God that my eldest son will never marry and have children, and that nothing will come between Bertie and Lilibet and the throne."[110]

However, Edward's private life was not the subject of comment in the United Kingdom's newspapers nor on its radio, and his amorous activities and affair with Mrs Simpson were unknown to most of the British public. The British press barons and the BBC had a pact of secrecy with the monarchy and the Government that they would not report on Edward's new liaison.

So when George Lancaster wrote from Gibraltar to his daughter in February 1936 after George V's death and commented, 'It is very possible that you may live to hear another Queen Elizabeth proclaimed to the Throne', had he heard rumours of the new King's affair and crisis that, unknown to the British public at home, was then playing out in London between Baldwin's Government and the new King? Was talk of the late King's own concerns about his son, expressed in his prayer 'that nothing will come between Bertie and Lilibet and the throne' circulating in the officers' messes of the Royal Navy overseas?

By the time of his accession to the throne in January 1936, Edward was determined to marry Wallis, who by then was seeking a divorce from Ernest Simpson. The proposal that a twice-divorced woman, who was also an American and a commoner, should become Queen was totally unacceptable to the Government, most of the British Establishment and to the leaders of the Dominions of the Empire. That she should be the King's consort was also anathema to most religious leaders, and particularly the Church of England, as the monarch was the head of the Anglican Church, which forbade a divorced person from remarrying in church if the former spouse still lived.

The British press and radio were not reporting any of this, but the American press was doing so to a US readership excited by the prospect of one of their own marrying the 'King of England'. Had naval officers stationed in Gibraltar, including George, seen these American newspaper reports and discussed the likelihood of Wallis becoming Queen? Many of those officers would have met Edward as the Prince of Wales, or observed him at close quarters, and probably discussed the activities, public and private, of their future King. Most Royal Navy officers, being conservative by nature with a strong loyalty to the Crown and Empire, would have been horrified by the idea of Wallis becoming their Queen – religious views apart, divorce was still regarded as socially unacceptable. She was also an American, which meant she was 'looked down on' by a significant element of the class-conscious officers of the Senior Service, and their wives.

Various proposals were put to Edward by Prime Minister Baldwin throughout 1936, including the concept of a 'morganatic' marriage – that he might marry Wallis, but she would not become Queen. The King had not yet been crowned and a solution had to be found before his coronation, which was set for May 1937. Still these discussions as to the future of their monarchy were kept secret from the British public, and the whole of the British press kept to the agreement not to publish any reports of this constitutional crisis.

One Wednesday evening in December 1936 the sixteen-year-old Beryl Lancaster was at home in Devonport when she heard the newspaper boy out in the street shouting about a special edition. The previous day, 1 December, Dr Alfred Blunt, the Bishop of Bradford, had made a speech to his Diocesan Conference in which he had commented on the King's need for divine grace, stating, "We hope that he is aware of his need. Some of us wish that he gave more positive signs of his awareness."

Although Dr Blunt had made no reference to the King's wish to marry Mrs Simpson, and later claimed he was only referring to the King's lack of regular churchgoing, the British press interpreted this as the first public comment on the crisis and a reason to break their silence. The King's situation made front-page news and special editions were rushed out, including the one by the *Western Evening Herald* in Plymouth on 2 December.

Incongruous as it may appear in our current world of constant celebrity exposés, paparazzi photos and phone hacking, this was the first time that most of the British public learnt of their King's intention to marry Mrs Simpson. Once the news was out, many supported the King, but the weight of public opinion was against him. Edward was still determined to marry Wallis Simpson, and on 10 December 1936, only nine days after the press had released the news of their relationship, he abdicated from the throne.

The next day he made a BBC radio broadcast to explain to the British people that he was unable to do his job 'as I would have wished' without the support of 'the woman I love'. He then left for France with the title of Duke of Windsor, married Wallis, and remained in exile from Great Britain for the rest of his life.

Edward's visit with his Duchess to meet Adolf Hitler in October 1937, and their alleged pro-Nazi sympathies, supported the commonly held view that he would have proved a most unsuitable and even dangerous monarch had he kept the throne. During the Second World War the British Government appointed him as the Governor of Bermuda and sent him with Wallis to that Caribbean island, probably to reduce the risk of Hitler making him the puppet king of a conquered Britain.

In the Lancaster family, as in many other British homes, Mrs Simpson was forever after referred to as 'that woman'. For George, who had had the honour of serving on a ship escorting Edward, Prince of Wales, to Canada, and who had proudly stood to attention as the Prince inspected him and his fellow crew members on HMS *Dauntless* in August 1919, this failure of the royal heir to perform his duty to the Crown and Empire must have amounted to a bitter betrayal.

In his letter to Beryl in February 1936 George had referred to his own 'long exile' and being 'fated to remain' in Gibraltar. It was the birthplace of his grandmother Ellen, but he clearly did not enjoy his posting of some twenty months based on the Rock, where the opportunities for off-duty recreation were much more limited than in Malta or Hong Kong. As an officer who had been promoted from the lower deck, he may have found it difficult to command crewmen from a similar social background, some of whom may have resented his promotion. As an engineering officer he would have been looked down on by some of the more snobbish 'deck' officers on the bridge who still regarded engineers as their inferiors.

George was now forty-nine, and after twenty-seven years in the

Royal Navy, including many long periods away at sea or stationed overseas, he was clearly wanting to return to his family in Devonport and looking forward to retirement. While in Gibraltar, George received news from his wife Ida that her mother, Mary Horne – Polly – had died at home in Devonport on 7 January 1936, aged sixty-nine, her husband David surviving her. The death of a parent, especially the first parent to die, is usually a difficult time. Although Ida was used to George's long absences away from home, grieving alone without her husband's support was hard, and he wished to be with her.

The report of his commanding officer on HMS *Shamrock* indicated that George had become rather withdrawn and was no longer finding naval life congenial. In September 1936, Commander J.H. McNair wrote that Lancaster was a:

> Thoroughly reliable officer, and has kept department in high state of efficiency. Is shy and consequently not of much assistance in the mess on cruises but with those he knows he is a very pleasant messmate – Cdr. Macnair.
>
> Concur with above report – Rear Adl. Pipon.

HMS *Shamrock* was George's last ship, and he received his discharge in November 1936 after returning to Britain from Gibraltar. On 4 February 1937, his fiftieth birthday, he was placed on the Retired List, fifty being the normal retirement age for naval officers and men. On 24 October that year his father, George Lancaster senior, died, aged seventy-nine, in the Royal Naval Hospital at Stonehouse, leaving Emma a widow.

George had mentioned his watercolours in his letter to Beryl, and once retired he was able to pursue his main hobby of watercolour painting. He had taken up sketching and painting as an ideal leisure pursuit while serving at sea as he needed only a pencil, a small paper pad, a few small brushes and a box of paints to keep on board ship. While in China he had sketched and painted a few local scenes and his ship, *Berwick*. Self-taught, he clearly wished to improve his artistic technique in retirement and purchased several instructional booklets on the subject, such as *The Art of Landscape Painting in Water Colours*; *How to sketch sea, town and country*; *Water Colour Sketching*; and *How to sketch from life*. He also tried out the very different medium of oil painting, and bought books called *Oil Colour Painting* and *Simple Rules for Painting in Oils*. His sketchbook includes several paintings of the Devon coast and of boats on the Barbican outside the Plymouth Customs House, sketches of Devon estuaries and of local buildings.

The Lancaster family had acquired a car by the mid-1930s, a 'Baby Austin', the Austin 7, which had become extremely popular and in 1931 sold for £118. George would drive Ida and the girls out on excursions to Dartmoor and the coast. They also joined the many locals who still flocked to the Hoe to watch warships sailing out into the Channel through Plymouth Sound or returning after a long tour of duty overseas. The Tinside open-air swimming pool, an Art Deco lido, was opened off the foreshore of Plymouth Hoe in 1935, just along from the Promenade Pier and below the bandstand next to Smeaton's Tower. Beryl enjoyed regular swims at the Tinside pool.

Other leisure pursuits included trips to the cinema, always popular with the Lancaster family, and with thousands of other Plymothians. Film audiences increased after the screening of the first talkies in Plymouth in 1930, and the Gaumont and Regent cinema houses, each with a capacity of over 3,000 seats, both opened in Plymouth in November 1931.

When her father retired in 1937, Beryl was in her last year at Devonport Secondary School for Girls. She was not as academic as Ida in her interests, but she did well at school, played in the hockey team and was awarded book prizes, one for being first in her Sunday School class in January 1934. She developed an excellent general knowledge, always listening to the radio, and was interested in current affairs, like her father. She enjoyed reading, although perhaps not such serious literature as her elder sister – Richmal Crompton's *Just William* stories, first published in the 1920s, were a great favourite of hers.

Beryl went on a school trip to Belgium in 1936, the girls travelling with their teachers from Plymouth to Kent by train and from Dover to Ostend by cross-channel ferry. They visited Brussels, and Ypres to see the Menin Gate which had been built there in 1927 to commemorate the British and Empire servicemen killed in the Great War. The school party also went to Bruges, where they toured around the medieval architecture and canals of that historic city. They visited the Béguinage, a Benedictine religious community for single or widowed women, where Beryl bought postcards and a little bronze bell in the shape of one of the

Béguine nuns. It was to be her last trip abroad for twenty-five years.

Ida was pursuing her teaching career, and in August 1937 she also went on a trip abroad, going with friends to Paris to see an art exhibition and to look at the shops – although, as she wrote on a postcard to her sister, 'of course we could not afford to buy anything'.

At home in Devonport, George was looking forward to a peaceful and calm retirement.

Young Ida

14 Beresford Street, Stoke, Devonport, 22nd July 1928

Dear Daddy,

I had your letter of the 29th yesterday. I am glad you stirred your stumps
about replying, it looks as though my sarcasm brought forth a little fruit.

(Ida, aged fourteen, to George.)

George's elder daughter, Ida – named after her mother – was born on 24
February 1914, and she was their only child until the arrival of Beryl in
June 1920. The photographs of the young Ida show a slightly chubby
fair-haired child who grew up into an intelligent and gracious young
woman who clearly knew her own mind.

What little we know of her childhood and adolescence comes
from various family snapshots. An early photo of baby Ida, taken in
1915, shows an infant with blonde ringlets sitting next to her rather
nervous-looking mother, Ida, who is dressed in a distinctly Edwardian
costume of a full-length skirt and buttoned long-sleeved blouse. Other
photos show Ida and Beryl together in Malta, where they lived with
their parents from 1922 to 1924. At this stage Ida was ten or eleven, and
in the photos she looks rather careworn and feeling responsible for her
younger sister, Beryl, then aged two or three.

In the late 1920s there are various family snapshots of Ida and
Beryl with their parents at the beach or at picnics on Dartmoor. Ida,
aged twelve, is enjoying the company of her cousin Miriam who was
the same age, and there was clearly an affinity between the two girls,
with Beryl, aged five, standing to one side of them and probably
being a rather naughty and annoying little sister. Snapshots of family
outings to the beach include one taken at Torquay that shows George,
in his long-sleeved shirt, waistcoat and hat, on the beach building
a sandcastle with both his daughters. More formal family photographs
taken by a professional photographer show Ida with her two daughters,
an adolescent Ida not looking straight at the camera but away into the

middle distance, while Beryl, aged about seven, and her mother look directly at the photographer.

From September 1924, after their return that year from Malta, Ida attended Devonport Municipal Secondary School for Girls (later Devonport High School for Girls).

Ida wrote every month to her father while he was in the Far East from 1928 to 1930, serving on the China Station. Two examples of these letters indicate that she was an intelligent and perhaps rather precocious fourteen-year-old.

14 Beresford Street, 22nd July 1928

Dear Daddy,

I had your letter of the 29th yesterday. I am glad you stirred your stumps about replying, it looks as though my sarcasm brought forth a little fruit.

We went to Sandway yesterday afternoon and Beryl and I went out bathing. It was the first time I had been in this year and it was a trifle chilly.

When I had your letter yesterday I thought from what you had written you would prefer me to take Arts and when Mummy had her second letter by the evening post I found out that you had said as much. Really, I think you might have told me which you really preferred instead of saying I had better do as I think. I cannot say for certain, but I expect I shall take Arts considering this term's results. Perhaps I had better tell you the list – Geometry 30.8% (all right you need not look disgusted it's not my fault), Arithmetic 65%, Algebra 77.5%. I was top both for Literature and Composition but I cannot remember the marks. I know I had A for each. History 82%, French 75%, Latin 77%, Botany 83%, Needlework 74%, Chemistry 79%, Drawing 41%, Cookery 49%, altogether I have about 68%. I expect you will answer this letter quickly enough, to blow me up. If I take Arts I shall take History, English, French, Latin, Arithmetic, not Geography or Algebra, Geometry. In Arts drawing is an extra subject, I think Botany is taken in any case until after the School Certificate. Yesterday morning Miss Watts asked us which we would prefer to take and I said Arts. She said we did not always take what we ourselves chose, they have to decide for us because it affects our whole career and they know much more about it than we do. I expect I shall know definitely which I am taking within a day or two as we break up on Wednesday.

Last Monday in History lesson Bessie was misbehaving as usual.

Miss Bodmin said, "Bessie come here and sit in the front."

Bessie picked up her books and marched to a seat in the back.

Miss Bodmin – "Bessie I said you were to sit in the front."

Bessie – "Well Miss Bodmin I'll be good here."

Miss Bodmin – "That does not matter, come and sit here."

Bessie picked up her books again with a sigh and said, "Strikes me I'm a blinking Pickford's van Miss Bodmin."

At this point in the letter there is a drawing of mother Ida, sitting in a deck chair. Ida (daughter) comments:

This is just to show how unfair Miss Bate was when she marked my drawing paper. I expect you can all see who it is. It is quite true to life, Mummy is sitting in the deck chair with those yellow sun goggles on saying, "Give me a piece of toffee Ida and I will not worry you any more." She has said it quite six times already. It is wonderful how thoughtful she can be; toffee is not good for my teeth you know.

Our red rambler is looking so beautiful now that I intend taking a photo of it when I get a film, with Beryl in her carnival gypsy dress underneath. By the way if you do not send Beryl a letter soon she will not write any more to you.

Please do not forget my remittance, I am still 'stoney' because I have not received it yet. Hurry up with my next lesson, China is really a wonderful place! Your loving daughter,

Ida xxx

PS I wish you could give your daughter a lesson in handwriting for I think it is vile. I have never seen worse.

PSS I wish you could give your wife a lesson in punctuation.

An interesting, perhaps rather cheeky, letter from a teenage daughter to her father on the other side of the world – but one in which there is clearly a warmth and a rapport between the two of them and a great importance placed on the value of education and doing well at school.

Ida, now fifteen, wrote another letter to her father on 3 March 1929, sent to 'Mr. G Lancaster CD. Eng. RN HMS *Berwick*, China, c/o GPO London via Siberia':

Dear Daddy,

Yesterday afternoon Mummy and I both had letters from you and Beryl her postcard. I must thank you for the bag you sent me; it came in plenty of time for my birthday and I was delighted with it. Beryl wants one for her birthday and Mummy also says she would like one but if I were you I should not buy any for them, I object to three people in the same family having identical bags, and as I received mine first, I think my wishes should be respected. Of course, I do not suppose they will be, and you will buy the bags, but you must not buy ones which are exactly like mine; because I say you must not.

I took my two certificates out to show Miss Kellow last Thursday, she has some of hers framed; and I was thinking, if I have my six framed, they would look quite imposing, especially if I decided to take pupils, which I most emphatically will not. I have started on that Chopin Album (that also sounds imposing doesn't it) and it now looks quite respectable as I have sewn it together and covered it.

Why have you given up smoking? This, my dear man, is a question to which I want an answer, and it is not to be completely ignored as were several on my previous letter. I think you had better unearth your pipe again, because I have made you a tobacco pouch at school and I am not going to have my money wasted, especially seeing I have none to waste. At present I am waiting to get something to go inside, you know the kind of thing, it keeps out air or water, I cannot remember which.

Several of us at school are beginning to wake up to the fact that we have to take 'General Schools' next June 12 months. I for one had not realised how close it was. You should hear the fuss Mummy makes over Beryl if she happens to have marks for her homework. It is "Beryl this" and "Beryl that", she is petted and pennies are showered upon her, but if as I remarked yesterday I by any marvellous chance happened to Matric[111] when I take the exam no fuss whatever would be forthcoming. I should come home, say, "Mummy I have got Matric." Mummy most interested, would casually reply, "Oh have you, lay the cloth for dinner will you." And that would be the fuss I should get.

Kathleen, Dorothy and Ralph Churchward were out here yesterday to tea. I don't think you realised I should be seeing Kathleen so soon did you? She said they had had an 8 page epistle from you; (whilst Mummy and I receive only 3!) And this is the important part; you said that you hoped

267

Kathleen was not as saucy as I am, and that it was a good job for me you were so far away. What, precisely did you mean by that? I think that it is a very good job for you that you are not nearer, because you would certainly hear more than you bargained for when you wrote that stuff. Another thing I don't think you would have said anything at all like that if you had had the remotest idea of my hearing it so quickly. It is not safe, you know to write anything about other people, because you never know where it will go to. I should like to enlighten you upon the subject of the picture which I drew of your cabin. It was not meant for a plan, and I do know how to draw one, it was merely meant to give you a general idea of it and I think I remember details rather well.

The photos arrived one day last week. They are quite good but I do not think the Officers on your ship are very good looking, with the exception of yourself of course. If they held a beauty competition on your ship you would be the winner; but I should like to know how you always manage to get in the most awkward positions you are right underneath one of the guns and consequently cannot stand up straight.[112] If ever you have another take a hop skip and jump for a place where at least it is possible to stand up straight. I am afraid I have exhausted all my news, what little I have, but before I close I should like to express my thanks for receiving a non-geographical letter from you.
Your loving daughter,
Ida xxx

In another letter Ida tells George of her mother's concerns about money:

The family exchequer is in a very bad way. Your timid wife is afraid to buy herself a new coat. I am always being told "I can't afford it, I must wait for the sales, because Daddy will be angry because I have not saved enough." Will you kindly cable home and order her to buy a new winter outfit…a cheque of £20 or over would be much appreciated…is my monthly allowance to be increased on the strength of your promotion?

Ida was taking her Royal Academy piano exams (the Lancasters had a piano at home, like many families in those days before television) and she writes to her father about her examination pieces, including ones by Bach, Mozart and Chopin – 'so you better begin to train your ear'.

In October 1928 she tells her father about her forthcoming confirmation at Advent, another of the events in his daughters' lives that he must miss:

Mummy said something about having my photo done so that you will be able to see how I look. If you are not present in person, you will be in spirit…

Ida's letters demonstrate a remarkable degree of maturity and fluency in writing, the product of a fine education at her girls' state school. They are also proof of her loving family relationships, despite the long absences of her father. As their photographs confirm she was close to her sister Beryl, who was six years younger, even though in her letters to her father Ida does assume the role of the superior sibling. She tells George that 'Beryl is as saucy as ever' and when it comes to their need to buy new clothes, 'Beryl of course does not count, she can wear my leave off clothing'.

Ida's School Matriculation certificate in September 1930 confirmed that she had taken the General School Examination (the equivalent of our current GCSEs) and had obtained credits in English, Elementary Mathematics, History (English and European), Latin and French.

Ida was a Prefect in the Sixth Form at Devonport Secondary School for Girls and pursued 'a course of Higher Study' (the equivalent of A Levels) from September 1930 to July 1932, and was awarded a Higher School Certificate in Latin, English, French and Modern History.

She went straight on from school to study for an honours degree in history at the University College of the South West of England in Exeter from September 1932 to July 1934. In the college photograph dated May 1933 she is sitting on the ground in the second row at the front, a serious-looking young woman in her college gown, surrounded by a hundred or so rather prim-looking young ladies and a rather greater number of very earnest-looking young men. That Ida had secured a place at the University College – the forerunner of the University of Exeter – was quite an achievement for a woman in the 1930s.

Soon after arriving in Exeter she decided not to continue her history course, and instead trained at the College to become a teacher after completing a two-year diploma. Her certificate, dated 17 July 1934, confirmed that she had completed the two-year course from 1932 to 1934 'satisfactorily' and had passed the Final Examination of the South West Board of the Examination and Certification of Teachers in 'the principles and practice of teaching Hygiene; theory and practice of Physical Training; English (advanced); History; Mathematics and Music (advanced)'.

A testimonial given to Ida in May 1934 from the University College reads:

> Miss I. Lancaster is just completing two years' training as a teacher in the Education Department of the above college, having given up an Honours Degree Course in History because she wished to become a teacher of young children.
>
> She is an intelligent student and her work in academic subjects, History and Mathematics, has shown her intellectual grasp and ability to plan her studies. She is conscientious and painstaking, prepares all her work thoroughly and has a growing appreciation of results and modification in methods necessary to secure them.
>
> As a teacher of young children, she is gentle, gracious and encouraging. She has a pleasing manner and voice and an easy flow of well-chosen words which would make her oral lessons specially successful.
>
> She has taken Advanced Music, is a good pianist and can teach singing. She is keen on games and has been Vice Captain of the Netball Club. With further study and training which she intends to take, she should become a very pleasant and effective Junior School Teacher.
>
> *S.Y. Mathias M.A.*
> *Lecturer in Education.*
> *Stanley H. Watkins M.A.*
> *Professor of Education.*

After Ida had left the University College she took a further one-year course at the Froebel Educational Institute in Roehampton, southwest London, where she specialised in teaching junior pupils, studied educational psychology and trained in First Aid. In 1935 she secured a job back in Plymouth at the Trinity J.M. & I. school (Trinity Junior, Middle and Infants School). She stayed there until 1937, and when she left at the end of the summer term the headmaster of the school, Charles V. Wilson, gave her this letter of reference dated 27 July 1937:

> Miss Ida Lancaster has served on the staff of this School as Certificated Assistant Mistress for two years. During that period she has had charge of the Nursery Class and has given satisfaction to His Majesty's Inspectors, the managers and myself.
>
> Miss Lancaster has specialised in the teaching of handiwork, speech training and singing and her ability to play the piano has been a great asset in developing the last-named subject in the whole of the Infant Section.
>
> She is a good disciplinarian and her quiet, gentle manner attracts boys and girls and enables her to bring out the best that is in them. Her work is well prepared, the lessons are taken in good style and quite a feature of her work is her aptitude for individual attention. She is zealous, painstaking and very devoted to her duties.
>
> Miss Lancaster has taken the greatest possible interest in the general welfare of these little children who come from one of the poorest districts in the city. She is well versed in the duties connected with Infants' School work and her contact with the parents is all that could be desired.
>
> Miss Lancaster's qualifications and abilities especially fit her Infant Sectional work and from my practical knowledge of her worth I can most confidently recommend her.

The letter came in an envelope marked 'Plymouth Education Authority', addressed to Miss Ida Lancaster as a reference that she could take herself to her next post.

Ida was a well-read woman, with a personal book collection that included several Shakespeare plays and Jane Austen's *Persuasion* and *Northanger Abbey*; tales from *Le Morte d'Arthur* and Longfellow's *Hiawatha*; and stories from *The Iliad* and *The Adventures of Odysseus*.

We have no record of where Ida went to teach after leaving the Trinity Infants' School in July 1937, although we know she was able to enjoy a brief holiday in Paris in August 1937. Some formal photos taken of Ida, two of her alone and one with her sister Beryl in Plymouth in 1937, show an attractive, self-assured and gracious young woman of twenty-three.

Beryl left Devonport High School for Girls in February 1938 at the age of seventeen with her School Certificate in English, History, Latin and French and joined the Naval Construction Department in Devonport Dockyard, where she worked as a secretary. Now that both their daughters were grown up and employed and George was retired, he and his wife Ida could look forward to a life of calm domesticity together in Crownhill after so many years of separation while he was away at sea.

At some stage in late 1937 or during the following year, their daughter Ida became seriously ill, and by the autumn of 1938 she had given up teaching and her parents were nursing her at home.

Ida had cancer. This was probably only diagnosed at an advanced stage, as there were then few reliable tests for the disease. A considerable bar to effective diagnosis and treatment was the fact that in the late 1930s, and for decades after, cancer was still the 'taboo' illness which few would discuss openly, and it was standard practice for doctors and families not to inform patients of the true nature of their illness.[113] Many people even believed cancer to be infectious. In such a climate of fear, Ida's parents told neighbours and friends that she was suffering from tuberculosis rather than identify her condition as cancer.

There were few options for the treatment of cancer in the 1930s apart from surgery, if the tumour was operable, or radiotherapy, a relatively new procedure, with high doses of radiation being risky and often ineffective. Although penicillin had been discovered in 1928, antibiotics were not available, and were not widely used until the Second World War. Chemotherapy drugs were not developed until after that war. Palliative care and pain relief were not used to support cancer patients until the 1960s through the pioneering work of Dame Cicely Saunders's hospice movement.

We do not know what surgery or other treatment Ida received, if any, or whether she was admitted to hospital during her illness. There was no National Health Service in England in 1939 and health care was very patchy, available in a range of charitable voluntary hospitals dependent on philanthropy and donations, or in expensive private institutions and nursing homes. Access to free treatment and medicines was fairly limited and depended on contributions to the scheme established by Lloyd George's National Health Insurance Act in 1911, a scheme which only covered wage-earners and did not extend to their family dependants.

Serious illness could cause real financial problems, and although George may have been able to afford some professional medical care for his daughter, it was her family who mainly looked after Ida at home.

While Europe was moving to the brink of war to resist Hitler's aggression, the Lancasters were coping with their own terrible personal crisis. In later life Beryl rarely mentioned that time. She did say that she was grateful to Neville Chamberlain for trying to appease Hitler and coming back from their meeting in Munich on 30 September 1938 with that piece of paper proclaiming 'Peace in our time', because it gave the family another year of peace to care for her sister.

On 27 July 1939 George's wife Ida heard that her widowed father David Horne had died, aged seventy-eight, at his home in George Street, Devonport, his son David by his side.

Three days later, on 30 July, her daughter Ida also died, at home in 14 Beresford Street. She was twenty-five. George's brother, Alfred Lancaster, registered the death, and on the certificate the cause is stated as carcinoma of the liver and ovaries.

Ida was buried in Weston Mill Cemetery in Plymouth. Her epitaph there reads:

Sacred to the loving memory of IDA.

Beloved elder daughter of George and Ida Lancaster.

Passed to the higher life July 30th 1939 aged 25 years.

In God's keeping.

Blitz

Just over a month after Ida's death, on the morning of Sunday 3 September 1939, the Prime Minister, Neville Chamberlain, announced in a BBC radio broadcast to the British public that 'This country is now at war with Germany'.

In the six years since Adolf Hitler had become Chancellor of Germany he had pursued a policy of rearmament of his country and had remilitarised the Rhineland area bordering France, both in contravention of the Treaty of Versailles. The Nazis had also embarked on their programme of violent persecution of Jews and other ethnic groups, as well as disabled people, homosexuals and others perceived as 'anti-social'. In March 1938 Hitler's troops marched into Austria to enforce its *Anschluss*, or union, with Germany, and that summer he proposed to take over the Sudetenland area of Czechoslovakia inhabited by three million Germans. At Munich in September 1938 Chamberlain, with the support of the influential appeasement lobby in Britain and the French Prime Minister, had agreed to Hitler's demands, expecting to secure 'Peace in our Time'.

But Hitler wished to extend his new order across Europe. In March 1939 he invaded the rest of Czechoslovakia and then set his sights on the Free State of Danzig, where its mainly German and Nazi-voting population wanted union with Germany. This was a direct challenge to the independence of Poland, because if Hitler obtained Danzig, Poland's borders and national sovereignty, as settled at Versailles in 1919, would be under threat from the Führer's ever-expanding territorial ambitions.

Great Britain, now recognising Hitler's threat to democracy and stability in Europe, agreed with Poland to guarantee its borders, and with France opened negotiations with Soviet Russia to try to form an alliance against Hitler. But in August 1939 Russia's leader, Stalin, astounded the world by making a 'non-aggression' pact with Hitler, together with an agreement to partition Poland between Germany and Russia.

Germany invaded Poland on 1 September 1939 and failed to respond to Britain's ultimatum that it would declare war on Germany if Hitler did not withdraw from Poland by 11 a.m. on 3 September. After Chamberlain's announcement that morning, mobilisation of Great Britain's armed forces, and the call-up of civilian men aged between eighteen and forty-one, began immediately.

In common with other naval officers who had retired before the war, under the National Service (Armed Forces) Act 1939 George was eligible for recall back into the Navy even though he was by then fifty-two. But the outbreak of war occurred less than five weeks after Ida's death on 31 July 1939. George's naval record states that:

7.9.39 – sent medical certificate stating that he is suffering from neurasthenia and is unable to follow his employment.

19.11.39 – medical certificate received stating Mr. G. S. Lancaster is still suffering from neurasthenia.

Neurasthenia was a commonly used medical term in the inter-war years to describe a nervous disorder or stress. No mention is made on George's naval record of the circumstances of his condition – the recent death of his daughter.

At that time many, and perhaps most, families of his generation would have lost a father, brother, son or other close relative in the Great War when nearly a million British and Empire servicemen died. Infant mortality was also very common at that time, as were adult deaths from heart failure and – the great taboo illness – cancer. Influenza was a major killer too, and the global pandemic of 1918–19 caused more deaths worldwide than the Great War, with some 250,000 deaths in the United Kingdom.

The rituals of death – the formal mourning, the drawing of curtains, the wearing of black for up to a year afterwards – were strictly observed, but in that less demonstrative era when emotions were kept firmly in check, dwelling on such a loss was discouraged and there was perhaps less support from friends and family than would occur now, let alone bereavement counselling. Then, as now, many people thought it more helpful, or less embarrassing for them, not to even mention the death, as if the person who had passed away had never existed. The bereaved were instead sustained by their religious faith and many turned to spiritualism, a movement purporting to be in touch with the departed in the afterlife which flourished particularly in the 1920s and 1930s after the Great War, and again after the Second World War.

George's sister Ellen told her own family at that time that she thought George and Ida would never get over their loss of Ida. Parents actually never 'get over' the death of their child, at whatever age, nor do they 'move on'. George and Ida were undoubtedly devastated by their daughter's death at the age of twenty-five and they would have lived every day with the enduring trauma of losing their child to cancer. But the Lancasters' grieving remained private, the damage internal, and their bereavement was quickly subsumed by the dictates and privations of another world war.

The period from September 1939 to May 1940, when there was little active fighting except at sea, is called by historians the time of the 'Phoney War'. But for naval families in Plymouth that early part of the war brought fear and grief. After leaving Devonport on 3 September, the aircraft carrier HMS *Courageous* was torpedoed in the Western Approaches on 17 September 1939 by a German submarine, the first British warship to be sunk by the enemy. She sank with the loss of 519 men, leaving hundreds of families in Plymouth bereaved.

In May 1940 the British Expeditionary Force was cornered in northeast France by the advancing German armies, and Plymouth was one of the reception ports for thousands of British, French and Belgian servicemen who were evacuated by the flotilla of little ships from the beaches at Dunkirk. Over the summer of 1940 Hitler's armies occupied the Netherlands, Belgium and France. As Germany's forces swept across France in May and June 1940, thousands of refugees from France and the Channel Islands also arrived at Millbay Docks in Plymouth.

Several warships of the French Navy escaped from the shipyard in Brest in Brittany just before German troops arrived, sailing to Portsmouth and Plymouth. France surrendered and concluded an Armistice with Germany on 22 June 1940, Hitler forcing the French leader Marshal Pétain to sign it in the same railway carriage in the Forest of Compiègne where Germany had signed its Armistice with the Allies after its defeat in 1918. In Britain the Government of Winston Churchill, who had succeeded Chamberlain, ordered that all the French naval vessels in

British ports surrender to the Royal Navy to forestall them sailing back to German control.

The French submarine *Surcouf*, then the largest submarine in the world, was berthed in the naval base at Devonport when a Royal Navy boarding party of some thirty men arrived on 3 July 1940 to take control of the vessel. The French naval officers on *Surcouf* were not prepared to take down their flag and surrender, regarding it as a betrayal of France's honour, and there was a brief shoot-out in which three British sailors and one French sailor were killed. This was allegedly the first time that crews of the British and French navies had engaged and shed blood since Trafalgar in 1805.

In September 1940 the threat of Nazi invasion of the British Isles was at its height, and it was largely prevented by the success of the British fighter pilots of the RAF against the Luftwaffe in the Battle of Britain. It has also been claimed by some historians that the number of Royal Navy battleships and destroyers in the English Channel would also have been an effective force in fighting any German invasion fleet, and so constituted an effective deterrent to Hitler.[114]

The fighting of the war had now become 'total' and the development of aerial bombing extended the combat to civilian communities across Great Britain – the Home Front. The winter of 1940/41 saw the start of Hitler's *Blitzkrieg* – 'lightning war' – against Great Britain, and the German air force, the Luftwaffe, commenced its attacks on strategically important cities such as Liverpool, Hull, Birmingham, Coventry, Bristol and Plymouth. George's home was no longer a place of safety and refuge.

The residents of Plymouth were now in the front line. As happened across the country, everyone was issued with a gas mask and strict blackout regulations were imposed so that no lights guided the enemy bombers as they approached the city. The windows of every home were covered with sticky tape to stop smashed glass flying around, and blankets were used to stop house lights showing through the curtains.

Motor vehicles had to dim or mask their lamps, and pavement edges, tree trunks, postboxes and other roadway structures were painted white to help people navigate along the streets in the pitch dark. The blackout was strictly policed by wardens and fines imposed by the magistrates for breaches.

Plymouth was one of the prime targets for the Luftwaffe as it was a port for the Royal Navy and the site of Devonport Dockyard where warships and submarines were built, repaired and refitted for the battle at sea. There were several military barracks across the city, including the Royal Marine Barracks at Stonehouse, adjacent to the Royal William Victualling Yard, which supplied food, drink, ammunition and other essential stocks to naval vessels. Many of those ships were engaged throughout the war on convoy duties, escorting across the Atlantic the Merchant Navy ships that brought essential food and other supplies from North America to keep the British population fed and alive through six years of war.

The possibility of a land invasion of the south coast of England by German forces, particularly after the fall of France in June 1940, completely changed the lives of the civilian population. Everyone had to carry a national registration identity card to produce when required by authorised officers. As a naval base and garrison city, Plymouth was a protected area where a close watch was kept on potential aliens, and the police carried out sporadic raids in public places to check everyone's identity. A Plymouth Invasion Committee was formed to co-ordinate the civilian response to a German invasion and to liaise with the military authorities.

The Home Office had established the nationwide Civil Defence Service before the war, which directed each local authority to set up its own civil defence organisation. This was responsible for the wardens of the Air Raid Precautions (ARP) Service, as well as fire-watchers, rescue teams, first aid posts, stretcher parties, and even the local fire brigades until the National Fire Service was created in 1941. Old veterans and adolescent boys too young to join up became Local Defence Volunteers, later the Home Guard. The recruits of the Royal Observer Corps, many part-time volunteers, manned headlands and hilltops to watch out for the approach of enemy forces.

Signposts and place names were removed, road blocks with machine guns were set up at strategic points, bridges were mined and huge barrage balloons placed over vital positions across the city, designed to make enemy planes crash.

The rationing of food and clothing was introduced with strict control of prices, and while this was of course the subject of many complaints and there was a black market in many commodities, the system for the distribution of goods was generally well managed and the population did not starve. Emergency feeding centres were set up at schools and community halls across Plymouth after the raids started, and the City Council soon established permanent catering facilities as part of the national network known as 'British Restaurants', which served regular customers with hot and reasonably cheap meals throughout the war.

Shortly after the outbreak of war George and Ida left 14 Beresford Street, their home for some twenty-eight years since their marriage in 1912. George bought a newly-built house at 8 Moreton Avenue, Crownhill – 'Anson', named after an eighteenth-century British admiral. The family needed to leave Beresford Street with its dreadful memories of Ida's illness and death, and George also wished to take Ida and Beryl to a place of greater safety. Crownhill was then a suburb on the northern outskirts of Plymouth on the road to Dartmoor, farther away from the city centre and certainly from Devonport and their former home's proximity to the dockyard and, it seemed, the risk of German bombing.

Anson in Moreton Avenue was also a superior property to Beresford Street. It was a three-bedroomed semi-detached house with a garden and a garage for their car, a Baby Austin which had been acquired in the 1930s. The house was on one of the many new estates that had been built in Plymouth (and throughout England) in the inter-war years for middle-class families moving up the housing ladder who could afford to purchase their own homes.

It was also a freehold property, so George and Ida no longer had to pay the much-resented annual ground rent due at Beresford Street to Lord St Levan's Estate. Lord St Levan had remained the freehold-owner of most of the houses let to occupiers on a long lease in that part of Devonport (a type of arrangement still prevalent in the late twentieth century in areas of Plymouth and in Bristol, Manchester, Liverpool and other large cities where the annual rents due to landed estates had not been redeemed).

George, his health ostensibly restored, rejoined active service on 1 April 1940, aged fifty-three, and the man who had started his working life in Devonport Dockyard as a fourteen-year-old apprentice fitter was raised to the rank of Lieutenant Commander (Engineer). He served at HMS *Drake*, the shore training establishment at Devonport known as 'Guz' to naval crew,[115] where he worked as an instructor on the technical training of naval cadets and Engine Room Artificer recruits. The war meant there was now an urgent requirement for trained engine officers and Engine Room Artificers in the Royal Navy, and in December 1939 the overall length of the apprenticeship for the rate of an ERA was shortened by six months to four years.

For over five years, from April 1940 until September 1945, George taught recruits the subjects of mechanics and engineering and instructed them in the practical operation of turbine engines. In December 1941 the Engineer Commander at HMS *Drake* wrote on George's naval report:

> Has done excellent work as Tech. Officer to Mech. Candidates. Appears to have particular aptitude for this kind of work and has been of greatest assistance in giving lectures and preparing sketches in order to keep apace of modern engineering practice. Reserved manner but excels in conversation on serious subjects.
>
> He has conducted himself to my entire satisfaction. A most painstaking and hardworking officer. Has achieved excellent results in the technical training of Mechanician Candidates.
>
> Loyal, valuable, retention in training service recommended.

After the fall of France to the German army in June 1940, the Luftwaffe was able to launch raids on southern England from air bases in Normandy and Brittany across the Channel. The first air raid on Plymouth took place on 6 July 1940, the bombs falling on a corporation housing estate in the district of Swilly and killing a woman, a man and a boy. Several further raids and fatalities followed over the next five days.

From then, and over the winter of 1940/41, the Luftwaffe carried out some thirty 'minor' air raids over the city, most of them comparatively small in scale compared with raids suffered elsewhere – although the loss of homes and the deaths and injuries caused by such raids were not minor to those who suffered them. The raids would usually start with the dropping of showers of incendiaries which caused widespread fires, followed by high-explosive bombs which destroyed large areas of the city. Land mines were dropped and low-flying enemy planes would sometimes machine-gun people they could see on the ground. During daylight hours the locals would sometimes be able to see dogfights between German and British planes over Plymouth and cheer when one of the enemy raiders was downed.

The Lancasters' new house, Anson, soon acquired another amenity: an 'Anderson' air raid shelter dug deep into the corner of the back garden to give them an underground refuge from bombs. These shelters were made of curved sections of corrugated iron bolted together and placed over an excavated dug-out in the garden, with the excavated earth covering the iron roof. They were available for purchase for a sum dependent on the family income, and were free to households that earned less than £250 a year. Several British homeowners also constructed more robust concrete shelters, many of which could still be found situated in Plymouth gardens or back yards for decades after the end of hostilities in 1945.[116]

An alternative form of protection during the Second World War was the cheaper but still strong indoor 'Morrison' shelter, a kit of steel and wire mesh which could be put up in the kitchen or dining room. Otherwise people relied on just the understairs cupboard to protect themselves, or went to one of the many public shelters constructed in Plymouth by the council or by larger businesses in the city.

The Lancaster family had another form of air raid alert. Their fox terrier, Danny, a new pet for Beryl and a comfort for her after her sister's death, could sense the approach of enemy bombers before the sirens went off. His barking would send Ida, with George and Beryl if at home, running early to the protection of the shelter.

If, as was usual, the attack was at night, they would scramble from their beds, quickly put on warm clothes and grab a ready-prepared flask of tea and perhaps some sandwiches. As they left the house, the beams of the Plymouth searchlights, the flashes of anti-aircraft fire and the guns of the Navy ships in port would light up the sky. The family stumbled in the blackout with a dimmed torch across the garden and climbed down the ladder into the shelter. Once inside, they closed the wooden door and placed a blanket across it to reduce the effect of any blast. The hours they spent in this cramped, dark, cold space, often staying there throughout the night with an oil lamp or just some candles for light, were often shared with neighbours such as the Bazeleys who lived next door.

George, Ida and Beryl listened to the drone of enemy aircraft engines overhead, the whistling of the falling incendiaries and the crashing explosions of the large bombs which would shake the shelter if they landed nearby. The fear for their own safety must have been compounded by the knowledge that their refuge would not necessarily protect them, for many in the city had been killed by direct hits on Anderson shelters.

What can George and Ida's thoughts have been while they sat there underground in the corner of their garden? During those interminable hours George might have reflected on his earlier active service in war, and recalled the terror of nearly drowning in the engine room on *Warrior*. Both he and his wife certainly each thought privately and quietly of young Ida, dwelling on their memories of her childhood and youth and the lost experiences and opportunities she would never have – the 'might have beens' of a life. However stoical they were, their bereavement was still so recent, and their parental grief so raw, that each must have at times felt overwhelming black despair in that dank shelter.

Did Ida have a silent conversation in her head with her dead daughter? Did George take her hand in his as comfort, both instinctively knowing at that moment they were holding the same person in their minds?

Once they heard the 'All Clear' siren, they emerged from their shelter in trepidation, fearing what damage had been inflicted on their neighbourhood or even their own home, and ready to deal with any burning fires. George had moved his family away from Devonport to escape the anticipated bombing, and indeed their former district of Ford, being so near the dockyard, was severely blitzed. On 27 August 1940 bombs falling there destroyed Ford House, a Public Assistance Institution for the poor where thirteen women inmates were killed. But the enemy planes also attacked Crownhill that same night, as they did during the heavy city-wide raids in March and April 1941, and again on 5 July 1941.

Even once a raid was over, there remained the constant danger to the public of unexploded bombs, some with deliberate delayed-action mechanisms. After the brave bomb disposal squads had located and extracted such a bomb, they took it by lorry, escorted by a police car, out to Dartmoor to be exploded.

At the outbreak of war in September 1939, Beryl was working as a secretary in the Naval Construction Department at Devonport

Dockyard. In common with the rest of the dockyard workforce, her post there was classified as a 'reserved occupation' in that it was regarded as essential war work. She was not allowed to transfer elsewhere, not even into the armed forces, and so she was thwarted in her wish to join the Women's Royal Naval Service (the 'Wrens') like her cousin Miriam Watson, who had been widowed just before the war and had joined the Navy. Miriam served in South Africa during the war, based at the port of Pietermaritzburg, where her father, Jack Ronson, a naval engineering officer, was also posted for a time while she was there.

Instead Beryl's wartime was spent in a vulnerable role in the front-line of the Home Front, and she also had to spend many evenings at the dockyard on fire-watching duty with colleagues. The Government introduced the compulsory nationwide fire-watching scheme for civilians in January 1941, with organised rotas and training in the use of stirrup pumps and buckets of sand to put out fires started by incendiary bombs.

After an air raid on 12 March 1941 that badly damaged houses and ships in the city, King George VI and Queen Elizabeth came to Plymouth on 20 March in recognition of the city's spirit in the face of aerial bombing. The King and Queen visited the dockyard and naval base, and they were escorted around the city by its Lord Mayor, Lord Astor, and his wife, the Plymouth Sutton MP Nancy Astor.

Three hours after the King and Queen's evening train left North Road station in Plymouth, the Luftwaffe arrived and bombed the city for two nights in succession, on the nights of 20 and 21 March. The Palace Theatre, where the band-leader Billy Cotton was performing, was hit, as were buildings along the whole of Union Street. The Guildhall was bombed, the naval barracks and victualling yard were left badly damaged, the main post office was destroyed and the mother church of the city, St Andrew's, was left a mere shell with only its walls standing. Most tragically a bomb landed on the children's ward and maternity unit at the Plymouth General Hospital, and at least twenty-five children, some mothers and six nurses were killed, including a seven-day-old baby boy called Harold Santilla and his mother, who was twenty-four.

The large department store, Spooner's, which was then on the corner of Bedford Street and Old Town Street, was destroyed, as were many other long-established shops in the city centre – Dingle's, Yeo's, Popham's and Goodbody's. The following day staff from Spooner's were sent to Exeter and Torquay to buy food supplies, and makeshift stalls were set up in the streets to provide parcels of essential foodstuffs to the local people. On the second night the Luftwaffe came again, and after two nights of bombing the death toll was 336 civilians, who received a mass funeral – many were buried in a communal grave. Fires continued to burn across the city for several days.

The following month, in April 1941, Plymouth endured three successive nights of terrible air raids on 21, 22 and 23 April. On the first night 35,000 incendiaries and 700 high-explosive bombs landed on the city.

At HMS *Drake*, where George worked, the Boscawen accommodation block for petty officers was destroyed, with seventy-eight men killed, and many others trapped in the building were not rescued until the following day when their cries were heard.

George also served as an air raid warden at HMS *Drake*. The air raid wardens' service was part of the National Civil Defence Organisation, and as with all other ARP wardens, it was his duty to be on constant alert for long periods during the day or night, and to ensure compliance with the blackout regulations. At *Drake* he had to direct the staff and servicemen and women working there straight to the bomb shelters when the air raid sirens started to warn of an imminent bombing raid. George would have been trained to recognise and deal with the consequences of high-explosive bombs and incendiaries, take anti-gas precautions such as fitting and checking gas respirators, and apply first aid to casualties. Wardens would also dig the wounded and the dead out of the rubble.

The Luftwaffe bombers arrived again on 22 and 23 April. More devastation was caused to the dockyard and much of Devonport itself, where hundreds of houses were hit. Five hundred and ninety-one people were killed during these three nights of air raids. Further raids came on the nights of 28 and 29 April, when 124 German planes arrived on the first night and 162 planes on the second. Saltash was bombed, along with Milehouse, Keyham and Torpoint. HMS *Raleigh*, the shore establishment at Torpoint, suffered the loss of forty-three sailors when two air raid shelters there were directly bombed.

During those dreadful air raids of March and April some 30,000 people would leave the city each night to escape the bombing, returning in the morning to go to work and look for food. They went out of the city on trains and lorries, by hitching lifts, by bike or on foot, to

Plympton or on to Dartmoor to villages such as Yelverton, and further afield to Horrabridge and Tavistock, or up the Tamar Valley to Bere Alston and Calstock.

On the night of 22 April 1941 a public air raid shelter at Portland Place on North Hill (now part of the Plymouth University site) received a direct hit from a German bomb and seventy-six people there were killed, with only a few survivors. Ena Payne, a young woman of twenty (the same age as Beryl), had gone to the Portland Square shelter with her boyfriend on hearing the sirens. After recovering consciousness, she found she was buried in the rubble, and her boyfriend dug her out using his bare hands. She survived, but lost her father and her grandmother in that raid, the only family she had.

Forty years later Ena described her experiences in a letter in April 1981 to the Plymouth *Evening Herald*, concluding:

> *I went through the Liverpool blitz, the Exeter blitz and the doodlebug raids on Southampton without a scratch. Lucky perhaps, but the best part of my life ended at the age of 20 in Portland Square shelter on April 22 1941.*

Four other families were wiped out that night at Portland Square. Another survivor was eleven-year-old Barbara Mills, who lost both of her parents, her grandfather and her sister. The wife and six children of a soldier serving away with his regiment were all killed, and he was recalled to Plymouth to identify their bodies.

Across the road on North Hill, Plymouth's Central Library was destroyed in those April raids. One hundred thousand books were lost, although the city's adjacent art gallery and museum were saved, including invaluable paintings by the famous eighteenth-century artist Sir Joshua Reynolds, who had been born in Plympton.

During these raids in the spring of 1941, thousands of incendiary bombs were dropped on Plymouth, causing raging fires in congested areas full of old properties which the inadequately equipped fire brigades – still managed by the local Civil Defence Service – were unable to control. Often the fires started by the incendiaries would burn for hours, even days, and the water supply for fire hoses would fail. Brigades that came from other parts of Devon to assist found that their equipment did not fit the Plymouth systems. It was only after the severe raids on so many British cities that a National Fire Service with standardised fire-fighting equipment was established later in 1941.

The business centres of both Plymouth and Devonport were destroyed by this conflagration, and for several months shop owners had to trade using stalls, Nissan huts and shop fronts in private houses. The destruction of the city centre meant that businesses had to move to accommodation in other parts of the city, notably to the previously disregarded thoroughfare known as Mutley Plain, which became the main shopping centre.

Officially the death toll in Plymouth during those March and April air raids in 1941 was a total of 926 people, the majority of them civilians. After the April 1941 raids the Prime Minister, Winston Churchill, visited Plymouth on 2 May, first touring the naval dockyard and Royal Naval Barracks where several sailors had been killed by bombs, and then the ruined city centre, accompanied by the MP Nancy Astor and her husband, Lord Astor. 'God bless you all…well done Plymouth' Churchill said at the end of his visit.

Plymouth may not have been the worst-hit city in the British Isles, but by comparison with London, Liverpool and Birmingham it was a much smaller city with a population of only 200,000. It has been calculated that more high-explosive bombs per acre fell on Plymouth than any other city apart from London and the Liverpool/Merseyside conurbation. During the Second World War, Plymouth had eight 'major' air raids (meaning raids when 100 tons or more of bombs were dropped).

H.P. (Pat) Twyford was the war correspondent for *The Western Morning News* daily newspaper in Plymouth throughout the war, and in 1945 he wrote a book, *It Came to Our Door*, about the city's experiences during those six years, when it had 602 air raid alerts and fifty-nine actual raids when bombs were dropped. He includes a chronological account, as recorded in his reporter's diaries, of each of those air raids across Plymouth, from June 1940 to April 1944, which attacked its naval and military installations, the waterfront and dockyard, the business centres and all its residential neighbourhoods. It makes for sober, even shocking, reading.

During the war, the Government set up a Mass Observation Unit (MOU) which produced reports on the attitudes and behaviour of the British population during wartime. In May 1941 the MOU produced its report on the April raids in Plymouth:

The civil and domestic devastation in Plymouth exceeds anything we have seen elsewhere, both as regards concentration through the heart of the town, and as regards the random shattering of homes all over the town. The dislocation of everyday life also exceeds anything we have seen elsewhere, and an enormous burden is being placed on the determined spirits of the people.

The MOU report was critical of the poor organisation of some of the authorities in Plymouth and of post-raid evacuation arrangements, particularly for the elderly, and, much to the annoyance of Government ministers in London, it expressed concern about the morale of the population. The report stated that the residents of Plymouth had 'strong local pride and tradition of toughness associated with the sea' and clearly wanted to show that they could 'take it', but they would have to have been of 'superhuman character to come through raids unaffected and unshaken'.

Shaken and badly affected they no doubt were, but for most Plymothians their wartime spirit and grim determination to survive were epitomised by the lady who, following an air raid, nailed a piece of scorched wood over the remaining door of the bombed fifteenth-century St Andrew's Church in the city centre with one word written on it – *Resurgam*, meaning 'I shall rise again'. There is still a plaque with that word fixed permanently above the 'Resurgam' door at the rebuilt St Andrew's Church.

Another show of good morale were the open-air dances organised on Plymouth Hoe during summer evenings, which were introduced after the heavy raids of spring 1941.

George's sister, Ellen (Nellie) Ronson, and her three youngest children – Alan and the twins, Betty and George – were bombed out of their home during the Blitz. Ellen's husband Jack was serving overseas. Her eldest son John was in India and Miriam, her elder daughter, was also abroad serving with the Wrens. George helped his sister to find a new home to rent across the road from the Lancasters in Moreton Avenue.

While George instructed cadets at HMS *Drake*, his wife Ida was occupied keeping house, making do, often trying to prepare meals without gas, electricity or water supplies and queueing interminably every day for food and clothing with her ration coupons. Ida helped to run the neighbourhood canteens and rest centres in Crownhill, and took her turn on duty as a fire-watcher. She also had to comfort others who had been bereaved, but this time through war.

In May 1941 many Devonport naval families lost fathers, brothers and sons when HMS *Hood* was sunk in the Denmark Strait by the German battleship *Bismarck*, with the loss of all but three of its crew of 1,418 men. On 10 December 1941 the sinking of HMS *Prince of Wales* and HMS *Repulse* following attacks by Japanese bombers near Singapore caused many more bereavements for Plymouth families.

Three days earlier, the Japanese attack at Pearl Harbor on 7 December 1941 had brought the United States into the war, and over the next three years this led to a huge influx of American servicemen to Plymouth to join the many other nationalities already based there. These included the men of the Royal Australian Air Force based at Mount Batten on the eastern edge of Plymouth Sound, who flew the flying boats from there on Coastal Command operations; the Royal Indian Army Service Corps with turbaned headdresses; Canadian, New Zealand, Free French, Dutch and Norwegian sailors serving with the Royal Navy; Polish and Czech pilots on patrol in the skies ready to attack Luftwaffe raiders; and a large contingent of Canadian fire-fighters.

Plymouth was a difficult, dangerous and tragic place to live for the six years of war from 1939 to 1945 with privations that we can scarcely imagine. Water, gas and electricity services were frequently cut by bombing raids, and Beryl remembered one wartime Christmas when the bird, probably a scrawny chicken, was somehow roasted in a biscuit tin over an open fire because there was no fuel for the oven.

After bombs hit the corporation bus depot at Milehouse in 1941, buses in Plymouth became scarce, and in any event there was no bus service to Crownhill until the autumn of 1942. Although the Lancasters had a car which only George drove, most motoring for private purposes was suspended during the war and there was strict petrol rationing. The family's move to Moreton Avenue meant that after work at the dockyard, Beryl had a very long and no doubt rather scary walk home of some three miles across the city in the blackout.

Then in late 1942 a national curfew was imposed on public transport services, intended to save both petrol and rubber, which in Plymouth meant that after 9.30 p.m. there were no buses available to Crownhill, or indeed to anywhere else. Accordingly, theatre and cinema performances finished at 9 p.m., but public houses kept open until 10 p.m., and their last customers joined the many other pedestrians walking home across the city.

After the heavy bombing in the spring of 1941, there had been sporadic raids during the rest of that year. In 1942 Hitler turned his attention to attacking historic cities in England with the *Baedeker* raids, named after the German tourist guide, and in May 1942 Exeter was severely bombed. The Luftwaffe carried out more serious air raids on Plymouth throughout 1943, and after a six-month break there was another heavy attack on 30 April 1944, mainly on the waterfront.

This was the final air raid on Plymouth, the last of fifty-nine raids on the city over a period of four years which killed 1,172 civilians and injured 4,448. The number of servicemen and women killed and injured in addition is uncertain as the figures were not released for security reasons.

There were 3,754 houses destroyed by the bombs, and some 18,398 were badly damaged. The city's shopping centres were destroyed, as well as nearly every public building, twenty-six schools, forty-one churches and eight cinemas, the Promenade Pier at Plymouth Hoe and Mount Edgcumbe House on the other side of the Tamar in Cornwall.[117]

The Lancasters suffered another family tragedy on 31 January 1943 when George's nephew, the elder son of his brother Alf, died of tuberculosis at the age of eighteen. This nephew, another George Lancaster, was the last of four successive generations of the family to bear that name.

There was also a family crisis for George and Ida during the war. Beryl, running for a bus, had jumped on to the platform, but had missed her footing, fallen and suffered a serious head injury. George, no doubt desperate to obtain the best medical treatment for his surviving daughter, arranged for Beryl to have an operation at the leading University College Hospital in London, where a procedure involving the grafting of some bone from Beryl's hip to her head was performed successfully.

By the start of 1944 the tide of the war was turning and top-secret preparations were being made along the whole of the south coast of England for 'Operation Overlord', the Allied invasion of France, the next vital stage in defeating the Nazi Third Reich. Devonport Dockyard, where George and Beryl both worked, was a hive of activity, and additional security restrictions were imposed. Plymouth Sound was full of naval vessels and craft of all types and sizes, many of unusual appearance and uncertain use, and long convoys of military vehicles and men drove through the city streets.

Some 60,000 American troops of the US Fourth Infantry Division were now camped at sites around Plymouth, including at the Seaton and Plumer Barracks in Crownhill, and at the Raglan Barracks in Devonport. For months they had been engaged in intensive training in and around the city, at sea and on Dartmoor, for the invasion of Europe. Despite the common refrain about the 'Yanks' that they were 'overpaid, oversexed and over here', the American forces were popular with the locals, and not just the young women. Plymothians invited Americans for tea and there was considerable goodwill in the city towards them, fostered by the Plymouth MP and Lady Mayoress, Nancy Astor, herself born an American.

Generally the conduct of the American servicemen was very good, and their own officers dealt strictly with any breaches of discipline, but their presence did cause some unexpected tensions. Beryl recalled a race riot in, of all places, the small Cornish town of Launceston, where white American soldiers, used to racial segregation back home, objected to the publican serving beer to black American soldiers in the same bar.

The American soldiers organised a baseball team called the Plymouth Yankees, which played on Saturday evenings at the Pennycross Greyhound Stadium, and the gate moneys were given to local charities. They also organised Christmas parties for thousands of local children in 1943, and gave them toys, candy and chocolate, which were otherwise strictly rationed.

A few American servicemen gave talks at local schools. Some 12,000 children had been evacuated from Plymouth in the early years of the war, especially after the terrible blitzes in March and April 1941. By 1943 about 8,000 of them had returned, even though by then some twenty-six Plymouth schools had been destroyed or badly damaged in night raids.

Frank Vass was a pupil at St Paul's Catholic Primary School in St Budeaux in Plymouth. Although not from a Catholic family, he had been moved there after German bombs had wrecked his two previous primary schools. He and the other ten-year-olds in his class were tremendously excited by the visit of an American soldier who was a real Wild West cowboy from Wyoming! Their cowboy performed amazing tricks by spinning and looping his lasso and throwing the rope around groups of two or three laughing, jumping boys and girls at a time, as if corralling cattle, leaving the children with a happy wartime memory that lasted a lifetime.[118]

Early on 6 June 1944 – 'D-Day' – thousands of the British and American servicemen based in Plymouth embarked on ships and landing craft at Cattedown and Turnchapel at the mouth of the River Plym, and at Saltash Passage on the River Tamar. With other Allied forces from ports along the south coast of England, they headed for the beaches on the Normandy coast, where thousands of them would lose their lives in the bitter fighting. Vicarage Road in St Budeaux in Plymouth, down which the soldiers marched, was renamed Normandy Way after the war.

George continued to work as an instructor at HMS *Drake*. In August 1944 his commanding officer, Engineer Commander Easterbrook, wrote on George's record:

> Most conscientious, is Technical Officer for Mech. Candidates, has carried out his duties in an exemplary manner, is tactful and takes charge of meetings in a firm but quiet manner.

The following year, Victory in Europe ('VE Day') was celebrated in Plymouth on 8 May 1945 as joyfully as elsewhere in Great Britain, with dancing and fireworks on the Hoe and street parties across the city. The celebrations were combined with the pain of so many deaths, and no doubt for George and Ida the poignancy that the new post-war world would not be shared by their elder daughter.

Victory in Japan ('VJ Day') followed on 15 August 1945, when Japan accepted defeat after the dropping of the first atomic bombs. George must have quietly reflected on his attendance at Emperor Hirohito's Coronation Fleet Review and his visits to Miyajima near Hiroshima and to Nagasaki back in 1928 and 1929.

1945

The year 1945 was a watershed in the history of Britain, a demarcation of eras when its people passed not only from war to peace, but began their long, slow transition from a rigid social structure of hierarchy and deference to a more egalitarian and diverse society.

Before the war against Japan in the Far East had been won, another battle was fought at home: an electoral battle in the General Election of July 1945, which Prime Minister Winston Churchill called once victory against Germany had been secured, ending the wartime coalition of the Conservative and Labour parties.

Churchill would have preferred to defer the General Election until the war against Japan had been won, and Attlee and the other Labour ministers were prepared to stay on in the coalition until October. But several Conservative ministers and Churchill's strategy advisers were convinced that an early election would favour him and that the British people's gratitude for his service as their war leader would sweep him to victory as their peace-time premier.

They were wrong. The Labour Party won by an overwhelming land-slide and its leader, Clement Attlee, became Prime Minister. Whether, as many commentators maintained, the votes of returning servicemen were the decisive factor or not, the majority of the British electorate voted for a new social and economic order in 1945 that would recognise and reward the sacrifices they had made during the war.

All of the three Plymouth constituencies elected Labour MPs, including Michael Foot, a future leader of the Labour Party, who was returned as the Member for Plymouth Devonport, beating the sitting Liberal/Independent MP, Leslie Hore-Belisha,[119] a former Minister of Transport and Secretary of State for War. Plymouth Sutton elected the Labour candidate Lucy Middleton, who was one of only twenty-four female MPs elected to Westminster in 1945. She succeeded the Conservative member for that constituency, Nancy Astor, who had been retired by her own party because her anti-Catholic and other increasingly eccentric views had made her a political liability to the Tories.

In the November 1945 municipal elections, the Labour Party also took control of Plymouth City Council for the first time. The defeat of Churchill at the ballot box and the victories of Labour in both the general and local elections in Plymouth were a huge shock to Conservative voters like the Lancaster family.

The Education Act 1944 of the wartime Coalition Government, the achievement of the Conservative minister R.A. Butler, was the precursor of major social change with the introduction of free secondary education for all. From 1945 to 1951 the Labour Government's radical legislation would establish the welfare state, advocated in the Beveridge Report of 1942, with a comprehensive system of national insurance. Attlee's administration also introduced the National Health Service; promoted a large council-house building programme; and nationalised the country's coal and steel industries, and the railways. All these measures laid the foundations of a post-war nation which would be radically different from the Great Britain of the first half of the twentieth century.

But in 1945, after six years of war at the 'sharp end' of the Home Front, there were bomb sites all over Plymouth, and most of the city centre had been devastated by the Blitz. There was a chronic shortage of housing following the destruction of nearly 4,000 homes in the bombings, plus serious damage to more than 18,000 houses. A large number of factories, business premises, schools and churches had also been destroyed.

Servicemen were gradually being demobbed, returning to wives and children after long periods of traumatic separation and often facing the challenge of rebuilding their domestic lives. The people were exhausted, and they were still coping with the strict nationwide rationing of food, clothing and petrol which would continue for several more years – food rationing did not end until July 1954. In 1943 the City Engineer, J. Paton Watson, and a leading town planner, Professor Patrick Abercrombie, had produced a new 'Plan for Plymouth', but the reconstruction of the blitzed city after 1945 in accordance with their designs would take most of the next decade, and beyond.

The end of the war brought major change for the Lancasters too. George carried on working at HMS *Drake* until his second retirement on 14 September 1945, when he received his Discharge Certificate and 'reverted to the Retired List'. At the age of fifty-eight, he had finally left the Royal Navy after thirty-five years' service.

Once the war ended, George was keen to continue his hobby of watercolour painting. His remaining book collection includes a booklet on *Drawing Trees* published in June 1945. He also painted a portrait of his daughter Beryl. Danny the fox terrier survived the war, as did the Baby Austin car, and peacetime life returned with trips to the coast and picnics on Dartmoor where George could sketch.

In 1944 Beryl had met a Royal Navy dentist, Surgeon Lieutenant Freddie Hunt, at a dance. He was twenty-three, a year younger than her, and was a Scotsman, the youngest child of Frederick and Helen Hunt. Frederick senior owned a drapery business in Crieff in Perthshire, and since 1936 and throughout the war he had been the Provost of the town, a position similar to that of a mayor in England. Frederick and Helen Hunt had also suffered bereavement. Of their five children, their son Archibald had died, aged three, of an unknown illness before Freddie was born. In 1936 their eldest child, Alasdair Malcolm, a land agent, had died of rheumatic fever at the age of twenty-eight.

Freddie had been at HMS *Drake* in Devonport since January 1944 serving as a naval dental surgeon. For Beryl he had one additional special quality in that he played with Danny, her adored dog – Beryl always maintained that she would not trust a man who didn't like dogs. George and Ida met Freddie, and at their first peacetime Christmas in December 1945 the talk must have been of Beryl's plans for their future.

Sometime after Christmas, George had a bitter row, possibly a political one, with the husband of Lily, one of Ida's sisters. As a Conservative voter, George was no doubt upset by the result of the 1945 General Election. Ida's sister, Lily Scott, and her husband still lived in Devonport (where she ran a public house until the late 1950s) and were more likely to be Labour voters. Whatever caused it, such a family row, particularly for a man of George's quiet and gentle temperament, undoubtedly caused him some stress.

On 28 December 1945 George was at home in Moreton Avenue, using a step-ladder in the front parlour for some purpose – changing a light bulb or taking down Christmas decorations. He suddenly suffered a massive heart attack and died immediately at the house, aged fifty-eight.

His brother Alf reported the death, which the certificate recorded as due to a coronary thrombosis. After two world wars, the demands of service overseas in the inter-war years and the tragedy of losing his elder daughter, George's heart had failed him.

George was buried at Weston Mill Cemetery in the same plot as his daughter Ida, and only a few yards away from the grave of Dame Agnes Weston – the Aggie Weston who had founded the Royal Sailors' Rest hostels.

George's mother Emma survived him. After living for a few years with her son Alf and his wife, she developed dementia and ended her days in a nursing home in Saltash in Cornwall, where she died in 1947, aged eighty-three.

Beryl married Freddie in September 1946 at Emmanuel Church in Plymouth, and they lived for a year in Fareham in Hampshire while Freddie was based at the shore establishment HMS *Collingwood*. They returned home after Freddie left the Navy in 1947 and lived with Ida for a few years while he established his own dental practice in the city and saved enough to buy their own bungalow in Charlton Road, Crownhill, next to Seaton Barracks. Beryl's much-loved fox terrier, Danny, died in 1950. Like most middle-class women of her generation, Beryl gave up her job on marriage, and as a housewife devoted her time throughout the 1950s and 1960s to bringing up her three children, Margaret, Rosemary and John.

Ida lived on at Anson on her naval widow's pension. In 1954 she managed to obtain an increase in the pension from the Ministry of Defence because George had achieved the higher rank of Lieutenant Commander when he returned for service in the Second World War. She never owned a fridge, let alone an automatic washing machine. Ida outlived both her younger sisters and her brother, and survived her husband for another quarter of a century, during which she saw her generation's sense of duty and loyalties to Crown and Empire change, to be replaced by different, more materialistic values. With Beryl's support, Ida somehow coped with the loss of her elder daughter and George, and with her long widowhood, and she enjoyed seeing her three grandchildren grow up in Plymouth.

After suffering a stroke in the late 1960s, Ida lived in a care home in Plymouth. On Easter Sunday, 14 April 1971, she died, aged eighty-four. She was buried at Weston Mill Cemetery in the same plot as George and their daughter Ida. Her epitaph reads 'Reunited'.

*

George left no memoirs. His few surviving letters confirm his literacy and fluency of expression, but this 'shy and simple' man was not one to write of himself – he left us little by way of a 'voice'. His alleged shyness was more in the sense of being reserved, and perhaps not feeling the need to speak unless he had something worthwhile to say – an undervalued quality. If he were 'simple' it was not in the pejorative sense, but in being straightforward, uncomplicated, with no side – reliable, trustworthy, loyal – as the reports of his commanding officers confirm.

Compared to most of us, George lived his life on a broad canvas. He served through two world wars, and in the interwar years his deployment as a serviceman overseas was determined by major political events. He travelled far and witnessed and endured much, and as an Englishman of his time he did his duty to his King and his country, to God and his family.

George also observed a duty to himself – a duty to improve his lot in life, to advance up the scale, for the sake of his children as much as for himself. George's father had been born into the poverty-stricken slums of mid-nineteenth-century Liverpool, where throughout her life his twice-widowed mother Ellen had had to take on menial jobs to feed herself and her family. George's father instilled in his son a determination to progress to something better in life.

The many gifts that George brought home to his family from overseas, and the sensitive care with which he chose those items for Ida and his daughters, say something about his values. The cream silk bedspread with embroidered Chinese dragons; from Japan, a pair of ceramic figures in traditional dress, a leather purse and two paintings of Mount Fuji; a set of ebony boxes with mother of pearl inlay; the cane chairs from the bazaar in Hong Kong – these were not mere tourist souvenirs, but finely crafted objects of lasting beauty from far-away places.

George's naval sword and medals are the tangible memorial to his service career. But perhaps an even more significant mark of his legacy to his grandchildren is contained within two rusty metal boxes, kept but forgotten for decades in the family's attics or in understairs cupboards. In one strangely shaped box is a black velvet naval officer's cocked hat with gold braid on one side; in the other box a pair of naval officer's gold epaulettes. George, who had started his working life as a fourteen-year-old apprentice fitter in Devonport Dockyard, had worn these as part of his full dress uniform as a Lieutenant Commander in the Royal Navy, a rank achieved after over thirty years of working his way slowly up the hierarchy of the Senior Service.

George Samuel Lancaster never saw his three grandchildren, or the rebuilt post-war Plymouth in which they grew up. Yet the values he observed and the knowledge he developed were influences in their lives. He achieved a considerable degree of what we now call social mobility through his hard work and self-sacrifice, and this enabled his grandchildren to have a far higher standard of living and enjoy greater opportunities for education, employment, home-ownership and travel.

George's story is the perspective of one man on many of the events of an extraordinary half-century. He was one of hundreds of thousands of men who served in the Royal Navy in the first half of the twentieth century, and like all those whom in our remembrance of war we now value more greatly, he was indeed a 'warrior'. The life of this particular shy and simple warrior is not 'top-down' history charting the actions, and inaction, of monarchs and politicians. It is his story, and their story: a story of uncommon people, and one that deserves to be passed on, not forgotten.

Acknowledgements

I am fortunate to live in a small Somerset village where I can sit in the Pub at Wanstrow with my neighbour Richard Pelham, and discuss the naval history of the Great War. On All Saints Day 2014 on the centenary of Coronel we both raised a glass in memory of the brave sailors who died at that battle.

Richard has helped with my research throughout, lending me books and supplying information on many technical points as well as photographs of *Warrior* and *Engadine*, Rutland's seaplane, and the programme from the 2003 service in Tallinn in memory of the British sailors who died supporting Estonia in 1919. He read the whole manuscript, and his extraordinary knowledge and ever-courteous comments and corrections have been an invaluable contribution to this book – even if we do disagree on the standing of that impetuous motorcyclist Admiral Robert Arbuthnot (whose Triumph motorcycle apparently went down with him on HMS *Defence*).

My understanding of naval matters was also enormously helped at an early stage by Commander Alick Moore and his wife Penny, who read sections of the manuscript and whose enthusiastic interest in my grandfather's naval career encouraged me to complete his story.

My introduction to Rear Admiral John Burgess by his daughter Sara following a chance conversation was extremely fortuitous. As a former Engine Room Artificer and distinguished naval officer, John's insightful and positive comments on the book and his explanations and clarification of many naval issues, including details of the life of a 'Tiffy', have been invaluable. His kindness in contributing the Foreword represented a vital endorsement.

Elisabeth Balfour, also one of the wonderfully eclectic mix of customers at the Pub at Wanstrow, gave me very useful advice on the publishing process, and her generosity in undertaking a full copy-edit of the manuscript was a major contribution to the process of producing a consistent and coherent text. Her kind comments on my story of George and insight into my reasons for writing it were also very heartening.

I would have made no progress at all in the lengthy process of writing this book without Jane Mayes's meticulous transcription of all my incoherent dictation, and her genuine interest in whatever she typed for me spurred on my efforts.

My cousin John Ronson in Toronto supplied a wonderful set of photographs of the Lancaster and Ronson families, many of which I had not previously seen. Steve Thomas, from our neighbouring village of Nunney in Somerset, kindly gave me photographs of Able Seaman Alfred Swain at the Pyramids in 1914, and of HMS *Warrior*. Keith Walton assisted my research into the Baltic operations in 1919, and Tim Dougall provided useful information on First World War cruisers. Frank Vass from my art class told me his touching childhood memory of the American soldier performing his cowboy lasso tricks before D-Day. My thanks go to all of them.

I am particularly grateful to the military historian Peter Hart for his permission to use the very extensive extracts from his own excellent book on Jutland, *Death in the Grey Wastes*, which I quote in recounting the experience of HMS *Warrior* at that battle.

I am obliged to the Plymouth historian Chris Robinson for permission to use material from his books on the history of Devonport and Plymouth; to Gordon Smith for approving my quotations from log books published on his encyclopaedic naval history website; to the librarians at the Plymouth Central Library for their assistance; to Dr Andrew Gordon for consent to use extracts from his book *The Rules of the Game*; to David Higham Associates for permission to use the quotation from Eric Hobsbawm's *Uncommon People*; and to Tina Rapinet for allowing me to quote from *Last Bastion* by her father, Eric Brockman. Her relatives, Martin and Lorie Scicluna, were also very helpful in giving me insights into life in Malta.

I have tried to ensure that I have attributed all other quotations and source material, and I apologise to any persons whom I have failed to mention through oversight or inability to trace the original author. I must also stress that this book is not intended to be an academic or authoritative study, and no doubt it will contain many errors of fact or interpretation, particularly as regards naval matters of which I have little direct experience. All such errors are my responsibility alone.

My long-standing friend Deborah Watts encouraged me greatly by her enthusiastic support for my project, and by twice inviting me to speak to her sixth-form history class at Bruton School for Girls on 'Operation Red Trek' in the Baltic in 1919, which I hope gave her students a different perspective on the Russian Revolution. I am confident that Deborah's interest in naval history will develop now that she has a grandson who is descended from Admiral Sir Reginald Tyrwhitt.

Quintilla Wikeley generously gave me the benefit of her very considerable communications expertise, supplying much useful advice on how to reach potential readers.

There are many other good friends who have encouraged my writing endeavours: I regret I cannot list them all but I am most grateful to Elspeth Richards, Kenneth and Patience Thom, Valerie Norton, Bridget March, Daria Stephens, Cali Smith, Angela Southern, and especially Anne Montague who has done so much to help me forward.

Helen Hart and Emily Heming at SilverWood Books have assisted greatly with my publishing journey and have given me the confidence to proceed to publication, and to persuade a book market that this is a story worth reading.

My sister Margaret Bishop and my brother John Hunt have been encouraging and supportive of my wish to tell our grandparents' story. All three of us owe a special debt to our great-great-grandmother Ellen Lancaster who, widowed and impoverished, successfully raised her children, and at the end of her life was still trudging through the streets of Everton at dawn to wake up Victorian workers by knocking on their windows.

My late and very much missed mother Beryl carefully preserved her father's papers and correspondence and transcribed his diary, no doubt hoping that one day we would recognise his contribution in life. Without Beryl's care, and her amazing interest in people and events, I would never have been able to write this story. I remain so grateful to her and my late father Freddie for giving me such a wonderful upbringing and education in Plymouth.

My greatest debt is to my own family. My husband Malcolm has been unfailingly patient and encouraging, even when being dragged around the streets of Senglea in Malta as I searched for the location of my grandparents' married quarters. I have received constant loving support and a range of good ideas for the book from my indefatigable daughter Alexandra and her husband Jag, and from my son Iain, who has inherited his great-grandfather's engineering ability and artistic skill in painting ships. My family's faith in my project has been more important to me than I can possibly say.

Finally, I wouldn't have written this story of my grandparents, George and Ida, were it not that I now share with them an uncommon bereavement – the loss of a daughter to cancer.

Our daughter Sophie died on 14 December 2009, aged twenty-four. This book is my tribute to her love, her laughter and her courage, and also to her great-aunt Ida. Two lives of much achievement, much promise, both cruelly curtailed.

Yet both Sophie and Ida left their own imprint on the world, and in the enduring memories of their family and friends.

Sources

Original Sources

Lancaster family papers, photographs and book collections

National Archives Naval Service Records for George Lancaster ADM/188/74 and George Samuel Lancaster ADM/196/136

Plymouth City Reference Library – Naval History Section: Navy Lists; Maps; Plymouth Directories

Plymouth and West Devon Record Office – log book of Royal Military and Navy Free School

The Horseshoe magazines of St John's Recreation Club, Devonport, September 1909 – February 1910

Imperial War Museum:

R.C. Church Collection of Jutland accounts

Charles Howes CPO, HMS Diligence – Account of Smyrna 1922

General Register Office records

HMS *Warrior* log book 1915/1916 (www.naval-history.net)

HMS *Dauntless* log book 1919 (www.naval-history.net)

Devonport and Plymouth

Plymouth 1890 History and Directory, William White, Hindsight Publications, 1989

Days in Devonport, Gerald W. Barker, 1982–1984

A History of Devonport, Chris Robinson, Pen & Ink Publishing, 2010

Plymouth in the 20s & 30s, Chris Robinson, Pen & Ink Publishing, 2008

The Royal Navy and the Great War (First World War)

Devon in the Great War 1914 – 1918, Gerald Wasley

All About Ships, Lieutenant Taprell Dorling, R.N., Cassell & Company Ltd, 1912

From the Dreadnought to Scapa Flow 1904–1919 (volumes I–V), Arthur J. Marder, Seaforth Publishing, 1961

Fisher's Face, Jan Morris, Random House, 1995

www.dreadnoughtproject.org

History of the Great War – Naval Operations, volumes 1–3, Sir Julian Corbett, and volumes 4 and 5, Henry Newbolt

Naval Battles of the First World War, Geoffrey Bennett, Pan, 1974

The Escape of 'The Goeben' – prelude to Gallipoli, Redmond McLaughlin, Pen & Sword, 1974

The Price of Admiralty, John Keegan, Hutchinson, 1988

The Imperial War Museum Book of the War at Sea 1914–1918, Julian Thompson, 1997

Castles of Steel – Britain, Germany and the Winning of the Great War at Sea, Robert K. Massie, Random House, 2003

The Empire of the Deep: The Rise & Fall of the British Navy, Ben Wilson, Weidenfeld & Nicolson, 2013

First World War at Sea, David Wragg, The History Press, 2014

The Sailor's War 1914–1918, Peter H. Liddle, Blandford Press Limited, 1985

Lost Voices of the Royal Navy, Max Arthur, Hodder & Stoughton, 2005

Sober Men and True: Sailor Lives in the Royal Navy, 1900–1945, Christopher McKee, Harvard, 2002

This Great Harbour – Scapa Flow, W.S Hewison, Birlinn Ltd., 2005

Selection and Early Career Education of Executive Officers in the Royal Navy c 1902–1939, Elinor Frances Romans, University of Exeter thesis, 2012

Jutland

Battle of Jutland, 30th May to 1st June, 1916: Official Dispatches with appendices, Admiralty, Great Britain

The Battle of Jutland, Geoffrey Bennett, David & Charles, 1964

The Rules of the Game – Jutland and British Naval Command, Andrew Gordon, John Murray, 1996

Jutland – The German Perspective, V.E. Tarrant, Arms and Armour Press, 1995

The Continuing Argument over Jutland, Louis D. Rubin, VQR Online essay, 2001

The Battle of Jutland 1916, George Bonney, Sutton Publishing, 2002

Jutland 1916 – Death in the Grey Wastes, Nigel Steel and Peter Hart, Cassell, 2003

General Histories of the Great War

The First World War, John Keegan, Hutchinson, 1998

The First World War – A Very Short Introduction, Michael Howard, Oxford University Press, 2002

The First World War, Hew Strachan, Simon & Schuster, 2003

World War One – A Short History, Norman Stone, Penguin, 2007

The Sleepwalkers: How Europe Went to War in 1914, Christopher Clark, Allen Lane, 2012

The War that Ended Peace, Margaret Macmillan, Profile Books, 2013

Catastrophe – Europe Goes To War 1914, Max Hastings, William Collins, 2013

The Baltic

Northern Shores: A History of the Baltic Shore and its Peoples, Alan Palmer, John Murray, 2006

Communist Russia under Lenin and Stalin, Chris Corin and Terry Fiehn, John Murray, 2002

www.historicalrfa.org

The Smyrna Crisis

Paradise Lost – Smyrna 1922 – The Destruction of Islam's City of Tolerance, Giles Milton, 2008

Smyrna's Ashes: Humanitarianism, Genocide and the Birth of the Middle East, Michelle Tusan, University of Nevada, Las Vegas, 2012

Malta

Last Bastion – Eric Brockman, 1961

Malta Re-visited – An Appointment with History, Eric Gerarda-Azzopardi, 1984

China

Cambridge Illustrated History – China, Patricia Buckley Ebrey, Cambridge University Press, 1996

Generalissimo – Chiang Kai-Shek and the China He Lost, Jonathan Fenby, Simon & Schuster UK Ltd, 2003

1930s

King George V, Kenneth Rose, Macmillan, 1983

Edward VIII, Philip Ziegler, Collins, 1990

The Battle for Spain – The Spanish Civil War 1936–1939, Antony Beevor, Weidenfeld & Nicolson, 2006

The Second World War

It Came to Our Door – Plymouth in the World War, H.P. Twyford, Underhill, 1945

Plymouth: A New History, Crispin Gill, Devon Books, 1993

The Blitz – The British under Attack, Juliet Gardiner, Harper Press, 2011

The Road to War, Richard Overy, Macmillan BBC Books, 1989

All Hell Let Loose – the World at War 1939–45, Max Hastings, Harper Press, 2012

A Short WWII History, Norman Stone, Allen Lane, 2013

Notes

1. In 1842 Kitty persuaded the Liverpool authorities to set up the first combined public baths and washhouses for the poor in Great Britain, a pioneering measure which was then adopted throughout the country and saved thousands of lives from disease. Kitty became known as the 'Saint of the Slums', and in 2012 she was at last honoured by a commemorative statue of her which was placed in St George's Hall in Liverpool.
2. HMS *Cambridge* was a 116-gun ship launched in 1858 as HMS *Windsor Castle*. She was renamed HMS *Cambridge* in 1869 when she replaced the 1815 vessel of that name as the gunnery ship off Plymouth. She was sold in 1908. From 1956 to 2001, HMS *Cambridge* was a shore establishment at Bovisand near Plymouth for the R.N. Gunnery School.
3. Aggie Weston (1840–1918) co-founded with her friend Sophia Wintz this hostel and another in Portsmouth. They became the Royal Sailors' Rests, and Aggie was made a Dame of the British Empire for her work in promoting the welfare of sailors. There is still in 2015 a Christian charity called 'Aggie Weston's' which supports serving sailors, marines and their families.
4. The Bayley surname is sometimes recorded in records as 'Bazley' or 'Basley'.
5. Source: Devonport Street Directory 1890.
6. In the Plymouth and West Devon Records Office.
7. The Field Gun Run was a race between naval crews from Devonport, Portsmouth and, in later years, the Fleet Air Arm that from 1907 until 1999 took place at the annual Royal Military Tournament at Earl's Court. It had its origins in the Royal Navy's involvement in the relief of Ladysmith during the Boer War in 1900. Guns from HMS *Powerful* were hauled to Ladysmith by the ship's Naval Brigade to defend the town against the Boers' attack.
8. Discussed in more detail in 'The Navy' chapter.
9. Using guns with the same calibre instead of mixed artillery permitted more accurate ranging of a target by salvo-firing, as shells from guns of the same calibre with the same flight time would show by their simultaneous splashes whether the range was correct.
10. In the English Civil War in the 1640s, Plymouth had supported Oliver Cromwell and his Puritan Roundheads, in contrast to the rest of Devon and Cornwall which were staunchly Royalist.
11. In Greek mythology, Terpsichore was one of the Nine Muses and the goddess of dancing and chorus.
12. National Archives Naval Service Record ADM/196/136. The reports on George from his commanding officers quoted in this book are taken from this naval record.

13. George may seem unusually short – but as a survey in 2013 found, the average height of British men at age twenty-one rose from 5ft 5in in 1871–75 to 5ft 10in in 1971–75.

14. An incident satirised in the 1949 film *Kind Hearts and Coronets*.

15. This first HMS *Warrior* is now moored at Portsmouth and is open to the public.

16. *Imperial War Museum Book of the War at Sea 1914–18*, Julian Thompson.

17. The First Lord of the Admiralty was, until 1964, the civilian Cabinet minister responsible for the Royal Navy.

18. Opposition to the Selborne-Fisher Scheme led to its termination by the Admiralty after the Great War.

19. *Empire of the Deep – The Rise and Fall of the Royal Navy*, Ben Wilson, 2013, Weidenfeld & Nicolson.

20. *Fisher's Face* by Jan Morris is an enamoured and entertaining study of the formidable Admiral Fisher (Random House, 1995).

21. Source: The Fisgard Association, timeline of artificer trainings, www.thefisgardassociation.org/association/timeline. The rank of artificer was discontinued by the Royal Navy in 2010.

22. Renamed HMS *Drake* in 1934, HMS *Vivid* is now the Royal Naval Reserve Unit in Plymouth.

23. George's ship was later renamed HMS *Zealandia* as another ship was given the name HMS *New Zealand*, the battlecruiser built at the expense of the New Zealand Government for the Royal Navy and launched in 1911.

24. *The Imperial War Museum Book of the War at Sea 1914–18*, Julian Thompson.

25. *Sober Men and True: Sailor Lives in the Royal Navy, 1900–1945*, Christopher McKee, Harvard, 2002. This book also discusses homosexuality in the Royal Navy.

26. The Parish of Maker, including part of the Rame Peninsula, was in Devon until 1844, when it was transferred to Cornwall.

27. In 1924 these old baths were replaced by a corporation open-air swimming pool built on the water's edge, a pool in which generations of Plymouth schoolchildren (including myself) learnt to swim in very chilly conditions.

28. There seems to have been a continuing inconsistency in the spelling of both her family names in Ida's life. Spriddle is sometimes spelt 'Spriddell' instead and Horne is variably spelt with or without an 'e'.

29. *The Age*, 5 December 1913, Melbourne.

30. The Representation of the People Act 1928 extended the voting franchise to all women over the age of 21.

31. Lady Astor, a Conservative, was the first of a line of eminent women MPs, such as Lucy Middleton, Dame Joan Vickers and Dame Janet Fookes, elected by Plymouth voters in the twentieth century.

32. St Aubyn Estate Plans, 1909–1910, Plymouth and West Devon Record Office.

33. Marjorie Laxton, quoted in *Days in Devonport* Part II, Gerald W. Barker, 1982–1984.

34. The other *Warrior*-class armoured cruisers were HMS *Achilles*, HMS *Natal* and HMS *Cochrane*.

35. Despite having been a pre-war partner in the Triple Alliance with Germany and Austria-Hungary, Italy joined the war on the side of the Triple Entente powers (Britain, France and Russia) in April 1915.

36. The eminent naval historian Arthur J. Marder was inclined to agree with Fremantle, but considered that 'if Troubridge was guilty it was of erroneous judgement, no more, and even that with extenuating circumstances'. *From the Dreadnought to Scapa Flow*, Vol.II, p.36, 1965, Seaforth Publishing.

37. Now known as Bar.

38. Imperial War Museum, R. Church Collection.

39. *History of the Great War – Naval Operations*, Vol. 1, by Sir Julian Corbett. The Germans had sunk two British cruisers at the Battle of Coronel, off Chile.

40. I am grateful for this information to Steve Thomas of Nunney who has preserved this photograph and Alfred Swain's war medals.

41. Source: Conway's *All the World's Fighting Ships*, 1906–21.

42. The Grand Fleet had been formed in August 1914 from the First Fleet and some ships of the Second Fleet of what had previously been named the Home Fleet.

43. *From the Dreadnought to Scapa Flow 1904–1919*, Vol. II, p. 356, Arthur J. Marder, 1961, Seaforth Publishing.

44. HMS *Warrior* log book 1915/1916 – www.naval-history.net.

45. W.S. Hewison's *This Great Harbour – Scapa Flow* (pp.85–87) recounts the King's visit.

46. The future King George VI.

47. Quoted by Andrew Gordon in *Rules of the Game*, 1996, John Murray, London, p.24.

48. In 1908 Arbuthnot competed on a Triumph motorcycle in the Isle of Man TT Races, possibly the only serving Royal Navy Admiral ever to do so. The Arbuthnot Trial race was run in his memory until the 1930s in the Isle of Man TT Races. Since 1982 the Salisbury Motorcycle and Light Car Club has held an annual Arbuthnot Trial.

49. Andrew Gordon, op. cit. p.392.

50. 'Mi' was Nell's baby daughter Miriam.

51. *The First World War*, John Keegan, published by Pimlico Random House, 1999.

52. Steel and Hart, p.53.

53. The losses at Jutland caused by cordite storage did not prevent further needless tragedy. On 9 July 1917 at Scapa Flow, the dreadnought battleship HMS *Vanguard* blew up just after midnight, the explosion apparently caused by a stokehold fire overheating cordite stored against an adjacent bulkhead. Some 804 men were killed, with only two survivors, and the destruction of the *Vanguard* remains the worst accidental explosion in British history.

54. *Indefatigable* had been built in Devonport Dockyard in 1909 when George worked

as an engine fitter there. He had probably helped to build and install its turbine engines.

55. Some of Beatty's opponents argued that if he had ensured that the super-*dreadnoughts* were accompanying his fleet, this concentrated force would have launched a powerful offensive on the German attackers and at least one of his battlecruisers might have been spared its fate.

56. *Jutland 1916: Death in the Grey Wastes,* Nigel Steel and Peter Hart, 2003, Cassell.

57. *The Fighting at Jutland: The Personal Experiences of Forty-Five Officers and Men of the British Fleet,* H.W. Fawcett and G.W.W. Hooper, Macmillan, London, 1921.

58. See *The Sailor's War: 1914–1918,* Peter H. Liddle, Blandford Press, 1985. In the 1960s Dr Liddle began collecting an archive of personal experience documentation and memorabilia connected to the First World War, which he continued to build for the next thirty years. The Liddle Collection is available for public inspection at the Brotherton Library of Leeds University.

59. Except where stated, all the following accounts from the officers and men of HMS *Warrior* are taken from Robert Church's collection, many of which are quoted in Steel and Hart's book.

60. To get an idea of the size of these ships' guns, the two huge naval guns, each weighing 200 tons, which are permanently situated in front of the Imperial War Museum in London are 15-inch guns developed in 1912 for the *Queen Elizabeth*-class battleship. Four of these ships comprised the Fifth Battle Squadron at Jutland and their guns could fire shells over a distance of sixteen miles.

61. Steel and Hart, op. cit., p.198.

62. Steel and Hart report that the several contemporary descriptions from witnesses of the *Defence* being apparently blown to smithereens have been slightly undermined by the discovery (shortly before the publication of their book in 2003) of the wreck of the *Defence* by divers and marine archaeologists who found it in remarkably good condition.

63. Steel and Hart, op. cit., pp.199–200.

64. Dr Peter Liddle, *A Sailor's War: 1914–1918,* p.114.

65. This photograph of crew on HMS *Warrior* is published in Liddle, op. cit., p.114.

66. Recounted in Liddle, op. cit., p.114.

67. Earlier that day, 31 May, Rear Admiral Beatty had ordered a Short seaplane piloted by Flight Lt Rutland with an observer to take off from the sea plane carrier *Engadine* on a reconnaissance mission, with reports of the position of the enemy ships being sent back to the *Engadine*. This was a piece of significant naval history as it was the first time ever in naval warfare that a 'heavier-than-air' machine had carried out a reconnaissance of an enemy fleet in action. *Engadine's* aircraft had participated in the Cuxhaven Raid on Christmas Day 1914 when British planes attacked the Zeppelin sheds at that German naval port. *Engadine* returned to ferry service after the Great War and was sold and renamed *Corregidor* in 1933. In the Second World War she was still sailing as a commercial ship, and as she was leaving Manila in the

Philippines in 1941 was sunk by a mine with heavy loss of life.

68. At the age of eighty, in reply to the 1972 questionnaire sent to him by Robert Church.

69. Frederick Rutland was awarded the Albert Medal for his pioneering flying mission and for this rescue attempt, and became known as 'Rutland of Jutland'. But after the Great War he went to the Far East and was recruited by the Japanese as a spy. When the war in the Pacific started in 1941 after the attack on Pearl Harbor, Rutland was arrested for collaboration with the Japanese and he was imprisoned in England until 1944. After that war he committed suicide.

70. *Engadine* had sailed from Rosyth on 30 May with Beatty's squadrons.

71. In fact seventy-one of *Warrior*'s crew had been killed at the battle or died later.

72. In the 1970s Mr Poole presented his pair of semaphore flags and his binoculars which he had rescued from *Warrior* to the Imperial War Museum.

73. Third Light Cruiser Squadron.

74. Official Dispatches for the Battle of Jutland.

75. The DSM was the 'other ranks' equivalent to the Distinguished Service Cross awarded to commissioned officers and warrant officers. In 1993, the DSM was discontinued, and since then the Distinguished Service Cross has been awarded to personnel of all ranks.

76. A personal connection here. My grand-daughter's great-great-grandfather George Lancaster served on HMS *Warrior*. Her paternal great-grandfather Dhian Singh was one of the 125,000 Sikh warriors who served in the British Indian Army in the First World War, in his case in Mesopotamia. He also fought in the Second World War in Burma, retiring in 1954 as a subedar-major.

77. *From the Dreadnought to Scapa Flow*, Vol. II, Arthur J. Marder, Seaforth, pp.9, 14.

78. Supplement to the *London Gazette*, 7 June 1918, Issue 30730, p.6771.

79. www.nationalarchives.gov.uk/pathways/firstworldwar/spotlights/blockade. This figure did not include some 150,000–200,000 deaths in Germany from the global Spanish 'flu pandemic of 1918/19.

80. Liddle, op. cit., 1985.

81. HMS *Dauntless* log book 1919 – www.naval-history.net.

82. The Women's Royal Naval Service had been founded at the end of 1917 and recruited some 7,000 women, but was disbanded shortly after the Great War ended. It was re-founded in 1939.

83. See next chapter.

84. Petrograd was renamed Leningrad in 1924, and reverted to its pre-revolutionary name of St Petersburg in 1991.

85. Libau is the German name, Liepāja is the Polish name for this city.

86. In 1919 these islands were within the territory of Finland – they are now within Russia.

87. Apparently the second aircraft carrier ever built.

88. Source: www.historicalrfa.org.

89. This Armenian genocide in 1915 is still denied by the Turkish Government, as was

evident on the centenary of the massacres in April 2015.

90. A full account of the background and these events at Smyrna is given in *Paradise Lost – Smyrna 1922 – The Destruction of Islam's City of Tolerance*, Giles Milton, 2008.

91. The Cheetaks were Turkish irregular soldiers.

92. Royal Navy sailors.

93. *Paradise Lost – Smyrna 1922 – The Destruction of Islam's City of Tolerance.*

94. Self-government in Malta lasted only until 1933 when the British withdrew the 1921 Constitution and Malta reverted to Crown Colony status. This followed disputes between the Maltese Constitutional Party and the Catholic Church in 1931 when the General Election was suspended.

95. See previous chapter.

96. The Three Cities of Vittoriosa, Senglea and Cospicua are still also known by their original Malti names of Birgu, Isola and Bormla.

97. A plaque in Triq Irlandizi marks the birthplace there in 1916 of Dom Mintoff, the future Prime Minister of Malta, unpopular with the British press and whom Beryl Lancaster considered to be anti-British. It is ironic that as children they would have lived and played only a few streets away from each other.

98. *Last Bastion*, Eric Brockman, 1961.

99. The Navy, Army and Air Force Institute.

100. The British became concerned in 1933 over the Maltese Government's support for the teaching of Italian in schools at a time when it was becoming clear that the Italian Fascist dictator Mussolini had designs on Malta.

101. Warrant Officers v. Engine Room Artificers – George was now a Warrant Officer.

102. Now the well-known Shanghai Bund or quayside area of the city.

103. Five years earlier the Great Kanto earthquake on 1 September 1923 had devastated Yokohama and Tokyo, with a death toll of about 140,000.

104. *Nagato* was a Japanese battleship launched in 1919 which survived the Second World War as it was mostly in reserve, apart from serving as Admiral Yamamoto's flagship during the Pearl Harbor attack. It was sunk during US nuclear tests in 1946.

105. This tomb near Nanking is the tomb of the first Ming emperor.

106. This was jai alai, a variation of the ball game Basque pelota. It was a popular gambling sport in Shanghai but was banned when the communists took power.

107. The *Rawalpindi* was converted to an armed merchant cruiser in 1939, and was sunk in an engagement with the German battleships *Scharnhorst* and *Gneisenau* later that year, when it was under the command of Captain Edward Kennedy, the father of the broadcaster Ludovic Kennedy.

108. The term 'Chief' or 'Chiefy' was a common informal form of address by officers to an engineering officer, regardless of the rank of that officer.

109. *The Battle for Spain – The Spanish Civil War 1936 –1939*, Antony Beevor, Weidenfeld & Nicolson, 2006.

110. Bertie was George V's second son, later George VI, whose daughter 'Lilibet' became Elizabeth II.

111. 'Matric' means 'Matriculation'.

112. This is the 1928 photograph of the officers on the deck of HMS *Berwick*.

113. It was not until well-known personalities such as the broadcaster Richard Dimbleby and the conductor Sir Malcolm Sargent died of cancer in the 1960s that the illness became more widely acknowledged and discussed.

114. *History Today: Europe*, Vol 56 Issue 9, August 2006

115. The origin of the nickname 'Guz' or 'Guzz' for the Devonport naval base is sometimes attributed to the 'guzzling' of Devon cream teas, although there is also a more prosaic claim that it comes from the call sign 'GUZZ' of the nearby naval wireless station at Devil's Point.

116. Perhaps optimistically kept through the Cold War in case 'the Bomb' was dropped by the Russians. The concrete air raid shelter in the garden of the house where I grew up is still there, in 2015.

117. Source: *Plymouth: A New History* by Crispin Gill, Devon Books, 1993, pp.259–262.

118. I am grateful to Frank Vass for this memory.

119. After whom 'Belisha beacons' were named.

Index

Lightning Source UK Ltd.
Milton Keynes UK
UKOW04f2154191015

260905UK00001B/1/P